A LEGACY OF MADNESS

Endorsements for *A Legacy of Madness*

A Legacy of Madness breaks down the barriers of silence that shroud mental illnesses within families for generations. It also details the larger problem of stigma and the failures of a system ill-equipped to provide adequate treatment and support. By sharing the story of his family history and his own personal journey, Tom Davis provides hope and inspiration to others.

—Rosalynn Carter, Former U.S. First Lady and Chairperson,
the Carter Center Mental Health Task Force

This is a book from the heart, and for any family with somebody who has mental illness, this is a must-read.

—Former New Jersey Governor Richard Codey,
Mental Health Advocate and Author of *Me, Governor?*

A LEGACY OF MADNESS

Recovering My Family
from Generations of Mental Illness

TOM DAVIS

HAZELDEN®

Hazelden
Center City, Minnesota 55012
hazelden.org

Library of Congress Cataloging-in-Publication Data

Davis, Tom, 1967–
    A legacy of madness : recovering my family from generations of mental illness / by Tom Davis.
      p.   cm.
    ISBN 978-1-61649-121-5 (softcover)
    1. Davis, Tom, 1967–   2. Davis, Tom, 1967—Family.   3. Mental illness—Social aspects—United States—Case studies.   4. Mentally ill—Family relationships—United States—Case studies.   5. Children of mentally ill mothers—United States—Biography.   6. Mentally ill—United States—Biography.   7. Suicide—Social aspects—United States—Case studies.   8. Families—United States—Case studies.   9. Intergenerational relations United States—Case studies.   10. Hillside (N.J.)—Biography. I. Title.
    RC464.D38A3 2011
    362.196'890092—dc23
    [B]

                                      2011031933

Editor's note
The names, details, and circumstances may have been changed to protect the privacy of those mentioned in this publication.

This publication is not intended as a substitute for the advice of health care professionals.

13 12 11 1 2 3 4 5 6

Cover design by David Spohn
Interior design by David Spohn
Typesetting by BookMobile Design and Publishing Services

CONTENTS

Preface   VII

Chapter 1   The Awakening   1

Chapter 2   Awareness   21

Chapter 3   Paradise Lost   47

Chapter 4   The Working Life   69

Chapter 5   The Sobering Life   95

Chapter 6   The History   127

Chapter 7   The Blues   151

Chapter 8   Eating Disasters   175

Chapter 9   Deliverance   201

Chapter 10   The End Is Just the Beginning   221

Epilogue   255

Acknowledgments   271

About the Author   275

PREFACE

A CENTURY AGO, THE SYMPTOMS of mental illnesses such as schizophrenia and multiple-personality disorders, among others, were well-known. But there was a dearth of treatment options that could have saved the millions who suffered. Many people with mental illness were locked away in psychiatric hospitals—or facilities commonly known as "asylums"—and treated in decrepit, inhumane conditions.

At the time, on October 4, 1928, my great-great-grandmother, Lydia Winans, and her son, Frederick, ended their long, yet troubled lives by flipping on the gas jets of their kitchen oven and suffocating themselves. Five years later, Lydia's other son, Edward, did the same thing, taking painstaking care to make sure that he was more successful in death than he was in life. They found a way out because there was no way back in, since their only alternative was evaluation, medication, and then a world of confinement or mistreatment.

All three were believed to have suffered from symptoms that would eventually be identified as obsessive-compulsive disorder or neurosis: perfectionism, low self-esteem, depression, and fear. None of them were ever diagnosed, because all of them likely feared the consequences.

In the 1950s and 1960s, psychotropic drugs that could have alleviated my family's symptoms of mental illness became more prevalent. My grandfather, Richard, who was Edward's son, saw many of these advances while serving as personnel director at Greystone Park Psychiatric Hospital in Morris Plains, New Jersey. Ironically, he was a sufferer himself; some say he took the job because he saw much of the same sickness in the patients that he saw in his family—and maybe even in himself.

Instead of seeking treatment, however, Richard, who was known as Dick, chose the path of his ancestors, using alcohol to suppress his own symptoms of obsessive-compulsive disorder (OCD)—particularly his perfectionism and fear of germs—that would eventually overwhelm him too.

As my mother Dede battled postpartum depression in the late 1960s, she became an alcoholic, and her fear of germs became much more pronounced after her third pregnancy. She was the first member of my family to be treated for mental illness; as a result, she was the first to be diagnosed with obsessive-compulsive disorder. Like her father Dick, she was ultimately overwhelmed by those symptoms. She died in 2003, decrepit physically and emotionally, never having fully recovered after two long stints in Ancora Psychiatric Hospital near Camden, New Jersey.

As my mother's condition steadily deteriorated, my brother and I suffered from anorexia and bulimia, and I have been diagnosed with obsessive-compulsive disorder. I have, at times, found myself heading down a familiar destructive path, and I've sought assistance through counseling, psychiatric treatment, and medication.

But I feel like I'm on the back end of a long, perilous ride that came to a head on January 18, 2003, the day my sister found my mother dead.

I never feel safe.

Even after generations of my family suffered, and died largely because of their inflictions, my family had very little contact with mental health professionals, and we read very little material that could have guided us as we battled the symptoms of mental illness. We knew my mother's repeated hand washing, her fear of germs, and her stubborn possessiveness were signs of neurosis. I knew my tendency to force myself to vomit as a way to relieve stress and fear didn't seem right. But we followed the path of self-destruction rather than treatment, largely because we chose the path of ignorance and fear. Treatment and the unknown, downright scary consequences of it were, as many say, a fate worse than death.

We knew that many of the same problems that existed when my grandfather was personnel director at Greystone, from 1949 to 1979, remained. Housing at mental health facilities was still overcrowded. Treatment options and insurance coverage to pay for them were lacking. Psychiatric facilities that took insurance, and provided what could be considered the right level of care, were scarce.

Perhaps most important, the stigma of diagnosis has been, and still is, the kind of thing that could destroy a reputation, kill a career, and ruin a life.

Since I was a child, I've often wondered why I am so imperfect, why my mother wasn't a so-called "typical" mother, and why my father was so stressed about it. I had the belief that other people didn't experience the same issues. I'd see people participate in sports or Cub Scouts and they just seemed too perfect. To me, they always seemed to have "perfect" clothing, to be "perfectly" groomed, and to be "perfectly" mannered. My family was jealous, because we knew we'd never be like them.

Now, as a parent, I've come to understand that the so-called perfect people are often more imperfect, more ignorant, and more helpless than I had ever imagined. Standing on a playground for an hour and talking with parents whose children play with your children can lead to some interesting revelations. You find out things about others that are surprising, if not shocking.

I still encounter people who don't fit the image of people who are suffering through mental illness. But, once I get to know them, I ultimately learn that they're experiencing some sort of dysfunction that is very familiar to me, and they're suffering through the same sort of crises.

In fact, as a person who won a Rosalynn Carter Mental Health Journalism Fellowship and has written extensively on mental illness in families, I'm viewed as sort of a sage on the subject—particularly since my mother died and I sought ways to learn more about why we are what we are. What I tell my friends is perhaps the first lesson I learned after my mother's death:

Knowledge is power.

I write to the people who feel powerless because of their inability to understand or help others suffering from mental illness. I want to connect to the compassion people have for others who are suffering. Those who are dealing with mental disorders may be people in the reader's family or someone they know.

They're definitely in my family.

CHAPTER 1

THE AWAKENING

March 2003

"WOODY GUTHRIE AT GREYSTONE" was a photo exhibit of the folk singer's stay at Greystone Park Psychiatric Hospital in Morris Plains, New Jersey. While looking at the photos, I was struck by the hospital's Gothic-style architecture, so different from another psychiatric hospital that once housed my mother within its bland, concrete walls.

In the photos, I saw vast expanses of grass and trees, long sidewalks that snaked through the hilly campus, and stately nineteenth-century buildings with Romanesque columns. The mountainous backdrop made New Jersey look more like Utah, with large white clouds hovering just above the peaks. The "main building," as it was often called, had bars on the windows. You may never leave, the bars seemed to say.

I thought I knew everything about Greystone. My grandfather worked there for thirty years as its personnel director. I had heard about how my grandfather, my grandmother Dorothy, and my mother Dede lived there at the same time, paying cheap rent for a multi-family house, and about how my mother would look out her bedroom window and brood over the "lunatics running wildly outside." This was where she was forced to live her teen years, at an age when many develop their first perceptions of humanity. My mother had wanted to be anywhere but there. My grand-father, on the other hand, always spoke of the place with reverence, act-ing as though it was a castle and he was its king.

Even after hearing these stories, I never got a real sense of what it was like to be there, to live there and endure the despairing atmosphere that seemed to permeate through the aging, decaying walls. In those pic-tures, I saw it. In Woody Guthrie, the man who wrote the iconic song "This Land Is Your Land," I could see the pain of Huntington's Disease through his forced smiles as he struggled to survive there in the 1950s and 1960s.

The exhibit was at the Teaneck, New Jersey, headquarters of the Puffin Foundation, a nonprofit group that supports art and musical programs. The exhibit hung on the walls while an event on Mideast peace was tak-ing place. I was there for an assignment for my newspaper, the *Record of Bergen County*, New Jersey, but as speakers took to microphones and talked about the Arab-Israeli conflict, I was distracted. The black-and-white photos of the folk singer with the clenched teeth at the mental hospital transfixed me. *I wonder if my grandfather knew he was there*, I thought. *I wonder if my mother knew he was there.*

My grandfather had passed away in 1991, and my mother had died two months before I saw the exhibit. So I was left to my imagination. I looked at Guthrie's face and wondered if he endured something similar to what my grandfather and mother endured. They weren't patients, my mother and grandfather, but they were forced to look at the same things and make peace with the same elements as he was: barred windows and "lunatics."

When the event ended, I ran into a colleague, Mary Ellen Schoonmaker, an editor at the *Record of Bergen County*. I pointed at the pictures of Guthrie being visited by his family on the grounds of Greystone. "My mother lived there," I told her. "She was probably there at the same time he was."

"Wow—how did your mother deal with that?"

"I don't know if she ever did."

I then told her about my mother and my grandfather and about how the rest of the family put up with their bizarre behavior—severely obsessive-compulsive behavior, in fact—that wasn't diagnosed until it was much too late, but had dominated our lives for so long. I talked about how they both soaked themselves in alcohol as though they were numbing a pain. I told her about Ancora Psychiatric Hospital in South Jersey where my mother was committed twice. I told her that I had often walked around Ancora, my teeth clenched like Guthrie's, smelling the urine and observing the zombie-like patients. When my mother was there, dealing with the frequent screams of the residents and the constant stench of urine, I thought *I should write a story on this.*

"You should," Mary Ellen said. "Why don't you do one for us?"

Two months later, I did, writing an article on the last five years of my mother's life—beginning with her bladder operation in 1998 and ending with her death in 2003—which was published in the *Record of Bergen County* in May 2003. The article, "Trapped by Mental Illness . . . and a Health-Care System That Failed Her," followed my mother's journey through a series of assisted-living facilities, nursing homes, and Ancora as her illness clouded any sense of logic and prevented her from getting the care she needed. The writing went well as I easily found words to describe the pain and heartache of her final years. Recalling the scenes of her despair brought it all back to life for me and reminded me why I went into writing in the first place: to learn from others and to educate.

Afterward, I sent it to just about everybody I knew. "This was the best thing you ever wrote," some said. "I never knew you went through this," others said.

For me, the day I had that article published, a cause was born. I had fourteen years of service in journalism, but I had grown jaded by the changes in the field, the diminishing quality of news reporting, and the low pay. I felt as though I finally had some sense of purpose, and journalism would be my tool. I would discover what really killed my mother. I would discover the causes of mental illness—and, of course, the possible cures.

I had had many of the same impulses as my mother and grandfather, enduring years of eating disorders and obsessive compulsiveness. I wanted to know why we were the way we were, and whether there was some family curse that I was failing to stop.

The first way to learn, I thought, was to learn about others who have endured similar issues. After the article was published, I started writing a column on mental health issues for my newspaper that won praise from a variety of advocates and mental health groups. From there, I used my work as a springboard toward acceptance into the Rosalynn Carter Fellowships for Mental Health Journalism program, for which I completed a reporting project on the treatment of the mentally ill in jails.

༃

Ironically, I was motivated by people like Woody Guthrie and the singers he inspired, such as Johnny Cash and Bruce Springsteen. All of them sang about the powerless and the imprisoned and, to use Springsteen's words, how it's "more than this" that compels people to behave in an odd manner or to perform unspeakable acts.

Springsteen, in particular, was an inspiration: I was a Jersey Shore kid who always connected with his songs because many of them were about me—the poor working stiff who couldn't catch a break. He also wrote about how it's more than evil that drives people to go insane and kill people for money, drink, or drug to the point that they get behind the wheel and drive into a wall. He wrote about how it's more than sinister for someone to choose a life behind bars, and how the imprisoned often come to either regret what they did or fail to understand why they did it.

To me, Ancora Psychiatric Hospital was like a prison, and the patients were its inmates. The hospital looked very much like the jails I had visited in Texas and Alaska for the fellowship, and the patients who walked around in jumpsuits looked much like the prisoners who lived in jails in San Antonio and Anchorage.

The journey, however, never felt complete. After I wrote the Carter Center series, prisons continued to be the primary home for the mentally ill, and psychiatric hospitals continued to be decrepit, downtrodden shelters that—as they did with my mother—forced patients to leave long before their treatment was finished because they didn't have the space or the money to keep them.

I entered the Columbia University journalism master's degree program in 2007 and was accepted into an acclaimed book course taught by Sam Freedman, a respected author and Columbia professor, in the spring of 2009. He was struck by my story of a family that could never get out of the way of itself. He saw me as a person who wanted to lift the curse by educating himself and others.

We both agreed that the best way for me to begin this journey was to look back on that day, January 18, 2003, when we found my mother. That event, more than anything, was the "awakening" of my life. It was the moment that illuminated every little suspicion I had of her and her illness, and that brought back all the troubles my family suffered through, going back to when I was three years old and used to think to myself, *Mommy's crazy.*

January 2003

I let my four-year-old son Tommy call my parents' house in Point Pleasant, New Jersey. It was a whimsical thing to do, something to erase the boredom of a January day, just weeks after Christmas, when the wet, ten-degree weather in New Jersey leaves a kid's skin chapped and itchy. Having him call seemed right, and cool, because it was something that could always make the grandparents say, "Oh, how cute."

I wanted my son to get to know his grandparents and see them in ways he hadn't before. I wanted him to know them away from the mental health facilities, doctors, and patients who had dominated my mother Dede's life in the years before he turned four. I often took him to the nursing homes and assisted-living facilities where he'd see these people, and then hide beneath my chair and wait anxiously for the visit to end. Or I'd take him to my old home, in Point Pleasant, where my mother's moods ranged from chipper to downright gloomy to, on occasion, plum drunk. Sometimes she'd be sitting in her living room chair, passed out after drinking from the case of Budweiser cans she stuffed in the refrigerator.

In 2000, I took Tommy to see her on Mother's Day at Ancora Psychiatric Hospital, where she spent two months before moving, reluctantly, to Rose Mountain Care Center, a nursing home in New Brunswick, New Jersey, just a few miles from my home in Metuchen. At Ancora and at Rose Mountain, Tommy played around my feet, rolling cars along imaginary roads on the carpet while my mother ranted about the food, the people, and the care, repeating, over and over, about how much she desperately wanted to go home. Tommy jumped to my side and grasped my arm every time he saw people hunched over, moaning, or talking to themselves.

By January 18, 2003, my mother had been in Point Pleasant for sixteen months since leaving the nursing home—her longest stay at her home in nearly five years. Finally, she was showing signs of stability, even recovery. She was still obsessive, filling the freezer with five or six containers of Breyers vanilla ice cream, and only eating an occasional spoonful every few days or so while leaving the rest to freeze. She still felt the need to shove cold, creamy food down her esophagus to quell the burning sensation of acid reflux that constantly tinged her throat.

At home, Dede still peppered my father Stan with repeated questions: "Am I going to be okay? . . . Are you sure I'm going to be okay? . . . Do you still love me best of all?"

She was still drinking coffee out of oversized mugs, filling them to the top, to the point that drips were spilling over the side. My father got a health care aide, and then another, and yet another, all of them eventually leaving because they couldn't deal with my mother.

But the fears she had about her debilitated body—all of which had finally forced my father to take action and seek help from an endless list of counselors and physicians—had finally abated. She no longer stuffed the refrigerator with six-packs of Budweiser and Michelob—cans she drank to numb herself from herself and the world. She stopped fretting about her bladder, the one that was successfully fixed in an operation in 1998, but had initially left her worried about the post-operative effects.

"I think there's something wrong with me," she'd said for years after the operation. "I think they didn't fix it right."

She also stopped taking medication that, in the rare times she had taken it, seemed to stabilize her mind and personality. Whenever she stopped, she'd plunge into a depression that would compel her to take a taxi to the liquor store, buy two cases of beer, bring them home, and drink until she passed out, with her head hanging off the side of the living room reclining chair. Or her moods would swing so wildly that we fully expected to get a call from a neighbor—as we did once—reporting that she was in her stocking feet, standing on somebody's lawn, fretting that the nurse's aide was out to kill her. All those incidents usually led to another visit to the emergency room and, if she talked of suicide, would land her in a nursing home, assisted-living facility, or, on two occasions, Ancora Psychiatric Hospital.

Once she left New Brunswick's Rose Mountain Care Center in September 2001, she finally seemed to tire of that life of getting pulled out of her favorite chair in the living room, where she spent countless hours watching news programs, to be hauled into a treatment program that would never treat her. For those sixteen months, she was showing flashes of her old charm, smiling through her tired face, crumbling legs, and shrinking arms. She seemed safe—and sane enough to be the grandmother she never really was. She even tried hard to connect with my boys Tommy and Jonathan whenever they came to visit, using much more effort than she had earlier when Tommy would play around my chair at the nursing home.

On January 18, 2003, around 5 p.m., I instructed my son on what numbers to push. Usually, either my father or no one answered, because my mother always refused to answer the phone. She sat in that same reclining chair all day, even though she never reclined in it. Her knee was too wobbly, and the muscles in her thighs and calves had atrophied, making her legs look like sticks. It was just too painful for her to get up, even though the phone was ten feet away, hanging on a wall.

This time, Tommy heard a click, and then wondered aloud why a panicked woman's voice was coming from the other end. "I don't know who it is," he said, handing me the receiver, his brown eyes opening wide. "It sounds like a woman."

I moved it closer to my ear and heard the voice of my older sister Carolyn.

"Thomas," she said. "Mommy died!"

"What?"

"She died!" she said, sobbing. "You've got to come here."

I hung up. Tommy looked at me. "What? What happened?"

I looked at him and his sweet brown eyes. He had seen enough of the tragedy of my mother in recent years. *Should I tell him?* I wondered. *Does he really need to know this?*

"Grandmommy died," I said.

Tommy looked at me, his face pale, and walked into the living room. He bowed his head, but didn't cry. He didn't seem to know what to do. Frankly, I didn't know what to do either.

ॐ

That day was like most others of the previous sixteen months. My mother woke up early, no longer staying up until 3 a.m. and passing out over beer and potato chips as she did as far back as I could remember.

No longer was she waking up at noon and getting dressed at 3 p.m., tired and hungover from her own little parties with booze and chips. On this day, as she had been doing lately, she was in the reclining chair by 8 a.m. and in day clothes by 11 a.m., wearing everything but socks or stockings for her feet.

The television was on as soon as she got up, with the sound low. She used to enjoy the conservatives who yakked a lot on the cable news programs. She'd watch them and bash Bill Clinton, yearning for the days of her favorite president, Ronald Reagan. She'd watch the faces of Pat Buchanan and Wolf Blitzer on the screen, staring at them for hours, only shifting her attention when my father or the nurse's aide walked by.

At the time, my father was mostly sleeping in my sister's room. For many years my parents shared the same bed, even when my mother's behavior filled him with rage. The bladder operation in 1998 was the tipping point—the final straw for my father. My mother's repeated questions and obsessions increased after her operation, so much so that my father couldn't handle it.

"There's something wrong with my bladder. . . . Don't you think there's something wrong with my bladder? . . . I don't want to get another operation. . . . Is there something wrong? . . . I think there's something wrong with my bladder."

He appeased her and took her to several doctors who all said the same thing: "Your bladder is fixed. It is no longer a problem."

But she didn't believe it.

"Dear, what if they're wrong? . . . Something doesn't feel right. . . . There's something wrong with my bladder."

Like the nurse's aides, my father threatened to leave a number of times; he even visited with a divorce lawyer. He ultimately stayed with her, saying the divorce lawyer warned him that he stood to lose a lot of money by leaving her, particularly if she needed long-term care. But he also grudgingly admitted that he never stopped loving her, even when she drove him crazy. He never gave up hope that the woman he had married in

1959—a sweet, loving, and charming woman who had had many boy-friends before him—would return. Whenever she flashed her smile, he saw the same woman he fell in love with, and he always hoped that that person could somehow resurrect and rebuild herself.

As soon as he woke up, he was usually out, heading up to the Ocean Grove beach cottage that my mother inherited from my grandfather after his death, and disappearing until night. He took long walks on the boardwalk, went to the movies at a second-run theater in Bradley Beach, watched television, and worked as a part-time desk clerk at a nursing home. He enjoyed being alone, but even more so, he yearned for a life without someone being as dependent and obsessed with him as my mother was. Even as my mother showed signs of stability, he still wasn't getting the life he wanted, the one he had hoped for when he married her more than forty years before.

After my father retired from his school principal job in 1996, he tried to play the role of the domesticated retiree, spending much of the day with my mother. He began to experience many of the things we as children had dealt with when we came home from school: she turned the heat up to eighty degrees on a sixty-degree day, taped the cookie boxes with electrical tape so we couldn't share, fussed whenever we were in the kitchen hovering near her food that sat on the stove or the kitchen counter and breathing our germs near it. He began to escape to Ocean Grove, about ten miles to the north, rarely taking my mother with him. If he needed to communicate with her, he spoke with her on the phone.

꒜

On January 18, my mother woke from her bed in the Point Pleasant house, waddled on her wounded leg to the living-room recliner, while my father headed out to the movies. It was a Saturday, not the typical day for news shows. My mother got up from her chair once, around 3 p.m., leaving a message with my father at Ocean Grove to pick up the mail there.

She also got her coffee in the kitchen and walked toward the mailbox that hung outside. She would sit in her recliner, like she did every day for hours at a time, and look through the mail.

She opened the heavy door, then pulled out the screen door, feeling the frozen breeze of the ten-degree day on her bare feet. She leaned her small, rickety frame on the wobbly hydraulic closer as she reached for the mail that was sticking out of the box, being very careful not to touch the cold cement porch with her feet.

The closer snapped and my mother fell face-first on the cement. She didn't stick out a hand to break her fall. The force of the fall was so strong that blood gushed out of both nostrils.

A neighbor who saw her lying on her face hustled across the street and helped her back up, supporting her as she reentered the house and helping her to her chair. The neighbor got some paper towels from the kitchen, which my mother used to blot the blood coming from her nose.

"You okay?" the neighbor asked.

My mother waved off any additional assistance. "I'm okay," she said. "It's okay. I'm okay."

The neighbor left as my mother continued to sit and blot her nose with the towels.

Within the next half hour or so, something—we don't know what—compelled my mother to get out of her recliner and rush toward the telephone in the family room at the far end of the house. She ignored the one that was closest to her, choosing the phone that sat on the old dusty bar. There she leaned against the rim of the bar while she pushed the buttons on the phone, trying to reach my father in Ocean Grove.

She called my father, I thought later. *She didn't call 911.*

My father still wasn't home from the movies. My mother left a panicked message on the answering machine. "Dear, something has gone terribly wrong!" she said in a rushed, breathless voice. Then there was more heavy breathing before the message ended.

She left the phone off the hook and made it across the kitchen before she collapsed on her back on the couch. The phone receiver dangled in the family room, making the loud buzzing noises with an operator message: "If you'd like to make a call, please hang up. . . ." No one was there to hear it.

ॐ

Around 4 p.m., my father returned from his movie in Bradley Beach to the Ocean Grove house. He listened to my mother's message and then tried to call home, getting only a busy signal. He called my sister.

"Could you go to the house and see what's going on there?" he asked.

On this day, in 2003, Carolyn was the natural choice to check on my mother. My brother, Edward, lived three hours away in Maryland. I lived an hour to the north. Carolyn stayed the closest to the family and our history, never moving more than five miles away from my mother or father. Carolyn lived in Manasquan, so she was much closer than my dad to where my mother was. She drove a few minutes to get there, pulling into the wide driveway around 5 p.m. and seeing the dark house.

Of the three of us, Carolyn was the child who suffered the most. She was the oldest and the one who was beaten the most by my mother when my mother started to show signs of illness. She struggled to have a relationship with my father, since my mother would often act nervous whenever she saw them together, just as she did whenever we were near her food in the kitchen. My mother didn't want my father near any women except her, and if he did spend time with Carolyn, he was subjected to the routine interrogation.

"What did she say? . . . What did you two do together? . . . What did she say, dear? . . . Can you tell me what she said? . . . Are you going to do anything with her later? . . ."

To Carolyn, the long, burnt-blue ranch was still home, even if it reminded her of everything she went through growing up. It was the darkest home on a street filled with 1950s ranch houses, a little slice of modest Jersey Shore suburbia that had recently become one of fastest-growing regions in the country. Beginning in the 1980s, the wealthy began to buy what property was left, building two- and even three-story mini-mansions that they claimed as "beach houses," even if those homes were three or five miles from the water's edge. On our block, the small, single-floor houses remained, reminding people of what Point Pleasant once was before the wealthy came: a blue-collar, middle-class refuge for people looking to escape the growing crime and ugliness in Newark and New York City.

When my sister arrived, she saw my mother lying on the couch, almost directly in front of the picture window. Carolyn rushed over to her and tried pick her up. She couldn't move her, or even bend her.

ᘓ

Tommy had called just minutes later. Tommy and I, as well as my one-year-old boy, Jonathan, had spent the day doing little of anything. I was deterred by the cold weather and my own exhaustion, having just returned from a reporting trip to Fort Drum near Watertown, New York, where I had interviewed troops who were gearing up for the upcoming invasion of Iraq.

My father arrived just as I called back again and heard my sister's heavy words. "Here—talk to Daddy. . . ."

"I did everything I could!" my father cried into the phone, sobbing.

"I know you did," I told him.

I then called my wife, who was at work. On Saturdays my wife worked in the city running an acting school for children. I always hoped that on Saturdays she could avoid the stresses of parenthood. Not on this day.

"Oh my God," she said. "I'm so sorry, Tom." She arranged for a neighbor to come to the house and watch Tommy and Jonathan, our youngest, who had been napping through all this. The neighbor arrived minutes after I got off the telephone, and I immediately headed south.

Throughout the hour-long drive, my mind raced. *Wow. I can't believe it. What do we do now? What does this mean?* I was still tired after the long, four-hour drive I'd made from Watertown, New York, the day before.

I yawned, but I couldn't cry. At times, I thought, *Why am I not crying?* I never felt the urge. I asked myself repeatedly *Why? Why? Why?* but never asked *Why did she die?* I asked myself *Why did it have to be this way? Why couldn't we be normal?*

When I got closer to Point Pleasant, I found myself on Route 34 and other roads I used to take when I drove back and forth to school in Rutgers in the late 1980s. My mind drifted back to those times, when I used to take those lonely drives home—especially after Jessica, my old girlfriend, left me.

Jessica was my first love, and I loved Jessica as much as I loved my mother; her leaving me sparked a fifteen-year battle with eating disorders that I could never completely shake. I saw those exit signs that pointed to roads that led to Jessica's old house. I felt chills. Again, I asked myself *Why? Why? Why?* It was the same question I asked myself when Jessica left me, when I felt as though my soul had been ripped out of my chest. It was the same question I asked whenever I made myself vomit in the months after we broke up and I lost nearly sixty pounds during a sixty-day stretch in 1988. *Why? Why? Why?*

The wide four-lane roads near Jessica's house that led to my parents' burnt-blue home in Point Pleasant were always so dark and empty in the winter. The darkness only fed my loneliness and pain. Other than the radio, there was little that could fill or replace the emptiness I felt around and inside me.

I arrived in Point Pleasant around 6:30 p.m. The house was now the best-lit one on the block, with a police car spinning its red lights and the big picture window fully lit and exposed. I pulled behind the cop car and got out. The cold air had a sharp, wet bite to it. But I barely felt it, even though I was wearing the same thin, blue sweatshirt I had worn the day before on my trip from Watertown.

⁓

My mother lay there on the couch, her legs stiff as wood, eyes closed, and mouth wide open. She looked like one of my children's dolls after they'd finished with them: lifeless and done. *God*, I thought, *if only my mother could see herself now.* She hated people knowing about her health problems. How could she hide being dead?

It was hours after she collapsed when I saw her. She was on the couch, but apparently she had been on her way to the bathroom, where she always hid in times of crisis. She always hustled to get there, pumping her arms as she dragged her weak right leg across the kitchen and living room floors. She'd slam the door and run the water for an hour, washing her hands until they were red and flaky. Then she'd sit on the toilet, and try to force out every drop of urine from her swollen bladder after drinking nearly a half-gallon of coffee.

By this time, the streams of blood from her nose had created streaks of red that had dried up under her nostrils. Her arms were locked at her sides and the heels of her feet dug into the carpet, preventing the rest of her stiff, ravaged body from slipping off the couch.

I screamed.

My sister and brother-in-law grabbed me and pulled me into the family room, through the patch of police officers who were carrying notebooks and listening to their radio calls. My father stood to the side, watching as my face contorted into a scream.

"If she would only take the damn medicine" was one of the first things I heard him say, minutes after I had entered the family room.

I'd heard him say that a hundred times. It was always his cry for help. Going back to November 1998, when my mother's thirty-year battle with mental illness was first addressed and we made our first visit to a psychiatric emergency room after she threatened suicide, my father would rant and rave about his inability to solve her problems. He hoped that whoever was in the room at the time was listening. No one ever seemed to be.

My head was so blurred with confusion, anger, and sorrow at that moment that I couldn't yet feel what was probably the most logical feeling: relief. It was the end of five years of hell, five years of bouncing around mental health facilities, assisted-living facilities, and nursing homes. It was the end of five years of fighting over psychiatrists, medicines, doctors, healthcare aides, and nurses.

It was the end of a life that never quite fit in the world. My mother had spent her life tolerating it, but never really accepting it. Her aversion to pills and doctors, her incessant repeating of questions, her constant worrying about spots or pimples she saw on her hands and arms, and her drinking at the kitchen table, keeping empty cans of Budweiser and a bag of potato chips at her side as her head fell to the table's surface—it was all over.

It was the end of decades of suffering from obsessive-compulsive disorder and its bedeviling symptoms that divided a family and destroyed a life.

At sixty-five years old, she was finally at peace.

ᘓ

After seeing my mother, stiff and lifeless, I felt something I didn't expect: fear. I had a bond with my mother that transcended bloodlines and, to some extent, sheer logic. I often felt as though I was my mother, just as she, too, probably felt like her father, as we both embodied his quirky obsessions and mannerisms and struggled to live the "normal" life that always seemed so distant.

My grandfather, in turn, was like the people before him, suffering from the same self-destructive urges that were nearly impossible to control for him and his ancestors—some of whom killed themselves. I felt that my mother and I had the same compulsions, urges, and quirks that forced us to confront and, sometimes, succumb to the worst challenges of life, and we dwelled on the lingering, ugly certainty of obsession, pain, and death.

When I saw her cold, stiff body, I remembered how I could feel her sense of isolation whenever she obsessed, and how everything she did made her different from all the other mothers I heard about at school. I felt fear because I saw my future, because I realized I had many of these same obsessions that had caused my grandfather to resort to drinking more than a half-case of beer each day.

They were the same obsessions that had challenged and doomed the lives of his father, uncle, and grandmother, all of whom died when they isolated themselves in their houses, turned on their stoves' gas burners, and breathed in the fumes. These same obsessions nearly compelled me to take my own life when I threw my guts up in college four to five times a day, ripping the will to live and succeed out of me.

In my mother's final years, I felt her pain and weaknesses, but I also shared her strength and stubbornness. In the end, her body was contorted and twisted, with a leg that was as stiff as a wooden plank and a face and hands that looked as if they had been scraped with Brillo pads. But she kept holding on, limping on her leg even after she fell several times on the sidewalk and scratched her face. She refused to let her ailments change what she was or what she wanted to do.

I felt her love, even when that seemed nearly impossible. She could be mean, even brutal, as well as distant and perverse. But the hard mask covered a soft soul. She wouldn't let us kiss her face, forcing us to plant one under her ear. But she wanted us to kiss her anyway, even if the germs from our lips may have, in her mind, endangered her health. She had a loud laugh that was infectious, and she often worried or even cried when any of her three children—or even her dogs—suffered.

She loved pets and young children. She held them tightly in her lap despite her fear of germs, dirt, and anything that normally drove her away. When I sat in her lap as a young boy, I could feel the touch of her palms as she rubbed them up and down my spine. I could sense her loneliness when she felt cold and she hugged me tighter. I could feel her fear whenever she descended into a raging argument with my father, and I climbed into her lap, worried that she would go.

I hold my children the same way. Even as they grow older, I keep them close, just as she did with me when I was small.

I also fear for my children, because they, too, could have inherited what seems more genetic than coincidental. My wife and I worried about it before we had them; we worry more about it now that we have three, and we worry we'll see certain signs and symptoms arise that will give us reason to believe that history could repeat itself.

If those symptoms do arise, we will keep holding our children and never let go.

⌇

In my mother's final years, I didn't need her hug, but I tried to show my love anyway. I scouted around and found a nursing home close to my house that I hoped would bring her the stability she needed. My wife and I visited her twice a week, and even as the decline of her body and obsessions kept others away, it was a way for us to stay as close as possible.

After she died I wanted to be the one to do something, or something more. I wanted to be the one to do something about this curse, to do the research and discover the background of our life. While I had long known something was amiss, something about that moment on January 18, 2003, and the events that led up to it, would force me to address what it was about this family that made us seemed destined for self-destruction. I would have to find out more about my family, because that was the only way to find out more about myself. I would have to find out what brought me there, with my mother in the other room, dead, and what could have been different.

Indeed, the events of January 18, 2003, were a metaphor for my mother's life, and those before her. Even in her moment of need, she couldn't get help.

ॐ

By the time I was whisked into the family room, I felt nothing and saw nothing. My eyes were closed shut. After my brother-in-law and sister took me in, I slowly opened them.

"Is it over?" I asked.

"Yes, Thomas, it is," Carolyn said.

"Good," I said.

I stayed in the family room with the family, waiting for my brother, Edward, to arrive and for the cops to leave. "I don't want to go back in there," I told everybody several times. "Don't," they told me.

Even when the police removed the body, and when Edward arrived, I stayed in the family room, sitting in another reclining chair and hanging my feet off the side, far away from the spot of her fall. My sister and brother-in-law left to take my ten-year-old niece back home. My brother and I sat alone in the family room, leaning back in our chairs, analyzing the day.

ॐ

I always felt comfortable talking to my brother. I always felt he was the one who was most like my dad: disciplined and determined. He succeeded in school better than all of us, and he had a common-sense approach to life. He was the only one among us who could fix a wall, build a bike, or chop down a tree. Only three years apart, we were friends as well as brothers.

We talked about how we'd seen it coming, even though it still came as a surprise. We talked about everything that had happened, even before the previous five years, when her behavior went into a tailspin after that bladder operation. We talked about our guilt and how we felt we could have done more. We talked about how we felt we had not done enough for her, even though, in those last years, we did a lot.

We talked about how we saw ourselves, and how we would have to deal with our own lives and prevent the same thing from happening again. I talked about myself and my own battles with eating disorders, and as I did every time I brought it up, I felt a little relieved to be talking, though a little embarrassed too.

As I looked at my brother, I saw a person who bore the brunt of my mother's illness but always seemed strong enough to take it. Unlike me, my brother Edward stood up to our father whenever my mother's obsessions drove our father into rages. Because of this courageousness, Edward took the whacks to the face.

On this night, however, Edward didn't seem like his typically confident self. In the family room, he sat far away from me in a stiff metal chair he had brought in from the kitchen, and he held his head low. As I talked about myself, after a few minutes he finally looked at me kind of sadly, wrinkling his mouth, leaning back in his chair and taking a deep breath as he waited for me to finish.

"You know what, Tom?"

"What's that?"

"I've never told anybody this before," he said. "But I used to make myself throw up too."

CHAPTER 2

AWARENESS

March 1970

My journey of discovery began when I was three years old in 1970. I sat in the living room, watching *Sesame Street*. My mother was fussing with the thermostat, just as she always did unless there was blazing heat outside.

Her playing with the dial almost always drove my father into a rage, and they'd launch into a Vaudevillian routine that rivaled anything from Abbott and Costello.

"What do you think? I own the oil company?" he'd say.

"I'm cold," she'd say, flashing her bright smile as a way to charm him away.

"We don't need to turn it up to eighty," he'd say.

"How about seventy-five? . . . Can we keep it at seventy-five, dear? . . . Can we keep it at seventy-five?"

"Okay, fine, seventy-five."

"Let's keep it at seventy-five, dear."

"Fine! Seventy-five!"

"Can we keep it at seventy-five forever and ever?"

"Look, don't start with me!"

"Can we keep it at seventy-five forever and ever?"

"Yes!"

"Do you promise to be nice to me? . . . Do you promise that we could keep it at seventy-five?"

"Stop repeating!" he'd yell. "You don't need to repeat it, okay? I heard you."

"Do you promise to love me best of all?"

"Yes, yes."

This time my father wasn't around, so my mother got to fuss with the thermostat at will. As she fussed with it and drew her face close to the dial to get a better look at the small, black numbers, I blurted out what immediately crossed my mind as I watched her.

"Mommy?"

"Yes, Thomas?"

I paused, waiting for her to turn away from the thermostat so I could look at her face.

"Why do you repeat?"

My mother's mouth popped open. I couldn't tell, at the age of three, how she planned to respond. Would she grab a garbage can and hit me—as she often did with Carolyn and Edward, my older sister and brother—to make me understand how naughty I was? Or would she let it go so that I could resume being—as she said again and again and again—her "favorite"?

Even at that age I knew we don't talk about *these* things. My sister and brother knew it, because if they ever talked back or questioned anything, it was usually met with a yell, a scream, a garbage can, or a backhand across the arm or face. Or at the very least, they would have to endure the repeating, which could be as painful as any punch or slap. "Talk nicely to me. . . . Promise? . . . Promise to love me forever and ever? . . ."

This time, my mother paused shortly, seeming a bit flustered. She came up with an answer that, perhaps, she thought sounded good, at least to a three-year-old.

"Because people can't hear me," she replied.

Then she walked away, disappearing into the bathroom and, as always, running the water for what seemed like an hour. She always went in there after fights with my dad or after yelling at my sister and brother, as though she were washing away all the tension she could feel in her body.

As she washed away, I sat there, blankly staring down the hallway at the shut bathroom door, trying to piece it together. I knew we had tension and trouble. I knew people said things to each other they didn't really mean. I didn't think anybody was trying to be anything other than what they were—loving, caring, and respectful, especially my mother, whom I worshipped to the point of adulation.

I didn't think anybody *lied*.

But right then, I knew my mother had lied to me, and by going into the bathroom, she wanted the lie to live, without guilt or consequence. Even at the age of three, I knew: if what she was doing was so innocent, then why would people react so angrily?

Feeding me that line firmly established the protocol for behavior in our family: ignore it, and it will go away.

I loved my mother more than anything. I trusted her and took sides with her always. But as the years went by, I often reflected back to that moment when I was three. I saw what was happening to my father as he raged and yelled at my mother for the repeating, her hand washing, her less-than-stellar cooking, her constant questions, her long bathroom visits, and her thermostat fussing. I saw my brother and sister despair over their lives and bear the brunt of my father's frustration. I always thought it was their fault, that they unfairly made my mother the target of their venom. With me, it was always "mother knows best," even when my mother washed her hands until they were flaky red or made me wash my hands whenever I touched the floor. *Why are they so upset?* I would ask myself. *She's just looking out for us. She wants us to be healthy.*

But as I grew older, I started to see everybody else's point of view, and I became more curious than trusting. I also knew that it was better to shut up than speak out, even as I watched our world falling apart. If I did speak out, I knew the best thing that could happen was that I'd be lied to. The worst thing was a beating. Ignore it, and it will go away. That seemed to be my family's credo, the foundation of our life together.

Back then, my mother would whisper to me, from time to time, that I was her "favorite." For some time, I believed it. For some time, I saw her more as the victim of the tension and never *really* the cause. I was the one who still got to sit on her lap and be hugged when my mother had long given up doing the same to my brother and sister. I was the one she smiled at, about whom she said, "He's so smart" while my brother and sister were standing right there, seething as they watched me get the princely treatment.

I was the one who screamed one time, pounding my fists on the table when my mother dared to go outside for five minutes to talk to a neighbor. Afterward, she came in and picked me up and promised to never do that again. She didn't, and she let me sit in her lap even more.

Sometimes she made me repeat too. "I'm sorry," I would say. "I love you best of all."

Sometimes I would get upset because I didn't get a toy I wanted or get a cereal I wanted to eat for breakfast. But when I told my mother "I'm sorry" and "I love you best of all," I meant it, and I was willing to say it over and over until I forgot about the toy. She was my protector. She was my soul mate.

At a certain point I started washing my hands if I merely touched the floor. I started to worry and fuss over dying, crying over fears that I was going to die of some disease caused by a germ that I couldn't see or stop. I worried about this stuff because Mommy worried about it. Like her, I asked whoever was in the room whether I was going to be okay. "Are you sure? . . . Am I going to be okay, Daddy? . . . Why do I have a bump on my skin? . . ."

"You're going to be fine. Stop worrying," he'd say.

But I didn't. After all, I was my mother's son.

ༀ

Over time I developed more empathy for others in my family. My sister Carolyn could be funny and witty, always quick with a quip or riddle to break up the monotony of the fights and tension. My sister would opt for restraint in her battles with my parents, choosing to settle—as my father did—for answering my mother's questions and moving on. It was either that or take another round of laying in bed, gripping the bed post, and letting my mother hit her with a trash can.

My brother Edward carried the most angst. As I grew older, he and Carolyn would talk openly about how much my mother and father were driving them crazy. They were tired of eating hamburgers that were burnt because my mother, worried about exposing herself and her family to germs, burned the meat we ate until it was entirely black and gray. They were tired of being shut out of the bathroom while my mother flushed the toilet four times, ran the water continuously, and then suddenly emerged an hour later, leaving behind a sewer smell while her hands and face looked redder after each visit.

Edward and Carolyn, like my father, were tired of the repeating, of being forced to affirm her constant questions.

"Do you love me best of all? . . . Promise? . . . Promise to be nice to me forever and ever? . . . Promise to love me forever and ever? . . ."

My brother, at a certain point, openly declared war. He frequently challenged my mother and her quirky behavior, fearlessly questioning her for taking so long in the bathroom.

"Um, talk nicely to me, Edward, do you hear me?" she'd say.

"No!" he'd answer.

My mother would then chase him down the hall and grab him.

"Do you want me to tell your father? . . . Talk nicely to me, okay? . . . Promise? . . ."

He often questioned my father, challenging him even when he was furious after having another go-round with Mother. Edward had a scientific mind, putting everything into formulas and openly questioning when things didn't add up. He had a sense of social justice, and he sought to right the wrongs that were happening.

"I can't eat this hamburger," he'd say at dinner.

"Why?" my father would say.

"It's too tough."

"Eat it and stop being a crankpot!" my father would shoot back.

"I can't eat it," Edward would insist, cringing as he sloshed the hard crust around in his mouth.

"Just shut up!" my father would say.

"What did I do?"

"Just shut up or I'll knock you across the room."

My brother would keep going. And going. And going. My father wouldn't give in to my brother like he would with my mother. In the end, their exchanges would end in similar ways: my brother backed into a wall with my father's arm pressed against his neck. Or my brother would get slapped on the arm. And, as Edward grew older, take a backhanded shot across the face, leaving a bloody mess around his nose. My father displayed the same rage he showed toward my mother, only he followed through with Edward, doing what I long suspected he dreamed of doing to her: intimidating her to shut the hell up.

༄

My father often tried to divert attention away from our troubles, hoping against hope that he could create the all-American family. On some level, he succeeded. He took us on trips across the country—trips that were part hell, because my mother's obsessions would often prove to be too much for my father to handle on two 3,000-mile driving trips. But we had many moments of fun and intrigue. I was always a bit of a nerd, so I enjoyed my father's fascination with going to presidential birthplaces for Truman, Lincoln, and others out west. He was a history teacher, and although we preferred to go to amusement parks like many children, I had just as much fun sitting in an old chair that Calvin Coolidge had sat in. If it put a smile on my father's face—a smile we didn't often see—it put a smile on my face too.

My father could also be playful, usually when nobody else was looking. We'd be on some 500-mile stretch of road across Ohio, taking the long, hard way across the country. He'd wait until my mother dozed off, and then I'd look up and see my father making chimp faces in the mirror. I laughed, but I tried to never laugh too loudly. If I did, the others would wake up. Then the fun would stop.

As I grew older, I became more aware of what my mother was causing. No one could get past her, and the mood would often be despairing as my father, brother, and sister struggled unsuccessfully to deal with her. They took out their rage against each other, because they didn't have the stamina to do it against her.

At times, they could be charmed easily by her and warmed by her smile, her laugh, and her affection. But my brother and sister also felt burned by her every time she repeated, hit one of us, threatened to take the punishment further, or threatened to "tell your father."

My father also felt burned every time she asked for self-affirmation, and after years and years of this, he eventually saw what he once hoped would be the perfect family life slip away.

ᔥ

In August 1973, my mother's spirit and her ability to show love and comfort toward her family were virtually shattered by a visit to the beach.

The fact that it was the beach made it worse: The beach was the one place that provided comfort for my mother, the one place where she didn't seem to care about dirt or germs. She swam in the water and sat in the sand, never worried about what was in it. It was a love handed down from her father, my grandfather, who had treated the beach as a refuge from his own troubled childhood. Both were swimmers, often traveling with my grandmother to Bradley Beach, where they rented rooms for the summer when my mother was a teenager. There they took to the tides, often swimming far out—sometimes so far that the lifeguards blew their whistles to call them back in.

On this day, one of my last pleasant memories was watching my mother wading in the Manasquan, New Jersey, surf, laughing as water washed up on her ankles. Her smile was radiant on that bright, clear day. She was still a slender woman, even with the pounds she'd put on after she stopped smoking three years earlier. Her brown hair was starting to gray, but her playfulness and her beach-inspired spirit gave her the impression of youthfulness. On this day, she slapped at the water as the waves came up and laughed as Edward and I ran from the water that washed up on the shore, only letting it touch our toes before the tide pulled in.

Then for what seemed like a half hour, my mother disappeared.

"Mommy?" I asked as I looked around and tried to pick her out from the other women wading in the shallow water.

After splashing my legs through the waves and seeing others looking up the beach, I finally found her. My father was carrying her, walking up the beach toward our car. I could hear my mother moaning and, at times, screaming, "Don't let them hurt me! Oh, it hurts so much!"

A crowd hovered around as my sister grabbed my brother and me and rushed us toward the car.

Is she dead? was my first thought.

My mother had been knocked down, twice, by a body surfer. She had gotten up, albeit a little shaken after the boy with a big frame, probably a teenager, knocked her down the first time. The second time, he came roaring in and landed on top of her. He caused my mother to twist the bottom half of her right leg, from the knee down. Then he took off, leaving my mother behind while she sat in the cloudy water, crying for help.

As we left, sitting in the car, my mother was still moaning and crying as my father tried to reassure her.

"It's going to be okay," he said, struggling hard to be calm. His teeth were clenched as he looked at her and nodded his head.

"Are you sure?" she asked, sobbing. "Are they going to operate? . . . Are you sure I'm going to be okay? . . ."

He was driving my mother to the hospital, forsaking an ambulance because he thought the car ride would be faster. My mother seemed more concerned about the hospital than the injury.

"I don't want to go to the hospital. . . . Am I going to be okay? . . . Promise me that I'm going to be okay. . . ."

I sat between my brother and sister in the backseat, and started to sob slightly as I watched my mother fret. When my father dropped us off at a neighbor's house before heading to Point Pleasant Hospital, I cried. "I want to go! I want to go!"

"You have to stay here," my father insisted.

"But I want to go! Mommy! Mommy!"

I stayed, watching several hours of television with my sister and brother nearby. We sat passively as we watched cartoons and sitcoms. For the most part, the television screen was a blur during that time as I sat, worrying and fretting. *Is she going to live?* I kept asking myself. *Am I going to see her again?*

Occasionally during a commercial, my brother and sister would turn to each other and talk. Their tone was more resigned than stressed, each more concerned about what was going to happen after my mother returned from the hospital than how she was doing. "How's she going to handle this?" they asked each other. "You see how she handles things already. . . ."

My mother had suffered a severe sprain, tearing the ligaments around her knee. She spent much of the night in the hospital, getting a cast that wrapped from her foot to her waist.

For months she had that cast, which sometimes rendered her helpless, laid up and needy, while other times made her stubborn and even resourceful.

"Oh, dear, please have them take this off me!" she would cry to my father.

"They can't do that—you have to let it heal!" he'd insist.

She often asked for help with simple tasks, like having my father turn on the television and asking him one more time, "Am I going to get better? . . . Will you still love me? . . . Do you love me best of all?" Yet she often limped on her bandaged leg to the kitchen so she could get a big mug of coffee in the morning, or several cans of beer at night. She walked on it a lot, pushing her routines as my father sought remedies.

The only one that seemed logical was an operation, and as he saw her work through her injury by limping around and balancing on the plaster cast, my father started to see it as the only choice.

"I don't want an operation!" she would say. "Please, take it off."

"You have to have an operation!" my father demanded.

"Please don't operate. . . . Promise not to operate? . . . Please, I'll be fine. . . ."

At my mother's insistence, the doctors took the cast off before her injury appeared to completely heal. The bottom half of her leg was still twisted to the right, and her toes were pointing in the wrong direction. Her leg had become a corkscrew, probably caused by the excessive walking and limping that she insisted on doing, even though she had been told that was a bad idea.

The doctors' insistence on operating became stronger, as did my dad's. But my mother was even more stubborn.

"No! I can't do it," she told my dad. "I don't want an operation! Promise me? . . . Promise me that they'll never, ever operate? . . ."

Ultimately, she had some physical therapy, but she quit after a few sessions. She returned to her normal routines, limping around the house, favoring her right leg with the twisted toes and corkscrew knee. The bathroom visits became longer and the late-night drinking heavier. She often indulged in Budweiser until she passed out on the kitchen table at 2 or 3 a.m.

After the accident, germs were no longer a mere nuisance to her. They became her bitter enemies. If we wanted to kiss her, we had to plant it farther and farther from her mouth. I would manage to catch a piece of her cheek sometimes, causing her to pull out a towelette and wash that side of her face. With each kiss, however, I remember feeling how dry her face was, and scaly.

Still, I would often rationalize it, even as something about it resonated with me and made me remember it forever.

Maybe she'll live a long life, I thought. *She's germ free.*

My mother also started gaining a lot of weight, growing a big belly within a year after the accident. During the day, she ate an Entenmann's chocolate-chip loaf that she kept in the refrigerator, sealing it with electrical tape so she could have it all for herself. If one of us removed the tape and touched it, a new box would appear, with more tape wrapped around the box.

My brother grew concerned about her behavior. Once he broke into the garbage bags in the garage and counted the previous night's consumption of beer. There were six empty Schaeffer cans, my father's favorite. There were sixteen empty Budweiser cans.

"Holy shit," my brother said, after dragging me in to see it. "She drank more than a half-case of beer in one night."

Briefly, we considered a game plan or an intervention. Maybe we needed to talk to Daddy. We both asked ourselves *Is this right? Do people normally drink this much?*

Instead, we let it go. We knew the risks. Ignore it, and it will go away.

꙳

My father, Stan Davis, first saw signs of trouble after my birth, in 1967. Until then, in his view, my mother was the best mother. She doted over my brother and sister, spending hours hugging them or holding them in her lap. She sang songs to them and took them to the grocery store, usually taking turns carrying one so they wouldn't have to walk the whole way. She was charming, engaging, and outgoing, taking the children to the neighbors' houses where she'd drink coffee while Edward and Carolyn played quietly with the other children.

With my mother, my father thought he could create the perfect family that he had not had as a child. His father drank heavily and beat him, and his mother died when he was eight years old. His father remarried, but young Stan disliked his stepmother so much that by the time his father died of Lou Gehrig's disease in 1955, when Stan was nineteen, he vowed to never have anything to do with her again. A few years after he and Dede married, they saw Stan's stepmother browsing in a department store, and he refused to introduce his new wife to her.

Together, they moved to Point Pleasant, New Jersey, a Jersey Shore community then known more for its beach and weekend tourists than its small-town, family-oriented lifestyle that was quickly developing, just as thousands from North Jersey and New York moved in during the 1950s and 1960s. He bought a house on the cheap and they began a family immediately, with Carolyn, the oldest, born ten months after their marriage.

My mother was especially pleased to be free of my grandfather. He had always been a suffocating, overly paternalistic presence to her, rarely letting her make a decision without his approval. If she had a job he didn't like, she had to quit it. If she had a boyfriend whose hair was too long, she had to dump him. If she wanted to go out on a date at night, he'd wait up for her—and berate her if she came home too late.

Right after their 1959 marriage, my mother gladly moved to the mostly undeveloped beach town—where some of the main roads were made of dirt—that was two hours away from her home in Morris Plains.

She embraced the role as homemaker while my dad worked as a teacher and then as a principal beginning in the mid-1960s.

Right after my birth, my mother began to withdraw, refusing to leave the house—whether it involved driving or walking—for months. She refused to go shopping, forcing my father to go to the supermarket. She started to sleep later and later, wear her nightgown later into the day, and drink more heavily.

"Do you think I need a psychiatrist, dear?" she asked my dad. "Do you think I need one? . . . Do you think I need a psychiatrist?"

"No, no," he replied. "You're going to be fine. Stop worrying!"

As the years went by, her moods started to swing from delightful to violent. She mostly took out her aggression on Carolyn. My father, frustrated by her changes, focused his anger on my brother—particularly when Edward moved into puberty and began to question why things were the way they were.

The knee injury was the final hammer on the nail. The drinking that had been occasional became habitual. Her repeating, which had been a quirky tick, increased. The worrying and fussing over germs became a staple and a stamp on her character.

My father thought the best solution was to give my mother what made her happy: travel and restaurants. His solutions were true to his nature: dry, conservative, and pragmatic. He never sought any deeper solutions, such as medication or therapy. He also was forever thrifty, never believing that money could be thrown at a problem to solve it. His feel-good methods were intended to bring happiness and shut everybody up.

In 1975 and 1976, he drove us across the country—twice—stopping at low-rent motels along the way and, on our second trip, staying at campgrounds—some of which looked more like Mogadishu than Missouri or Minnesota. Some of them had black water coming out of the shower faucets and bugs that looked as big as small birds. But Dad saved enough money on the motels and campgrounds that he could pay for the restaurants, and we went to many of them from coast to coast, starting with Denny's for breakfast and moving on to Howard Johnson's for dinner.

༃

The more we traveled, though, the more the trips seemed to promote the problems that were there, even fan the flames of tension. There were deepening divisions in our family that prevented us from truly enjoying each other.

On our trip to Los Angeles in 1975, the car broke down an hour into it, in Pennsylvania. For nearly six hours, we tolerated each other in blistering summer heat as we stayed at a Pennsylvania Turnpike rest area, waiting patiently as the car was fixed and my mother indulged in repeating.

"Do you think we'll make it, dear? . . . Are you sure? . . . Do you think the car will make it? . . . We're not going to turn around, are we, dear? . . ."

After the eight-hour trek to Ohio, the loosely tied Samsonite suitcases that were attached to our roof rack slipped out and scattered all over Interstate 70. My father, full of steam and curses, jumped out of the car as we sat silent and scared in the car, watching him gesturing wildly to stop the trucks and the cars that nearly ran over the path of clothes and suitcases that lined the lanes of the road. When he returned, his face red with anger, he had to listen to my mother.

"Are the suitcases okay? . . . Should we find a laundromat? . . . What if the suitcases aren't okay? . . . What if I can't get the dirt out? . . ."

Along the way, my brother sat with his arms folded, his legs spread out, bumping me whenever I got too close.

Edward often complained about having to stay at trailer parks and passing by the signs for Busch Gardens and other amusement parks without ever visiting them.

"I can't stand this," Edward would yell.

"Shut up!" my father would yell back.

"Why can't we go there?"

"Just shut up."

Perhaps the lowest of the low moments came on the second trip, when we did an even longer trek, hauling a trailer nearly across the country, eventually finding ourselves in Seattle before driving 1,000 miles south to San Francisco. It happened when my mother burped at the picnic table at our trailer site, and my father shot my brother a look.

"Say 'excuse me'!" my father yelled.

"For what?"

"Say 'excuse me'!"

"I didn't do anything!"

Edward got up and left the table and my father ran after him and pinned him against a tree by pressing his elbow into his chest. My mother and I sat silently and watched, until I happened to meet my mother's eyes with my own.

I looked at her, incredulous. *You burped!* I thought and said with my eyes. *Do something!*

She then raised a finger to her mouth and formed a "ssh" with her lips, warning me subtly. Shut up, Tom.

If anything, the trips pushed my father closer to his *own* lunacy as my mother peppered him with questions while we rolled along the long, barren roads of Indiana, Wisconsin, and Montana for thousands of miles, usually only stopping for gas, eating, and sleeping.

"Can we eat out tonight, dear? . . . Can we eat at a restaurant? . . . I don't have anything to cook—can we eat at a restaurant? . . . Can we do that, dear? . . ."

My father would be so annoyed by the hassling that he could barely control himself, yelling, on occasion, "Shut the hell up!"

My mother would return the volley. "You shut the hell up!"

A fight would ensue that would last as long as it took us to drive across Colorado. In the backseat, my sister and brother would eventually fall asleep. Awake, I would worry as our parents both yelled "divorce" at each other, each threatening lawyers until my mother would ultimately get my father to make up.

"Do you promise to love me best of all? . . . Do you apologize for what you said? . . ."

Those fights would continue into the night as we took our bags up to the motel room or set up the trailer at a campground. Edward and I would sleep next to each other at one end of the trailer, and we would hear the two of them rage on until my mother began her "Do you apologize? Do you love me forever and ever?" routine.

I'd hear my brother slip into sleep. Once, I asked him, "How can you fall asleep when this is going on?"

"What else can I do?" he said. "They shouldn't be married anyway. Maybe they *should* get a divorce."

I didn't want that. I wanted my mommy and daddy together. While my brother snored in the background and talked in his sleep, I stayed up and listened, hoping and praying that my father would give in like he always did. Sometimes, that wouldn't happen until 2 a.m. But it would happen, and then, finally, I'd fall asleep.

~

Though he was cranky and frustrated about his life, my father could also be a generous soul. Even as he endured the trips with my mother and dealt with her obsessions, he agreed to take my equally obsessive grandfather with us to Florida in April 1976, just four months after his wife Dorothy, my grandmother, died. The six of us jammed in a station wagon and headed south, driving 1,000 miles, once again, only stopping for gas, motels, and restaurants.

Richard "Dick" Winans, my grandfather, had complained about being lonely and despondent over her death—though, based on his history of irreverent, drunken behavior, no one could ever be sure whether he was telling the truth. He had angered my mother by leaving my grandmother alone as she was dying of heart disease and he disappeared for hours at a time, taking two bottles of booze with him as he drove around northern New Jersey in his Chevrolet Impala. He spent much of his time either taking a shower—by the time my grandmother died, he was taking as many as six a day—or drinking. His antics never seemed to end; indeed, they only seemed to get worse as the drinking increased. Others in the family, and even friends who knew him, warned us about how Dick was just letting himself go.

My grandfather had always been the dapper, buttoned-down administrator who demanded the same kind of organization and respect from his employees at Greystone Park Psychiatric Hospital. By the 1950s and 1960s, however, as the stress of working there wore on him, he took to the bottle, developing a distinct taste for vodka and beer. My mother grew closer to my grandmother as Dorothy grew more distant from my grandfather. By the late 1960s, the once suffocating relationship between father and daughter became a tense one as my mother, then older and more strong-willed, began to despise Dick's increasingly irresponsible behavior.

Sometimes my mother blamed Dick for Dorothy's death, accusing him of neglecting her after she suffered a neck injury in 1969. The injury idled my grandmother, preventing her from taking the long walks she had enjoyed. After the injury, Dorothy's relationship with Dick, which was already icy, became irreparable. Dorothy, who had attained some wealth in inheritance, had grown so tired of Dick's drunken antics that when she died, she left my mother tens of thousands of dollars in bonds, but left her husband nothing. My grandfather was enraged, threatening to take my mother to court. He never made good on his threat, though, as alcohol took more and more of his focus.

Through it all, my mother and grandfather managed to stay in touch, even as each grew more suspicious of the other. Indeed, their relationship was impossible to fathom. Both whined every time they felt pain.

Both worried whenever they were dirty and washed themselves repeatedly. Both fought like cats and dogs, usually hurling insults at each other until they tired and descended into silence. Both also had a strong sense of family and worried—or displayed concern, at least—whenever they heard the other was sick. They were honest with each other whenever they talked. They made each other laugh, because they liked to tease, even if the teasing could be a little insulting.

Even I felt a kinship with Dick. He reminded me of my mother a bit, and not just because of his obsessive need to stay clean. Both could have a goofy but dry sense of humor, never afraid to needle somebody about something silly or stupid. My grandfather was always trying to win over my dad by using flattery, and even pomposity, flaunting the money he had attained from a rich cousin's inheritance he received years before.

"You're so smart," he'd tell me. "Someday, we'll send you to Princeton."

People told me that I looked a lot like my grandfather or that I was the spitting image of my mother. For much of my early youth, I took those comments as compliments.

My father sensed this kinship and had the notion that—despite the struggles we endured by traveling to California and Florida before—a trip could bring everybody together and have everybody love each other in a Waltons family kind of way.

Just months after my grandmother's death, Dick agreed to play nice, saying he would behave himself if only he could go to his favorite place, Florida, the place with the year-round beaches. Beaches were always his ultimate escape.

Seventeen years into their marriage, my father had a wife who washed her hands until they were as scaly as fish skin. He also had a father-in-law who took to beer like a baby takes to milk. With this trip, he was hoping to spark something in a family that was having a harder time, year after year, liking each other.

The best thing that can be said about the 1976 trip, which we took when I was nine, was that everything my grandfather did overshadowed—and practically negated—my mother's quirks. The first time we stopped at a restaurant, my grandfather ordered highballs. He got drunk and banged his knife against a glass, yelling at the waitresses: "Miss, I need help! I need help!" He sounded like a wounded animal. "Miiiiiiissss!!!"

Soon after we got to the hotel in Miami Beach, he went out for a jog in a park nearby, disappearing at a time when we were supposed to be getting ready for dinner. Edward and I ultimately found him. He had gone for a jog wearing his full suit, jacket and tie and all, even though it was eighty degrees. His shirt had been pulled out of his pants, but the tie still had a perfect knot, just as it always had been when he worked at Greystone and kept up his appearances.

Often, we had to wait to go eat because he was in the shower, taking his regular four to six a day. When he did show up ready for dinner in his full suit, he would wait for us by lying on the couch in the lobby of the hotel—passed out after drinking nearly a case of beer. One day, my mother confronted my grandfather as we waited in the car in the parking lot.

"He passed out," she said when she returned. "I woke him up and he said, 'Where am I?'"

One of the last straws of the trip came when Dick agreed to babysit. He kept me in his hotel room while he showered, dressed, and slapped aftershave on his cheeks. He left soon after, disappearing until 2 a.m. and forcing my mother, who had no idea that he would leave, to sit up with me.

"Where were you?" she asked when he finally walked in.

"I was out on a date," he said, his shirt pulled out of his pants again, although his tie still had a good knot. His speech was slurred and his gait was heavy.

"I can't believe you would do this," she told him. "It's so irresponsible."

"You just watch out," he said, his body hovering on his wobbly legs. "Remember that I'm your father."

On our next-to-last day in Florida, my mother and grandfather got into a big argument, which ended with my mother demanding to go home. Before it erupted, my brother and I had stayed with him and watched him get sloshed. He pulled beer after beer from the refrigerator, tore off each can's top and slugged down its "ale" in nearly one gulp. By the time he was done, he was waddling, trying to show us his gold watch and how it worked. He was drooling slightly as he talked.

Again, as we prepared to go to dinner, he was too plowed to move quickly. My mother was angry. "I can't believe this," she said as she paced outside his hotel room, where he was still drinking and showing us the watch.

When he finally emerged, he was carrying a can of ale and was bare-chested.

"When is this going to stop?" my mother asked.

"I'm sixty-two and you're thirty-eight and you can't talk to me that way," my grandfather yelled after my mother confronted him. She'd called him "irresponsible" and "nutty."

Dick never went on a family trip with us again. Instead, we went on trips ourselves, enduring the long hours and struggling to survive as we shared each other's quirks. Or we stayed home and watched television movies that showed some kind of life that wasn't remotely close to our own. These movies provided us with low-cost escapes that didn't require any driving, eating at restaurants, dealing with relatives, or listening to repeating.

The more we did it, the more we realized maybe *this* was our therapy.

ↄ

Often, I watched television with my father, who usually sat in the family room, silently sipping from a half-empty Schaeffer beer can as I sat next to him, his eyes fixed on the screen.

On one night, in 1977, when I was ten, I remember him being particularly quiet as we watched a movie called *The Amazing Howard Hughes*, a forgettable TV flick starring Tommy Lee Jones that, for reasons I never expected, I would never forget. I sat next to my dad, fidgeting every so often as I scanned the *Daily News* sports section, studied the baseball standings, and occasionally looked up at the screen. Every so often, the TV emoted sounds of screams, car crashes, and a plane humming through the sky and skimming tree tops. I tried to ignore it, but the noise was so loud and real that I wondered if it was coming from the street.

Occasionally, my mom passed through the small, dimly lit room with shadowy dark, brown panels to get to the garage, where she kept her sizable supply of full Budweiser cans packed inside a 1950s Frigidaire. I glanced at her as she waddled through, and then I refocused on the television.

"What's on?" I asked.

"Just some movie," my father said.

"What's it about?" I asked.

"It's about Howard Hughes," he said. "He was one of the first billionaires."

"Is it good?" I asked.

"Mm, hmm."

My father rested his chin on the palm of his hand, tilted his head, and clamped two fingers on his cheek. I focused back on the newspaper, flipping between the comics and sports. But I remained wary of the TV, struck by the sounds of death and destruction that always startled me, even if they weren't real. *Is that happening outside?* I'd think. *Could that happen to me?*

By then, my father had become both a loud and quiet man, showing little interest in middle ground. He liked to sit quietly in the chair while jacking up the volume of the TV and watching anything from soft, gentle flicks to shoot-'em-up gangster movies. He could sit at the dinner table and say nothing for an hour, but then vent and yell at anything and everyone for ten minutes, usually harping about politics—he was a fan of Reagan and an enemy of Carter—and his job. He raged about the parents whom he felt demanded too much of him at his elementary school in Brick Township, where he was known as a mild-mannered principal who was fair to everybody.

At home, however, he occasionally yelled and blamed us for making his life miserable. When the trips failed to solve his problems, he was resigned to the idea that he would never get the family life he wanted.

He would be out in the garage, installing a drop-down ceiling for an hour before realizing that all the panels were cut the wrong way. "No one wants to help me, goddammit!" he'd yell, usually at Edward, who would courageously offer advice only to get it soundly rejected, every time.

But he was also the steady rock in a home with a lot of unsteadiness. As my mother drank and ate bags of potato chips, her moods swinging up and down, my dad would be the one to talk to, even if what he had to say was little more than an "mm, hmm" or "that's good" as he watched television.

Sitting near my father while he watched television and I flipped through a newspaper was one of his quiet moments, a too-rare bonding moment in a house that was breaking apart. Usually, when we did this, I buried myself in a newspaper, shutting myself away from the bloody sounds from television movies such as *Helter Skelter*, the story of the Manson murders, or the censored television versions of *Serpico* and *The Godfather*. They were so brutal and violent that I couldn't bear to watch. The newspaper was my protection, and the comics reminded me that I lived in the sleepy Jersey Shore town of Point Pleasant, not the mean Manhattan streets depicted in *Serpico*.

This time the movie featured Tommy Lee Jones wearing a pilot outfit, flying around in an airplane, and crashing into buildings. Or he was sitting in a director's chair, reshooting scenes repeatedly because they were just never perfect enough.

Somewhere, halfway through the movie, I found myself fixated: Tommy Lee Jones, as Hughes, was running his hands under water, repeatedly. I heard the sound of soapy hands slapping and sloshing together. He rubbed and rubbed and rubbed, using a small plastic scrubber to get under his fingernails and scrape around his knuckles. Then he repeated it, running his hands under water, then rubbing the water between his fingers before applying the soap again, and then the scrubber, and then the water. The camera zoomed in on his hands, focusing on the soapy suds swishing around and covering his palms and his wrists. Then it zoomed out and showed the other characters with horrified looks on their faces as they intently watched.

I turned my head toward the kitchen, where my mother was sitting at the table, staring straight ahead as she chugged down Budweiser beers and grabbed heaps of potato chips, crunching on the chips with her mouth wide open. She had just retired a six-pack. She kept a box of Wash'n Dri moist towelettes in her lap that she used to clean her lips and all sides of her hands. The used, drying towelettes were slipping off her legs, landing on the floor, and creating a pile. She carried the towelettes everywhere, filling up her pocketbook and taking them into restaurants on those cross-country trips. In restaurants, she'd pile them on her knee and throw them on the floor when she was done with them, turning the floor under her chair into a compost pile.

I looked back at the television and then back at my mother, who was still sliding a hand-wipe around her fingers.

Oh my God, I thought. *That's Mommy!*

I wanted to blurt it out loud. I wanted to stand on the chair and thrust my finger at the screen. *That's Mommy!* I wanted to say. *She's got something wrong! There it is! Can you see it?*

For me, all those years of fights and name-calling and tension, all those years of wondering why she did what she did and why everyone seemed to get so mad about it, were illuminated in a manner of seconds. For so long, I had been led to believe that everything she did, or everything we did, was good enough. Sure, it was weird, and the more I saw her behave, the more curious I became. Sure, finding half a case of empty beer cans in the garbage bag was scary, and the more I saw her drink, the scarier it got. But I usually gave her the benefit of the doubt, even as I grew more curious. *Maybe all mothers do it too*, I always thought. *Maybe germs are a legitimate threat.*

I listened to my parents fight when my father would curse and scream for divorce and my mother would wear him down.

"Do you apologize?"

"Yes, yes."

"Will you love me forever and ever?"

"Yes, yes."

"Promise? . . . Promise that you'll love me forever and ever?"

"Yes, yes!"

Sure, it was weird. But, I thought, *Maybe everybody does that. Don't everybody's parents get into fights?*

At the same time, I felt my mother pulling away from me, isolating herself behind a wall of towelettes, no longer the person she had been when she called me her favorite. She had stopped calling me that by the time I was six. By the time I was ten, in 1977, she had kicked me off the one place I felt secure, her lap. As I got older and bigger, heavier and dirtier, she couldn't support me, especially as she nursed her aching bones and twisted knee.

She still grabbed my hand and rubbed my fingers. She still gave me a wide, charming smile. She still took me to stores, even the liquor store, and let me tag along as she bought clothes to overstuff her closet, clothes she never wore. Just as she did with my dad, she made me promise to love her, forever and ever. I promised and I meant it.

But it wasn't okay. Nothing was okay, and this low-budget TV movie was my epiphany. As I watched this TV movie, *The Amazing Howard Hughes*, I started to realize who my mother was. I started to think of my grandfather and how much he must have inspired her, because they were so much alike. He was the older, taller, and slimmer version of my mother. Like her, and like Hughes, he self-medicated until he was numb and washed himself until his skin flaked, while manipulating others into believing that he was okay.

I started to think about all the signs I had seen before, and how I, we, let each of these quirks slip by without doing anything to stop them—as if we could.

In the movie, an aged Hughes lay on his back and filled his body with drugs, numbing himself from pain just as my mother numbed herself with beer. I stared at my dad, who sat there, his chin still resting in his hand, expressionless. *How could he just sit there?* I thought. I wanted to say something, even shake him. *Mommy's sick!* I wanted to say. I sat in the chair with my hand shaking and my heart racing. *Maybe he'll say something first,* I thought. *Maybe I'll just sit here and wait.*

That was the day I knew. That was the day I learned I lived a life that was different from others' lives. I vowed that someday some way or another, I would figure out why. I thought of myself. I could be another link in the chain as my fears of germs grew worse and worse. I could be my mother, and I knew I had to do everything in my power to prevent that from happening.

For that moment, though, there was little I could say or do. I thought of my brother being pinned against a tree, and being threatened to have his block knocked off after he was falsely accused. I was afraid of being punished for saying what was supposed to remain unspoken.

I was no longer three; I was ten, no longer cute and innocent enough to get away with a "Why do you repeat?" sort of question. I sensed that. Any thoughts I had of changing the way things were would have to wait, or else I'd risk losing whatever security I had in an insecure family.

I didn't say anything to my father that day. Instead, I sat with him and we quietly watched the rest of the movie. I felt that my father and I were conspirators in that moment, united in ignoring what was so clearly present. I almost felt close to him. Ignore the problem, and it will go away. In a way, it was a family tradition. Who was I, at ten, to break a tradition?

CHAPTER 3

Paradise Lost

November 2008

THE RAIN FELL LIGHTLY, creating little puddles alongside the narrow road. The sky at the Hillside, New Jersey, cemetery was dark gray, making the late November afternoon feel like night. I pulled my car to the side and looked out my window. Tombstones filled the lawn surrounded by mud and small streams of water that ran downhill, washing away the dying grass.

Evergreen Cemetery is where my book research began. My father told me about it, saying how he and my mother visited the vast graveyard right after they were married. He remembered it being unpretentious and bland, with markers too small to see unless you stood next to them. No markers honoring the military are allowed, and the tombstones are relatively modest and small. But there is a lot of history: Stephen Crane, the celebrated author whom some believe was a family relative, is buried there.

"Maybe there's something there," my father said. "Maybe they can tell us what happened."

The day before, my Columbia University professor, Sam Freedman, had accepted me into his acclaimed book seminar course. My proposal to him was to write a book on mental illness in my family and how three generations—at least that much—were brought down by things they couldn't control. I told him I suspected there were even more members of my family felled by the same kind of illness that destroyed my grandfather and mother. He accepted me, even though I told him that it was only a rumor—that I was working on a hunch, not doing formal research. When I was accepted, I was shocked. Sam Freedman is a professor known for being particular in his ways and a stickler for solid reporting, documented and well-guarded facts. All I had was a memory; somehow, he thought that was good enough.

I still felt that the subject matter had some big holes that needed to be filled, and I needed a solid foundation before I started digging too deep. I figured there were relatives somewhere who carried secrets to their graves, and I figured that I owed it not only to Sam, but also to myself to make sure my idea was fleshed out—and the family pattern exposed—before the writing began.

I was curious about Edward Winans, my great-grandfather, the one I had always heard about but never really knew. I wasn't sure whether the story of him I'd heard for many years—that he had stuck his head in an oven and ended his life—was real or some tale my mother or grandfather just made up to get attention. As I learned back when I was three years old, it was certainly possible that my mother was lying.

I knew I had to go to this Evergreen Cemetery. At the very least, Evergreen would provide atmosphere, and maybe a little inspiration. I would get a feel for a family that was an Elizabeth, New Jersey, mainstay since colonial times. Maybe I'd find out what eventually broke them down, and whether these were indeed graves for people in my family who, like my mother and grandfather, died before their time.

Neither my grandfather nor my mother was buried there. My grandfather Dick was buried by himself in a cemetery in northwestern New Jersey, just a few miles from the Pennsylvania border, in a plot near one that could be planned for his second wife, Dora. "I don't want to be buried near my relatives," he often told people. His second wife obliged.

My mother was buried in a small graveyard in Point Pleasant, just two miles from the house where she collapsed on that cold January day in 2003. Her plot is next to my dad's, and even though the two of them had their battles, my father declared that it will be his final resting place.

By the time I began the book research, my father had long moved on from the tragedy of my mother. He was even dating people and eventually moved to Manchester. But he was still hungry for answers and reasons why this seemingly normal American woman's life would end so tragically. He wanted some reason, some justification for why he stuck with her for so long, and why he never followed through on getting a divorce, even though he threatened it many times.

When I drove past the pillars that marked the cemetery entrance, I found the office and pulled off to the side to call my dad. As the wet drizzle worsened, I jogged to the door of the cemetery office, carrying my laptop computer bag on my shoulder. As I walked in, I saw two women sitting in cubicles, tapping on keyboards.

I asked about Edward Perrine Winans, a name that my father gave me, but wasn't sure of the spelling; the woman beyond the desk pulled out an index card from a box. She found it amid hundreds of cards that contained the names of the dead and the plots in which they were buried among the damp, rolling foothills of the Evergreen campus.

"Section I, plot 30," she said, pausing as she looked at the card. She gave me a strained look, with a crooked frown.

"Would you like to know anything else?"

"Um," I said, pausing slightly. "If you have anything, sure."

"It says, 'Edward P. Winans . . . Death by Gas Asphyxiation.'"

"*Really?*" I said, reaching for the card. "Let me see."

She slid the card on the counter and pointed to the words. The typing was from seventy-five years before, uneven and dark, but as clear as any computer printout. The words were as concise as they were incredible:

"Edward P. Winans/Death by Gas Asphyxiation."

I felt like slapping myself in the head. *What?* I thought. *Is this for real?*

Thoughts popped into my head, and passed through like a speed train. *How could I not know this?* I thought. To be forty-one and not know this? All these years, I could have just driven a few miles from my home in Metuchen and easily confirmed something everybody thought they knew, but weren't really sure. I could have confirmed something that not only satisfied my curiosity, but could have helped me and others who wanted to know why we are what we are.

I could have driven up there when I was at Rutgers, twenty years before, when I was in throes of eating disorders. I could have gone there instead of sitting in the Rutgers library, plunging through encyclopedias to find information about whatever disease I thought was affecting me, compelling me to make myself puke, because I thought puking was good for me and was the only way I could cure myself of whatever was making me feel sick.

I could have gone to Evergreen in the late 1990s, when my mother was bouncing around assisted-living facilities, unable to find the right care, or find anybody who wanted *to* care. I could have taken the photocopy I got of the cards to the nurses who gave up on her when they couldn't handle her repeating and her obsessive demands. I could have shown those people who refused to take care of her when we called 911, after she broke a coffee pot in a drunken rage or passed out on the reclining chair after drinking two six-packs of Budweisers. *See!* I would have said. *She is crazy, goddammit. Now do something about it!*

Even after seeing the card, with the evidence of some genetic curse more solid than ever, I still had a nagging doubt. I knew I had impulses that I couldn't control. I already knew I had a history, just as my mother had a history, of mental illness. I already knew my grandfather spent a third of the day in the shower, and the rest with either a bottle of beer or a glass of vodka in his hand. I knew that, whatever normal is, I wasn't it.

But I still wondered. *Doesn't every family go through this? Isn't there a little bit of wackiness everywhere?*

๛

I thought of my great-grandfather Edward's date of death—July 12, 1933—when the nation was knee-deep in poverty, unemployment, and despair. During the Great Depression, with nearly a third of the population out of work, suicide rates increased from 14 per 100,000 in 1929 to 17 per 100,000 in 1933. *This could be a fluke,* I thought. *Perhaps it was the Depression—sane people jumped out of windows after the stock market crashed. Maybe he thought the gas was just easier.*

I stood in the cemetery office, feeling a bit bewildered, not knowing what to do next. The lady behind the counter saw my stunned look and helped me along.

"There are a few more here," the woman said. "Do you want to know what they say?"

"There are a few more what?"

"There are other Winanses at the burial plot," she said. "Do you want to know about them too?"

"Sure."

She pulled out one for Edward's mother, Lydia, and another for his brother, Frederick. She looked at the cards and again looked stunned.

"Will you look at this?" she said as she read the inscription, raising her voice in surprise.

She pointed to the words on Lydia and Frederick's cards, just as she did with Edward's. Lydia was Edward's mother, and Frederick was his brother. Both lived in the same place, the cards said, at a home in Elizabeth, New Jersey. Both died in the same place, with the same cause.

"Cause of death: Gas asphyxiation."

Both died on the same day, October 4, 1928, just five years before Edward.

Two in one day, I thought. I pulled out my laptop and typed it into my notes. *Two in a day . . . two in a day . . . two in a day . . . That had to make news*, I thought.

Nothing about suicide was mentioned. But in my mind, it didn't have to be. Same day, same way. *What else could it be?* I thought.

"You've got to be kidding me," I said to the woman.

Again, she pulled out the card, slipped it to me and pointed to the words, affirming what she'd read.

"Wow," I said.

My first thought was to call my dad. I got photocopies of all the cards and ran outside, dodging the now heavy raindrops that fell on the grass and leaping over the puddles. I felt empowered, as though I had found some lost treasure. I had spent only two days researching my family's past and already every find was worth the effort. The foundation was building.

This was no fluke, I thought. *This is a curse. This is the proof.*

Suicide and mental illness are inexorably linked; approximately 95 percent of those people who commit suicide have a mental illness. Edward died in a manner that was similar to that of his mother and brother—on a warm day, when using the gas burners to help heat the house was unnecessary. They ended their sad, lonely lives when few treatment options, such as psychiatric clinics or psychologists, were available to those who didn't have the money to pay for them.

They ended years of perceived failure—likely triggered, in Edward's case, by the loss of thousands of dollars in the stock market crash of 1929, an event that ended whatever hopes he had of becoming a successful businessman. My father and other family members had told me about his life, how he had an uneasy and unsatisfied spirit that prevented his youngest son—my grandfather—from ever bonding with him in a way that my grandfather would have liked.

I thought of the movie *Good Will Hunting*, when the psychologist played by Robin Williams confronted a wayward MIT janitor with blue-collar roots, played by Matt Damon. I thought of what Robin Williams's character said when he couldn't get the Damon character to talk about himself. I thought about the way Matt Damon's character reacted when Williams's psychologist character seemed to tap into what he was repressing. He got him to realize that there are things that happen that we can't control. He told him, over and over, "It's not your fault," and as he did, the steely Damon character melted, losing his tough persona and dissolving into a crying mess.

It's not my fault, I thought to myself. *It's not my fault.*

⌁

As I headed back to the car, I stuffed the photocopies in my computer bag. I dodged the puddles and the drops falling between the trees as I zealously protected my stuff. I ran to my car, hunched over my bag, and called my dad on my cell phone from my car.

"Oh my God," Dad said. "He never told us that."

"He" was my grandfather, the cranky old man we had never liked. In just five minutes, I felt as though I had learned about half of his life, and way more than what he had ever told us. *No wonder*, I thought. *No one could be right-minded, growing up in that kind of life. No wonder he drove everybody nuts.*

No wonder he was nuts. He couldn't help it, but even if he could, look who surrounded him. Look who influenced him.

I listened to my father speak and remind me of everything that happened before. I remembered our Florida trip in 1976 and how my grandfather passed out on the couch and then took the jog through the park wearing a full suit. I remembered his yelling matches with my mother, and how she resented—until the day she died—the way my grandfather took care of my grandmother in her final years.

I remembered hearing about Greystone and the stress of living there, how my grandfather could be dapper-looking one minute, standing out as a solid member of the community, and then limply living as a sloppy drunk the next.

No wonder he was so screwed up, I thought. *Look at what he went through. Three people die around the same time. He made it to age seventy-seven.*

I got off the phone, turned on the car, flipped the windshield wipers to high, and followed the graveyard map to section I. The window was steamy, the air was dark, and the signs were so small, I could barely see anything on any stone and felt lucky when I saw an *I* on a small, white sign. I nearly screeched the car tires as I turned a sharp left corner and happened to see a flat stone in the ground with *Winans* chiseled in it.

I got out, put my jacket over me to shield from the rain that started to pour harder. I stayed there only briefly, because I couldn't read a word of anything, touching only the headstone for Frederick. I tried to turn it back over, but it had been tossed over so long ago that it was stuck in the ground with grass and weeds growing around it.

I saw other scattered tombstones, but I couldn't tell one from the other. Rain and darkness made them look like a colony of black and gray rocks. I tried to take pictures, but the frames were black. *I'll come back another day,* I thought. I headed out, but I knew I needed more. This was a start—a big one—but it didn't complete the puzzle. *When did the mental illness start?* I asked myself. *Who else had it? Who else died from it?*

That day, it was late, the local libraries were closing, and I needed to get home to my family, the one I knew I needed to protect, now more than ever. I saw the pattern and I knew it would force me to change how I approached them. I had a wife and three kids to worry about, but not only that, I had to worry that another generation of the Winans and Davis families would experience what I and my mother and the people before her went through. I had to worry about the potential for mental illness that led others to ruin. That night, the library could wait. I had to get home.

In the ensuing weeks, I went to libraries in Elizabeth, Bay Head, Hightstown, and Trenton, all places in New Jersey where my grandfather had lived. I talked to people in my family. I studied artwork that show-cased painted beach scenes in Bay Head, where my grandfather vaca-tioned with his family, even as the Great Depression took hold of the country and emptied the family's dwindling finances.

I read news articles on the deaths and discovered roles that my grand-father played courageously, if not heroically, to keep the family together. I learned of the hell he went through when his father died, trying to res-urrect a family that was lost. But I also appreciated how he maintained hope and managed to survive and start his own family.

At home, I looked at old pictures, pushing the dust off them. I found no pictures of Dick, my grandfather, when he was younger than twenty. All I saw were the pictures of him as an adult, having a family and try-ing to live the life that he hadn't had as a youngster—just like my father tried to do with our family. I saw the pictures of him smiling as he stood next to my grandmother and mother with ocean waves collapsing behind them.

I didn't see the cranky man I knew; I saw a person who had discovered his own ways of coping with the tragic events of his life and who sought to forge on and forget everything that had happened before.

At the Hightstown library, I found an article from the microfiche files of the defunct *Hightstown Gazette*. I thought I had little chance of find-ing anything, knowing that newspapers typically shy away from report-ing on suicides. But there it was, in the July 13, 1933, edition of the paper, a brief story on the front page: "Edward P. Winans Kills Self with Gas at Home."

In the story, I found information that had never even been part of the family rumors. I discovered that my grandfather not only knew about his father's death, but also had a profound role that must have created a memory he carried to his grave.

But Dick, like his father, was the perfectionist, and he obsessively sought to portray the perfect family life, even if his family's real life was far from it. He never talked about what was in the newspaper, and he never wanted us to know about it. He never wanted us to know that he was as screwed up as we were. But there it was, the story to be told, on a fading, scratched-up piece of microfiche. It was the story of a family and self-destruction.

Soon, I would learn the only place that would provide Dick any salvation was the beach. From the time Dick was little until the time he died, it was his favorite place to be.

July 1933

Outside Dick Winans's cottage, the ocean waves splashed on the soft sand, washing up to the tourists' bicycle tires as they pedaled along the Bay Head, New Jersey, shoreline. Along the beach, men dressed in suits, hats, and ties spread out their blankets and pulled food from picnic baskets. Some would arrive at sunrise, enjoying the orange glow that wrapped around the Bay Head horizon every morning.

In 1933, Dick spent his summer weekends there, jumping into the waves and swimming out so far that the lifeguards had to call him back. He often walked door to door carrying buckets of fish that he bought at a nearby wholesaler and then sold to the tourists who rented the six-bedroom mansions and the three-room cottages that lined the beachfront. Some politely declined; others pitied him and obliged.

Dick, then twenty, dreamed of attending Princeton University, even though he knew his family couldn't afford it. He wanted to be a successful businessman, even as his father suffered through the worst effects of the Great Depression, losing much of his money in the stock market crash and struggling to keep his insurance brokerage afloat.

Dick wanted to emulate his brother Robert, who was eight years his senior and with whom he often clashed. Robert had graduated from Yale University, parted ways with his family, and experienced some early business success. Dick, however, thought he could be successful without having to abandon his mother, with whom he'd often stay, lie on her lap, and stare into space. He liked to be with her, cook with her, hug her. When she got sick, he chose to take care of her and was willing to put aside all of his dreams until she got well.

He also didn't want to abandon the beach, where he dreamed of setting up a fish market that served the Bay Head rich.

The shore was Dick's refuge, a weekend escape from a life that was often unsettled and uneasy. It would be his one constant, the place that offered few surprises as his family moved three times during the early 1930s, eventually settling in the small but busy farming community of Hightstown, New Jersey, fifty miles north of Bay Head.

The beach was far away from the trees and the irritating dust that always seemed to be lurking in the air in Hightstown. There Dick seemed to detest the smell of the local farm life. He worried about the germs that came from the people who lived and farmed there. He avoided shaking hands, he showered two or three times a day, and he cleaned his hands every hour.

Dick worried about his nose, and he felt that he had to constantly empty even the smallest amount the bacteria-filled mucus that was lodged in his sinuses. He kept a handkerchief in his shirt pocket and blew into it constantly.

But at the beach, the smell was only of salt water and the fish from Dick's bucket. At the beach, Dick's nose would miraculously clear, and he often left his handkerchief behind at the cottage.

⌇

In Dick's life, the beach would be an enduring symbol, serving as a resting place for his mother Grace (Smith) Winans, as she recovered from the effects of a stroke that she suffered around 1930. The beach's elegance would remind him of the stories he had heard about his family, but hadn't had the opportunity to see: a prominent, successful colonial family whose members were among the first settlers in Elizabeth, New Jersey.

Ultimately, the shore would become a saving grace for Dick, helping him move past tragedy that forced him to put his ambitions of going to Princeton and opening a fish market on hold.

On July 12, 1933, a month after his high school graduation, Dick departed Bay Head and left behind his ailing mother so he could be with his father, Edward. Earlier in the week, his father gave simple, but short instructions: arrive at the South Main Street house at 3 p.m. on Wednesday.

No reason was given. Just come home, Dick was told.

Once there, Dick discovered what his father had planned: Edward, his arms folded and his head tilted over, but still wearing his eyeglasses, was sitting on a chair that was close to a gas range.

In the cracks in the walls and the ceiling of the century-old house, cotton batting and paper had been stuffed, sealing off any chance of leakage. Cotton and paper were also stuffed inside the keyholes and anything else that would give even the smallest amount of gas a chance to escape.

When Dick arrived, Edward Winans, age sixty-two, had been dead for twenty-four hours.

Emotionally, Dick was much closer to his mother than to his father, doing everything he could to cater to her wishes. But in death, he sensed a kinship with his father that he didn't have with anyone else. He saw a side of his father that perhaps he saw in himself. From that day on, Dick did all he could to avoid emulating the choices, the mistakes, and the heartaches that ultimately brought down Edward.

Dick found it haunting and even spooky that his father died the way he lived: demanding perfection from himself, with no mistakes or leaks that could steer him away from his goal. It was the way he wanted those close to him to live, and when they didn't, he shut them out and turned to his work, hoping that someday he could make the perfect living with the perfect family and the perfect lifestyle.

Edward demanded perfection even as his insurance business became *his own* refuge, the one place he could turn to when everything went bad, where he could throw himself into his work. When he wasn't at work, he would go to New York City, where he drank and caroused until late at night.

He demanded success even when the money stopped coming in during the Great Depression and he had nowhere to turn for support. He set high standards for himself, even though he died the same way his imperfect mother and brother, Lydia and Frederick, had when they turned on the gas jets in their small apartment in Elizabeth five years before.

Like Frederick, Edward would die feeling that his family was abandoning him, especially after his eldest son moved out, his peaceful wife suffered in silence from the stroke, and his youngest son, Dick, pulled further away from him, repelled by his aggressive behavior, his demanding personality, and his inability to be satisfied.

Unlike Lydia and Frederick, Edward's death would be labeled a suicide. Like so many others, he chose to kill himself rather than get rid of the car, the beach cottage, the private school educations for his children, and the stylish clothes that once made the Winans family members feel whole. He began to feel that he—like those before him—was failing the legacy of a family that was already disintegrating.

☞

Edward was an anxious man who was never satisfied with the money he had, the family he cared for, or the job he worked. In the years leading up to his death, he found success as much as he found failure, but it was the failure that mattered the most.

In almost every aspect of his life, whether it was his personal life or his job, something stood in his way that prevented him from having the life he wanted for himself and his family.

In the late 1800s, Edward first sought success in the city of Elizabeth, where his father, Elias, made a meager living as a house painter as he recovered from ailments—perhaps Civil War–related—that made it difficult for him to walk. The ailments made it almost impossible for him to continue the legacy of wealth and success in a family that had included authors, doctors, and even politicians who helped run the city. Elias raised his family in a small apartment on Liberty Street, where immigrants were cramming ten at a time into tiny dwellings that would normally fit four or less.

Growing up, Edward developed an interest in numbers and money. As a boy, he was a fan of collecting old coins and dollar bills, and he hoped to transfer the success he had in finding rare pennies and nickels to real life. He wanted to start an accounting business, but he took an interest in insurance as the industry gained popularity in the industrialized, post–Civil War era.

Even as a young man, Edward had a plan for everything. He wanted to move to the wealthy neighborhoods of Elizabeth—or perhaps a richer suburb of New York City, such as Livingston, New Jersey—and be like the cousins his father and mother talked about who owned large tracts of land in Rahway or were successful farmers and businessmen in Elizabeth. They had attained their wealth as northern New Jersey grew and manufacturing plants replaced the local farm life as the region's main industry.

As an insurance broker, Edward wanted to meet those lofty standards, and he began to live the life that he expected would lead to wealth, riches, and even power.

In the late 1800s, Edward started to enjoy some success as he worked in a small office in downtown Elizabeth, where he employed his brother Frederick as a clerk. People viewed Edward with a sense of trust. To many, he was gregarious and outgoing, even charming, always trying to sell his business. He always dressed to the nines, wearing a suit and bow tie whether it was icy cold or intensely hot.

He was slender and fit, largely because he didn't find the time to eat. People called him a "playboy" because he often left the family behind and spent the money he made in New York City, drinking and carousing at expensive hotels and clubs. For much of his career, he made a lot of money, working with Lenox china and other big companies based in the

New York area. He often met with clientele in the city—meeting, greeting, and socializing with big business—because his sole objective was wealth and success.

At home, however, he could be dour, dry, and demanding of his stay-at-home wife, Grace, whom he married in 1895. She was a small woman who came from an upper-class family in Elizabeth. She followed the housewife role typical at that time, staying home to cook and raise the children. She seemed to appreciate not only Edward's toughness; she also seemed impressed with his ability to draw up a plan for his life to make a lot of money, move the family into a big house, and live the Winans lifestyle of wealth and prominence.

As he gained success, Edward began to adopt the role as the family's wealthy caretaker. He helped Frederick, who had struggled long after he left school and had difficulty holding down a job. After working for his father Elias, Frederick married in 1892, three years before Edward, and had all three of his children before Edward had his first, Robert, in 1905.

Edward hoped that marriage would turn Frederick's life around. He hired him as a clerk, hoping he would stick to a schedule that would assure his punctuality, effort, and willingness to be responsible at work and at home.

While Edward's workload increased, however, Frederick took to the bottle, became unreliable, and ultimately spent much of his day at the Elizabeth train station, eventually forcing his frustrated wife and three children to move away to California.

With Frederick falling apart, Edward grew distant from him and their mother, Lydia. Lydia was said to be shy and reclusive, particularly after Edward's father, Elias, died in 1903 of heart disease. Lydia had been totally dependent on Elias for support, even as he spent his last years wheelchair-bound. She moved with Frederick to a small apartment in downtown Elizabeth, where they spent the next two decades by themselves, rarely venturing outside.

ᘒ

Frustrated, Edward made himself busier and moved his own family to Asbury Park, where Dick was born in 1913. Now with two children, Edward worked even harder to maintain his lifestyle, never settling for making only a small profit from his business. He spent more time in New York City, using his drinking and carousing as business opportunities that helped him reel in high-priced accounts, such as Lenox. He moved his family often, hoping to find whatever success he could in the big and small suburban communities of central and northern New Jersey.

By the late 1920s, he rented a cottage in Bay Head so his family could live a comfortable life that he couldn't have when he was living in a crammed apartment in Elizabeth. He also rented sizable Victorian houses in Lawrenceville and Hightstown, where he sent his youngest son, Dick, to Peddie, an exclusive and expensive high school that allowed Dick to live at home while going to the boarding school, so he could help take care of Grace.

Edward chose Peddie for Dick because he was impressed with its demanding curriculum and its brick and stone buildings with ornate rooftops that gave the campus a Princeton-like aura. Dick was compelled to wear shirts with high collars, silk ties, and knickers, giving him a classic look that rivaled any of the shirts, shoes, and socks worn by his fellow students.

During the summers, Edward encouraged Dick to drive his mother to Bay Head, hoping the warm sea air and the rich culture would inspire Dick to be like his brother and develop enough ambition to get himself into Princeton University.

Even during the Great Depression, the people of Bay Head still wore their expensive knickers and wide-brimmed hats as they walked or rode bicycles along the shoreline. To Dick, the atmosphere made him feel elegant and wealthy. He often went for long walks along the boardwalk that extended into Point Pleasant Beach, adoring the sunrises that glistened on the water. The area was surrounded by an ocean, bay, and canal, magnifying the orange glow that came from the sunlight.

৲৴

When his mother and brother died, Edward was fifty-seven and living with his family at the Stacy–Trent Motel in Trenton, a ten-story high-rise in the city's downtown that—after spending much of his money on the high life in New York—he really couldn't afford. His insurance business was profitable, but his expensive tastes made it a struggle as he found himself working harder and longer to live what closely resembled an affluent life.

When Lydia and Frederick died on October 4, 1928, Edward was doing what he normally did: working, traveling and, some believe, carousing in New York City with clients. The official word, at the time of the deaths, was that he was traveling and "couldn't be found." Police tried to telegraph Edward, hoping he would get the message.

He got the message a day later, but when he did, he didn't go to Elizabeth to take care of the remains. He left that job to his sister, Mary, who was married, lived in nearby Westfield, and rarely talked to Edward.

By then, Edward talked less and less with his oldest son, Robert, who was twenty-three, had graduated from Yale, and was starting his own family. Robert eventually became a successful businessman, but he became estranged once he ran into problems with Dick, arguing with him over the direction of the family, Grace's illness, and who should take care of her, especially when Edward was away. He saw Dick as a spoiled mama's boy who did little to raise the family's status, and who—despite his lofty pronouncements of wanting to be an Ivy Leaguer—seemed more interested in spending time in Bay Head than working hard enough to follow his brother's path.

৲৴

By 1929 as the nation fell into the Great Depression, Edward's dream of wealth and success died. He lost tens of thousands of dollars in the stock market crash, forcing him to work constantly, hoping to replenish the money he lost. But as he approached his sixtieth birthday, Edward found it difficult to escape hardship and tragedy.

His wife's stroke left her unable to walk and barely able to speak. Sending Dick to Peddie was a move toward stability, giving him an opportunity to be close to her and take care of her while Edward worked longer hours.

Just before Dick enrolled at the school in 1930, the family relocated from Trenton to Lawrenceville before settling on the Victorian house on South Main Street in Hightstown, across the street from Peddie. The family's home was part of a string of nineteenth-century houses that had five or more bedrooms.

Despite their worries, the Winans family still sought to fit in with the rich, spending all their savings on clothing for Dick that would match what the Bay Head wealthy were wearing—as well as what was popular among the high-achieving, high-income-level student body at Peddie, from which Dick graduated in June 1933.

By 1933, however, Bay Head had become a place that Edward could no longer afford. His money was virtually gone, yet he kept the car Dick used to drive his mother to the shore. Edward refused to buy a home, worried that he never knew where he was going to live next. His insurance business was dying as the Great Depression deepened, so he didn't want to get wrapped up in a long-term mortgage that he couldn't pay off.

Still, he continued to pay the rent at the Bay Head cottage, believing that it stabilized his family better than any job could. He also kept Dick in Peddie School, where tuition was more than $250 a year, even as other private schools—particularly Catholic schools—charged less than half the price.

With Dick, however, Edward was distant, having allowed his son to develop an even closer relationship with his mother, Grace, especially after her stroke. Grace had kept Dick out of school until he was seven, choosing to tutor him while the family moved from town to town. Grace also taught Dick how to cook; he liked to say his "specialty" was pineapple upside-down cake.

Before her stroke, Grace catered to Dick's fears and whims, washing his handkerchief almost every day. She wanted Dick to feel at ease whenever he had panic attacks, whenever he felt sick, or whenever he had a cold or even the slightest sniffle. She tried to calm him, allowing him to take more than one shower a day whenever he worried that a slight sniffle could lead to pneumonia or worse.

When Dick enrolled at Peddie, Edward's concerns grew as his son showed little interest in sports, afraid that games like football were too rough and too dirty, forcing him to come into contact with bacteria-laden dirt.

Unlike his brother Robert, who was active, ambitious, and gregarious, Dick joined no clubs at Peddie. He had few, if any, friends. Few thought he was on Robert's "genius" level or worked hard enough to be there.

Edward worried, in particular, about Dick's masculinity. He sent him to boxing lessons, hoping the experience would toughen him up and win him some friends. But Dick hated to come in contact with others, keeping his distance from sparring partners whose skin and sweat were full of the germs he hated so much.

Dick generally chose to keep to himself while at school, and he continued cooking with his mother at home. As the family struggled with illness and financial problems, Dick showed up looking sullen for class photos. In his high school yearbook, when each student was asked to describe himself or herself, Dick wrote, "An innocent, retiring floweret."

꒰꒱

Eventually, as Grace's physical health declined, Edward had to move his office into the house on South Main Street. He had hoped to retire by the time he was sixty. Instead, he was working even harder. He was hardly eating at all and became skinnier; his normally well-fitted suits started to look big and sloppy.

Grace's family, the Smiths, offered help, but Edward had a long-standing rivalry with Grace's brother, Chet, who made a lot of money as a landlord of tenement houses in Elizabeth. Chet was also beginning to strike it rich in the fledgling automobile industry, opening the first Cadillac dealership in the area. He often invited Edward and his family over to his mini-mansion in Elizabeth, where they sat in wicker chairs, drank, and said little to each other for hours.

Chet was like his sister Grace in size—small, even skinny—but opposite in mannerisms. He liked to boast about the money he made, which made Edward seethe as Chet talked about his dreams of buying more tenements—some may have called him a "slumlord"—and making himself the richest landlord in town. Edward would say little, privately maintaining the same goal he had thirty years before: restoring the Winans' affluent pride.

But the older Edward grew, and as his family fell apart, that goal was no longer possible.

ॐ

When Dick's father summoned him home from Bay Head on July 12, 1933, he didn't say why. Dick often argued when he viewed the reason Edward gave as insufficient. Dick was known to be stubborn and unwilling to accept contradiction or change. He often verbally sparred with his father whenever he criticized him for taking multiple showers each day and constantly washing his hands.

This time, however, no reason was apparently given. This time, Dick couldn't argue about what he didn't know.

That day, the sky was cloudy, but the seventy-degree temperatures made the air feel cooler than usual. Despite the threat of rain, not a drop fell as Dick made the hour-long car trip back to Hightstown, passing by the row of small shops and markets on North Main Street that catered to the local farming community. Had Dick stayed in Bay Head, he may have enjoyed the sea breeze that broke a recent hot spell, when temperatures approached ninety degrees.

Instead, he was in Hightstown, where the air was dusty and still, the kind of air that made him blow often into his handkerchief. As he stood a few feet from the door of his house, however, it was the smell of gas—not dust—that filled the air.

As soon as he smelled it, Dick turned around and hustled across the street, heading toward the Peddie classroom building, where he found the assistant headmaster, Ralph Harmon, and asked him to help investigate.

Dick often turned to the Peddie faculty for help. He had graduated from the school a month earlier, but even as an alumnus, he could still rely on them and trust them. Some of the faculty acted as surrogate fathers to students who lived on campus and felt homesick. Getting them to help was logical, he believed, and never impulsive.

In this case, Harmon was a natural find—he was a trusted math teacher to whom the Class of 1932 dedicated its yearbook. On July 12, 1933, Harmon readily left his place and followed Dick to his front door.

They opened it and followed the odor into the kitchen. There they found Edward.

They called the police, who found the cotton batting and the paper. As they discovered, Edward had again had a plan. Only this time, he had followed it through.

Weeks later, his Princeton plans on hold, Dick did the one thing his father could never bring himself to do: he sold off everything, dumping the Bay Head cottage, the Hightstown house, and all the furniture inside.

Then Dick left New Jersey, moving with his mother to Florida, where he enrolled at the University of Miami and gave his mother a gift as her health continued to decline: beach sand, warm air, and sunrises on the water.

CHAPTER 4

THE WORKING LIFE

November 2008

I LOOKED AT PICTURES in my grandfather's photo album, which I kept stored inside a crawl space in the attic of my house. The book was so dirty, and every turn of the pages sprayed black dust and an odor that was practically suffocating. I looked for pictures of my great-grandfather Edward or anybody remotely connected to him and his family. I wanted to see what they looked like. I wanted to see what they dressed like. I wanted to see whether there was any visual hint of the despair they went through.

I found a picture of Edward from about 1903, ten years before my grandfather Dick was born. Edward was sitting in a chair, his hair neatly combed to each side, with a bow tie tight around his neck. He had a stately, but skinny look, both prim and grim. His legs lay straight, and his pants seemed too wide and a little too long. His arms rested on the chair and his frown was flat, as if he thought that sitting for this picture was just a waste of his time.

He was sitting, but he looked so wound up, as though he was ready to jump out of the chair and get the hell out of there. His hands were folded neatly, but tightly, and his face was turned slightly to the side, as though he were giving himself some sort of princely look.

On the back was an inscription, written in pencil by my grandfather's cousin, Irving, who was Chet's son.

"<u>Dick</u>," he wrote, underlining the name. "This is your father."

What did that mean? I thought. *Didn't he know what his father looked like?*

It was the only picture of Edward in the entire album. Indeed, it was the only one I could find of anybody from Edward's side of the Winans family. There were many pictures of Dick's mother Grace and her family wearing elegant dresses and suits as they posed for professional studio shots that gave them an air of elegance.

But there was no Elias. No Lydia. No Frederick. No Winans, at least none of those before Dick.

I pulled the picture out, stuffed it into a folder, and kept leafing through the album. Dick, my grandfather, took a different approach than his ancestors, photographing nearly everything. There were many pictures of the beach, usually dating back as far as 1930. There were pictures of my grandfather looking as skinny as a pencil, wearing his swim trunks up past his belly button. There were pictures of him wearing his Navy seaman's outfit during World War II, posing with my mother.

Others showed the family at the house at Greystone, back in the 1950s, standing in a living room that seemed so colorless. A white wall held no pictures, tables held no flowers or pictures, and three small wicker chairs sat near a television set. The most colorful object was the Christmas tree, but even that had no more than three or four ornaments. My grandfather Dick, grandmother Dorothy, and mother Dede stood in front of it, looking stiff but smiling as they attempted to show Christmas joy.

When the setting was the beach, however, the pictures told a different story. My grandfather often showed his colorful side, whether it was playing with my mother's hair when she was twelve or showing off his bare, hairy chest just after he just got out of the water. He reminded me of the man I knew when I was little, the one who laughed whenever he told stories of selling fish to rich people in Bay Head when he was a teenager, telling how he was able to clinch the deal once he put on a sad, pathetic face. "It worked every time," he said, chuckling to himself. "There's a sucker born every minute."

It reminded me of the man who sang the verses of "U.S. Air Force" over and over on the way to Florida in 1976, drawing chuckles from me, Edward, and Carolyn but stern looks from my mother. He was as drunk as a skunk, but that time it was funny. Every time my mother showed a look of disgust, he'd turn to me and wink.

As I went through these pictures, I knew where I had to go next. I needed to move away from the places of despair, at least temporarily. I had to see a fuller picture of my grandfather, one that went beyond the man who had dealt with much heartache before he turned twenty-five. I had to go where he was happy. I had to find that laugh. I had to go to the beach.

ॐ

One day in November 2008, I played hooky from work and visited my mother's grave in Point Pleasant, just a mile from the beach. It was another rainy, windswept day. I felt like I did the day she died: I felt guilty. I had nothing to give her. I had nothing to say to her. I was never religious, so all I could see and feel was the cold, hard ground and the gray tombstone.

I did have visions, though, just not spiritual ones. I thought of how she used to obsess over the cold. I thought if anything "soulful" was down in my mother's grave, she was probably shivering.

I could still see her when I was three, in the middle of the winter turning up the thermostat and hearing it from my father. "What the hell are you doing? Do you think I'm made of money?" he'd say. But, as she always did, she flashed her smile and got his repeated assurance. "Yes, seventy-five. Okay, dear," before she hid in the bathroom.

Then the rest of us would sit in the living room and feel the sweat gradually cover our arms and legs as the house would drastically heat up. But we'd let it go, just as we always did. Let it be hot or watch her suffer and plead with my father to turn the dial up even more. Let it be hot or hear the repeating. Protest the repeating and get hit—or worse yet, hear more repeating.

As I stood there, on the cold, dying grass, I remembered how much she longed for summer whenever rain fell or snow covered the ground. She would remember Bradley Beach, where she spent her summers as a teenager with her father. "I wish we could go there now," she'd say in the middle of winter. She'd have these recollections the same way she still felt the cold chill of the outside air even with the thermostat turned up. As she grew older, the chill got worse as her memories grew longer.

On the way out of the graveyard, I looked around and watched the wind blow through the few trees that lined the side streets. I looked behind my mother's headstone at a tall grave monument about the size of a small flagpole.

It had no inscription. No name, no date. Not even a chiseled word that, perhaps, had faded over time. I looked around and saw that many of the tombstones were the same way. It was a lot like the Hillside Cemetery, only these stones were at least implanted in the ground.

What a cold, lonely place, I thought.

Toward the end of her life, I so much wanted her to avoid such a place. I wanted her to take the medication that would turn her around, turn her into the person she was when I was three, who lovingly hugged me back when I hugged her. I wanted to see the woman from the beach, where her wide, white smiles were never forced.

But there she was, in the ground, sealed away forever, never to feel the warm heat of our old, hot house again.

ॐ

I headed to Bay Head, the exclusive beach town about two minutes away, where my grandfather spent his youth. I drove past the cottages that lined the beach. I had passed them so many times when I was young, but now I could see my grandfather, carrying his fish bucket as he went door to door, flashing his sad, pathetic look as men and women, wearing tailored suits, fancy hats, and classic dresses, handed him money. Then I could see the tall, skinny kid stuffing the money in his shirt pocket behind his handkerchief and chuckling to himself as he walked away to find another sucker.

Just a few blocks from the beach, I saw the Anchor & Palette Art Gallery, where there were pictures of those same women with fancy hats carrying umbrellas as they stared out at the clipper boats sailing in the sea. The men wore long jackets, tucking the tails under their rear ends as they sat on the sand. Some pulled up their trousers as they waded in the water.

I was struck by the inscriptions that said "1930s . . . Bay Head." I talked to a woman who worked there, and told her how much I was confused by the scenes of wealth from the Great Depression era. "The rest of the country was struggling, but in the rich communities, they lived above that," she told me. "They weren't really affected by it."

I again thought of my grandfather, chuckling to himself as he carried his fish bucket. *This was his escape*, I thought. *This is what he wanted to be. He didn't want to be with his dad. He didn't want to be depressed. He didn't want a depression . . . He wanted to stay here.*

As I looked at the pictures, I thought of my own youth and how we soured on the beach after my mother's knee injury. We treated the beach as though it were another country, even though we lived only two miles away from the shoreline. My grandfather Dick rarely came around either, and when he did, he was usually wearing his formal wear—not his swim trunks—as he stayed for lunch. He and my grandmother Dorothy would sit on the couch, keeping a safe distance from each other and leaving after only an hour or two.

From the art gallery, I called my father. I called him frequently as I went on these fact-finding trips. He was finding my research travels as therapeutic as I was. He had dealt with my mother for nearly forty-five years. He was still looking for answers, just as he had when she was alive, and he often bugged me for more information. I was happy to oblige.

His response to my findings often dictated whatever move I made next. If he was shocked, I was onto something. If he was confused, I needed to dig more.

I told him about the paintings and how they reminded me of my grandfather's photo album. He was more intrigued by the photos of Greystone, the fortress that was once one of the largest psychiatric hospitals in the country.

"You should go to Greystone," my father told me. "You'll see everything over there."

⌇

Weeks later I visited Greystone and saw the old brick and mortar buildings, as well as the home that my grandfather, grandmother, and mother lived in. Many of these dark, decrepit buildings were empty, but they still towered over the campus, casting dark dreary shadows over the layer of snow that had fallen the day before.

I saw the offices where the administrators worked, the creaky brick buildings with boarded-up windows and two-foot-long icicles hanging from the gutters. One or two security patrol officers wearing big winter hats and thick-layered coats roamed the campus, scaring the geese who occasionally flew in to pick at the snow before flying away.

Most of these buildings were closed nearly a decade before; the hospital had been downsized and moved to a more modern set of buildings elsewhere on the campus. But I could see why Greystone was once to Dick the perfect fit: the main building, where the patients were housed, had the majesty of a kingdom, with tall towers that gave the building its powerful, medieval signature. I could imagine him sitting in there, serving as the powerful personnel director, peering through the window at the vast campus and flashing that same smart look he had when he sold fish to the Bay Head rich. *He made it,* I thought to myself. *He went from dumping his furniture in Hightstown to sitting on a throne at Greystone. . . . He made it.*

Looking at the dungeon-like buildings with prison bars on the windows, however, I could also see why Greystone and the life he lived there ultimately started to wear on him by the late 1960s. Dick often told my father how he eventually grew tired of the despair that surrounded him. He started to feel trapped as he aged, and he developed a similar dissatisfaction that his father Edward had had back in the 1920s. Despite his success, he never felt as though he found the life he really wanted. He was never really sure what that life was. As much as he enjoyed the power of his position, he grew sick of being around despair. Much of his life was affected by it. Eventually, he found drinking to be the best way to ease whatever pain he had felt all his life, whether it came from an old memory or the present day.

I drove behind the main building, watching some geese scamper away from my car on a road that passed a fire department. I saw a dilapidated building, a duplex, surrounded by a broken, eight-foot-high wire fence.

I pulled out a manila folder from my computer bag, and from the folder pulled a picture I got from my grandfather's photo album. The image was of the house back in the 1950s, covered in solid white paint with tall trees standing in the front yard, a white Chevy Impala in the driveway, and my mother standing in front of the driveway, forcing a smile. In the background were the mountains and hills of Morris County, perhaps the most beautiful landscape in New Jersey.

That's it, I thought. *This dilapidated duplex in front of me was where they lived. This was the place that didn't have any pictures on the walls.*

I parked, pulled out my camera, and walked through the snow. The temperature had dropped into the twenties, and my boots made a "crunch" sound as I stepped through the thin cover of ice. I looked around the building and tried to peek through the windows; though it was around noon, the inside was as dark as night.

I snapped pictures of the outside, but I wasn't pleased. The outside was so old and rotten; I wanted to know the *inside* and see the rooms where they posed in front of the Christmas tree, or where young Dede posed before she went to the senior prom, again flashing what seemed like forced, flat smiles.

I walked around the tall fence and found a place where it was caved in and ripped. *This may be my only chance*, I thought.

The area around me was barren and empty; cars passed by only occasionally. I worried about being caught for trespassing, so I kept looking around, looking behind trees and buildings, seeing whether anybody was even remotely close to popping out and catching me.

I walked over the fallen fence, trying to weave around the jagged wire edges, until I tripped, dropping the camera in the snow.

"Shit!" I yelled. I could feel my obsessive urges come out, and I worried that if I kept going I would be going to jail. Somehow, the subfreezing weather couldn't stop my forehead from sweating. I took deep breaths, feeling the cold air in my lungs. I looked hard again for anybody lurking behind a tree, behind the fire department building, or anywhere else on the mostly barren campus. I saw nothing, and moved ahead, entering the house through the dark back entrance.

Inside, it was all dark with virtually everything ripped out. The only sign of recent life was a discarded Dunkin' Donuts cup. The internal, wood structure was still there, but the walls, the furniture, and the floors were barren, and everything else was all torn out and gone.

I walked up the stairs and looked at the row of bedrooms. The ceilings were somewhat low. Dick always seemed to be bending in so many pictures; this was probably why.

Downstairs, the living room was small, but certainly livable—at one time, at least. I snapped pictures, hoping I would find some clue, something that reflected the lives of a family that fell apart. I wanted to see if there was a trigger, something that could have pushed their insecurities to the surface and compelled my grandfather—and even my mother—to eventually turn to alcohol to relieve them.

But it had all seemed as though it was normal, so authentic, and so 1950s bland long before the walls and electrical wiring were torn out. And now, so much of it was gone that it was nearly impossible to see whether there was something about the house that made their smiles flat and their eyebrows heavy.

On my way out, I looked out the windows and saw the main building again with its bars on the windows, and its dark stone. The building blocked the sun and totally covered the scenery behind it.

This was their view, I thought. *Oh my God. This was their view.*

At Christmas, they didn't look out and see kids throwing snowballs at each other and decorated houses lining the street. They didn't look out in July and see fireworks or kids jumping into pools and playing baseball in the street. They saw only what my mother would call "the nuthouse," one of the largest psychiatric facilities in the country, staring them down every day.

I could imagine the picture of Dick, Dorothy, and Dede standing together for a picture, with Dick's head bending down slightly, barely fitting under the low roof. I could see them pretending to like this, even though they clearly didn't. I could see them giving that same contrived smile, just like Woody Guthrie did in that Greystone photo exhibit, clenching their teeth as hard as they could.

February 1970

Dick Winans wore a fedora hat, scarf, and an overcoat to keep warm from the cold ocean breeze. The wind at the Asbury Park boardwalk in February was chillier than it was at his home at Greystone and carried a damp, frosty bite that could turn the skin red. As he walked the boardwalk, he gripped his camera tightly and prepared to capture the look of the sand, the sea, and the few people who, like him, loved it enough to visit the beach in freezing weather.

As much as he loved the salt air and the sound of the waves, though, Dick hated winter. He hated it when the germ-filled mucus lodged in his sinuses and made him fear that a cold, the flu, or pneumonia was coming. That morning in 1970, he wrapped himself from his neck to his feet, worried that even the slightest exposure to air would make him sick.

Whenever he had a pain, cut, or a sniffle, Dick would find the nearest person—whether it was his wife Dorothy or a secretary at his office at Greystone—and pepper the person with questions: "How serious is this? How painful will this be? Can I get pneumonia?"

At fifty-seven, he still kept a handkerchief in his shirt pocket, stuffing it there with a pack of ballpoint pens and a pencil. But the handkerchief was no longer enough to give him relief from the mucus he worried about and tried so hard to blow out of his nose to be rid of forever. He took cold medicine, but the pills were as effective as the handkerchief, even when he took more than the prescribed amount.

Dick's only way to stop worrying was to drink. When he drank beer or vodka, February felt like July. By 1970, he was doing more than keeping a bottle of wine in his car or in a closet at the Greystone duplex and taking occasional sips from it. Whether the alcohol was in a bar in Asbury Park or the refrigerator in his Morris Plains kitchen, Dick drank and numbed himself to the point that everything that had bugged him before suddenly became irrelevant.

By noon on that February day, Dick had forgotten the freezing temperatures. He was ignoring the wife who anxiously waited for him in their Chevy Impala as he lingered on the boardwalk. He focused on the women who, even in their furry coats and scarves, looked radiant in the midday sun. Dick pulled out his camera, the cheap one he bought secondhand in New York City nearly thirty years earlier, just before his service began in World War II, and started shooting.

Usually, the fur-wrapped girl was far away, standing alone or with a friend on the sand, watching the waves roll in. But Dick could aim a camera better than he could drive a car or anything else he did after he drank a six-pack of Budweiser.

Nearing sixty, Dick wanted a life he could enjoy. He wanted the life his father tried to force him to have, but couldn't, because Dick was too worried that he would be pulled too far from his mother and be somebody other than who he was. Or he was too shy to go beyond the church socials and ballroom dances he used to enjoy with his wife and live the high life that his father once did. Or he was too embarrassed because he was always blowing his nose, making others keep their distance.

As he got older, he became even lonelier. He would go on walks with Dorothy on the beach and his mind would drift. He realized he never had the life others had at his high school, where many boys in the all-male student body excelled in sports and clubs he didn't join or dated women he couldn't get near.

When he drank, the women on the beach became prettier. He grew envious as he watched them snuggle with their boyfriends on the beach. He wanted the fun they had, or the fun others had when they went to college in their early twenties. But because of war service, his mother's illness, his father's troubles, and his growing fear of people, places, and germs, he couldn't get it. He couldn't get a taste of it at college, since he graduated from Rutgers University when he was thirty-six, married, and working in a full-time job, as well as the father of an eleven-year-old daughter.

Even at Greystone, where the staff cared for a population of people whose severe mental illnesses created an atmosphere of gloom and desperation, the employees boosted each other's morale by organizing softball games and other social get-togethers. But Dick, like his father, chose to engage only in his work, staying in his office until late every night. At home, he wore gloves as he worked in his gardens or sat and read the newspapers.

In 1970, Dick had been married thirty-three years, but to him marriage had become an obstacle, not a reward for years of setting what he believed was a good example of hard work and discipline for his family and co-workers. He grew tired of the temperate life his wife insisted they live. He started to drive to Morristown and stop at liquor stores where he'd pick up a few cans of beer and drink them on the way home. Eventually, a few beers became a six-pack, and then half of a case that he'd pack in the back of the Impala, slurping down as many as he could on the five-mile drive back to the Greystone duplex.

At first, he tried to hide it from Dorothy, drinking as much as he could before she had a chance to see it. By 1970, however, Dick didn't care; he'd take the case of beer he bought, stuff it in the refrigerator or cabinet, and drink each can, well into the night. As he drank, he'd look at Dorothy, who would be standing between the kitchen and the living room of their home, placing her hands on her hips and raising an eyebrow. "What?" he'd ask, as if to say, "What are you going to do about it?"

Dorothy, ever formal and polite, would walk out of the room and back into the kitchen, shaking her head.

On this February day, Dorothy got fed up. She had watched him pull out that camera for about a decade and take picture after picture of pretty girls. This time, she insisted, would be the last time. She had warned him before: if he continued with this behavior, she was going to go move in with their daughter Dede and her husband Stan, who lived in Point Pleasant, about ten miles south of Asbury Park.

A year earlier, Dorothy had suffered a neck injury that limited her movement. Her heart began to fail, ultimately causing her to be hospitalized and then mostly confined to a chair in her house. She could no longer go dancing or take the long walks that made her feel skinny and fit.

But Dorothy worried more about Dick and threatened to take him to a rehabilitation center if he didn't stop pulling beers from the fridge or cabinet, chugging the contents, and slamming the empty tin cans into the trash. She threatened to send him to a psychiatrist, or even Greystone, for an evaluation when he continued to drink and drive and then back the Impala into another car before driving away without leaving a note.

But the older and drunker he got, the more Dick ignored Dorothy, usually saying nothing or uttering "bitch" under his breath as he waited for her to calm down.

Dorothy had had enough. With her neck and back pain forcing her to hunch over as she walked, she got out of the car, limped over to a pay phone, plugged in a dime, and called her daughter's house. Dede's husband Stan answered.

"He's loaded!" she said. "I don't know what to do. Please help me!"

Dorothy had made similar calls before, but she had never requested a direct intervention. With her neck stiff and her heart failing, she made the plea directly to Stan: please come and get me.

Stan left Dede and their three children behind, getting into his car and driving the ten miles north to deal with Dick and Dorothy. As Dorothy limped to the Impala, Dick ignored her and stayed where he always felt more comfortable—standing on the boardwalk, staring at the sea, and ogling at the women walking by.

ℨ

For all his life, Dick believed he had been a good man, a person who projected class, something he had learned as a student at the exclusive private high school, Peddie, in Hightstown, New Jersey.

Following his father's 1933 suicide, after he sold his furniture at the Hightstown home and moved with his mother to Florida, he still wanted to do right by his family. He hoped he and his mother, Grace, could find the peace of Bay Head, a year-round beach-like calm without the cold air, blinding snow, teaming rain, and dreariness of New Jersey's winters.

Dick hoped she could turn herself around and bring back the connection he had with her. He missed sitting there, when he was a young boy, watching his mother make cakes, pies, pot roast, and of course, pineapple upside-down cake. As he grew older, he went from standing at her side as a boy and occasionally mixing the ingredients in big bowls to fully cooking the family meals as a teenager.

He missed sitting next to her, leaning against her arm, and feeling the warmth of her body. He enjoyed her gentle touch. After she suffered her stroke, he could find little to replace that. He felt as though he lost the only person who could tolerate his obsessive worrying whenever he felt the slightest pain or a cut. She became his best friend when he had no interest in being with others.

She seemed to be the one person who truly loved him, because more than anybody else, she was the one who made him feel special. Even after his father's death, when Grace was unable to walk or speak, he felt a certain closeness to her as he lifted her in his arms and carried her to her bed every night.

In Florida, however, Grace's health continued to fade. Dick's outlook toward life hardened as a result. His commitment to being successful became stronger. His feelings about love and family became more acute.

After seeing his parents physically, mentally, and emotionally struggle their way through life, Dick wanted to have what his father had struggled to accomplish: to be successful, have a stable family, and live the great American life. He wanted ultimately to be a good husband and father to somebody and find a way to protect not only the family's health and well-being but also its security. He had to do the opposite of what his father did: he had to protect his money.

In 1935, Dick moved with his mother back to New Jersey and, when he was unable to find work that could help his brother support her convalescence, he moved into an apartment in Trenton. Grace moved into the Home for the Incurables in Newark, where she spent the last seven years of her life.

Although he mostly avoided his brother, Robert agreed to pay the bills as he developed wealth as a manager for Monroe Calculating, a business that served as an original developer of computer technology.

At twenty-two, Dick was finally on his own, living in an apartment and eager to move on with his life. He felt something he hadn't felt since he spent summer weekends in Bay Head: he felt free.

He started going to church socials, where he found himself socializing with some of the same people he had gone to school with in Trenton. Now by himself, and feeling little to no attachment with anyone, he started to look for something that could replace what he had before with his mother.

Still, he was a little shy. He needed something to help him break the ice. Much like how his father turned to booze and caroused in clubs in New York City whenever the stress of his job and family became too much, Dick started to buy bottles of liquor, and he would sip from a glass before heading out to the socials.

The liquor made him feel looser and more confident. He also thought less about the mucus in his nose, and he was less interested in pulling out his dirty hanky that he knew others would find distasteful.

He discovered his talkative side, and he put women at ease as he sat next to them and boasted about something most other men at that time didn't do—cooking. When he started to sip more liquor, he could finally connect with women.

At the church socials, Dick ran into Dorothy DeLacy, another acquaintance from his days growing up in Trenton. Unlike Dick, she was social and active, always participating in church activities and school clubs. She was a joiner and a leader, a member of the student council and other leadership positions at her school. She made herself so busy that she rarely had free time for anything, let alone to eat.

Dorothy offered what Dick wanted out of his own life: she grew up with wealth and attended exclusive private schools that taught her grace and charm. Dorothy, however, had been sheltered from the problems that had saddled Dick's family, never touching a drop of alcohol her entire life, and establishing her own comfortable sense of stability. She went on long walks every day, keeping herself skinny even as she continuously worried about her weight. She could be moody. Sometimes she was very talkative and engaging, but other times, she was cold and not very outgoing or friendly. She demanded perfection and formality from others, including her own family.

Three years older than Dick, Dorothy sought companionship in the local scene. She worked for the child welfare services division of New Jersey state government and went to the occasional Presbyterian church socials, where the drinks were no stronger than soda and grape juice. She was charmed by Dick's jocular but sensitive nature, and during their short courtship, they danced several nights a week, staying away from restaurants and bars that would offer something Dorothy disdained: alcohol.

Even when she was social and friendly, even as her family helped sustain their lives for years, Dick would eventually discover that Dorothy didn't provide what he really wanted. As social as she was, she could be detached. She could be prim and proper and not very willing to be touched or hugged. Dick never had the emotional connection with Dorothy that he had with his mother. That, he would soon learn, was a situation he could never correct.

ॐ

Dick and Dorothy married on February 12, 1937, exactly nine months before their first and only child, Dede, was born. After they had Dede, they moved into Dorothy's parents' house in Trenton, where they had built-in babysitters so both Dick and Dorothy could work during the day and go dancing at night.

Dorothy tried to have another child, but she miscarried. For Dick and Dorothy, the miscarriage was difficult, but it also brought some relief. Dede was a precocious blonde who demanded constant attention. She grew especially close to her grandparents, since Dorothy insisted on continuing with her job with the state and Dick struggled to make a living with his first job, as a salesman in the publishing industry.

For much of the time, Dick wasn't even around; he stayed in a boarding house in the Elizabeth area, where his work was based, coming home only on weekends. He considered moving the family to Elizabeth, fulfilling the dream his father had long before and living in some of the city's exclusive, though declining, neighborhoods. But Dick also wanted to avoid repeating his father's mistakes; he didn't want to spend money he didn't have. In Trenton, he lived rent-free and he was close to his wife's work.

When Dick was home, he, Dorothy, and Dede went on trips to his mother's relatives in Elizabeth and Westfield, staying in touch with them long after his mother's stroke and her death in 1942. As he felt the pressures of making a living, he increasingly turned to alcohol for relief and often mixed it with social events. Knowing his wife's temperance, he kept a bottle of wine hidden and sipped from it before getting in the car to visit with others.

He would often ham it up with Irving Smith, his cousin from his mother's side, who took over the family's Cadillac business that was thriving in Elizabeth. Like his father Chet, Irving boasted about his ability to make money and constantly tried to sell Dick a Cadillac. Dick would laugh and pretend to appreciate the needling. Privately, however, he resented everything Irving was about and he grew jealous of Irving's ability to have success without even trying.

They would also socialize with Dick's cousin, Edwin Baldwin, an artist trying to stake his claim in New York City, who visited Dick's family in Trenton. Baldwin liked to paint scenes of the sea, and he crafted simple, fading sunset scenes and pictures of boats sailing. Whenever Dick saw them, he could see Bay Head and perhaps his mother and the life he left behind after his father killed himself. Dick was so moved by what he saw that he did something he never did with anybody else, not even his mother: he gave Edwin money to help his art business, and he didn't ask for the money back.

At first, as a husband and a father, Dick tried to be everything his father wasn't: available. On weekends, he went on long walks with Dorothy. Sometimes he took Dede and Dorothy to the ocean—particularly Asbury Park, where they'd walk, enjoy the beach, and eat ice cream.

World War II pulled Dick even further away from his family. He worked as a doctor's assistant and was stationed in Long Island, assisting surgeons who worked on battle-scarred soldiers who were on their way home. He was able to go home every few months or so and take Dede and Dorothy to the beach where he posed for pictures—using his new, but inexpensive camera—in his sailor uniform.

Back then, with her mother working and Dick even farther away, young Dede grew closer to her grandparents. As she grew older, she started to dread her father's trips back home. Dick tried to make up for all the parenting he lost while serving in the Navy during the war. He would be stern and blunt, telling Dede whenever she gained weight and harping on her about what she ate. He would get on her case about her homework and grades, even though she was one of the top students in her school. He would warn her that she would never get into the college of her choice unless she worked as hard as she could, even though she already was. They only warmed up with each other at the beach. Dick would display the same sense of humor and sensitivity he showed at the church socials, especially after sipping from those liquor bottles before a family vacation or a visit with the relatives.

When the war was over and Dick had completed four years of Naval service, he decided to find a way to merge his worlds of money and family. He finally finished college, graduating from Rutgers University in 1949, and, after working a few years as a statistician at the New Jersey Department of Labor, scored high enough on his civil service test to be considered for an administrative position in state government. He scored so high that, despite his lack of management experience, he was recommended for some of the top positions.

Dick accepted an offer to become personnel director of Greystone, one of the largest psychiatric hospitals in the East. Greystone, an aging, isolated facility on a hilltop in Morris Plains, promised something he never had before: security. Dick had a civil-service job, which carried protections that to him made it virtually impossible to get fired. He had a 100-year-old Victorian home on the Greystone campus that, because of his administrative duties, cost him little to rent. Instead of dealing with the high-strung world of sales, he would have a busy but stable job that required little contact with people other than his secretary and assistant. He also had a job that, he was promised, would rarely go beyond the nine-to-five schedule.

His first office was in the main building, the large locked-down structure with a French-style mansard roof that resembled a dome. Patients were housed in separate wings, separated from the administrative offices by thick metal doors that echoed whenever they slammed closed. Dick had two assistants who dutifully served him and feared him whenever his "peculiar" moods and obsessive behavior—which grew increasingly severe as he got older—caused him to lose his temper.

Every so often, Dick would do something few others would do: he walked through the thick, metal doors that separated the administrators and the patients and he would talk to people. He made sure to shake as few hands as possible, and he washed his hands repeatedly afterward. But Dick could empathize with their plight. His grandmother, uncle, and father suffered fates that were very similar, even though they were never physically institutionalized. He never would say it out loud, but as he grew older, he started to feel more of the same impulses, insecurities, and tension the patients felt.

He often defended the people who lived in Greystone's dirty, cramped conditions, which the hospital's founders created in 1870 to establish a secure way of life. Others mocked him and his family for living at the "nuthouse," but Dick defended the patients much the way he defended all people who were disadvantaged, often speaking out for civil rights for African Americans and the disabled.

ꝫ

At Greystone, Dick typically earned a few thousand dollars a year, at most $27,000 during the year he retired. But, throughout his tenure, he had little desire to leave. After earning a master's degree at New York University in 1953, Dick had offers from companies throughout the country to work as an administrator. He turned them all down. Those jobs didn't give him the opportunity to walk home and have lunch at his cheaply rented house. The hospital had a staff cafeteria with inexpensive food, where he and his wife ate dinner on most nights. He didn't feel the need to move away from the brick North Cottage that housed a much larger office that he and other administrators moved into in the late 1960s. There, he had a view through his window of the main building's north patient wing, with crossed steel bars in every window. But he also had a working fireplace and tile floors that were regularly cleaned.

Those other jobs also didn't have a nearby home where Dick could shower three, four, sometimes five or more times a day. They didn't have a refuge from the filth in the outside air and the Greystone buildings, which filled his nose with the thick, gray mucus he hated so much. He also wouldn't have a place where he could stash his booze, the stuff that could make him forget about the smell of urine that filled the air whenever somebody opened the doors to the patients' wings.

For a while, Greystone was the perfect fit for Dick. The same stubbornness that made him bump heads with his father suited him well as an administrator. The man whose father thought he was too much of a mama's boy and wanted him to toughen up ultimately developed a reputation as a no-nonsense boss who had little patience for people he believed couldn't match his levels of discipline and effort at work. In his North Cottage office, he worked with a chair, a metal desk, and little else, representing his passion for minimalism and frugality.

He carried that air of frugality into his personal life, even when he had the good fortune that had escaped his ancestors. When his cousin Edwin Baldwin died, Dick struck it rich, getting what may have amounted to hundreds of thousands of dollars in inheritance from the artist, who never lost his gratitude for what Dick did to help him. Dorothy and Dede hoped that they could spend the money on travel, perhaps going to restaurants and visiting places like the Grand Canyon. But Dick didn't see the money as something to spend. He didn't want to be like his father and lose whatever he made. The money merely allowed him to continue at Greystone and erased the need for a higher-paying job. The money gave him wealth, but more importantly, it bought him even more security.

While at Greystone, Dick and his family still went to the beach as much as they could, renting a room at a Bradley Beach boarding house and spending their summer weekends there. Dick and Dorothy also kept dancing, joining the local Senior Assembly that allowed people in their forties and fifties to enjoy activities they had enjoyed in their twenties.

But their lives grew more complicated and they grew more distant as both Dick and Dorothy started to worry about getting old. It wasn't only Dick, who started to worry more about the pains in his gut that he got after heavy drinking, not to mention every other little pain he had as his lean body aged. Dorothy missed her parents, who stayed behind in Trenton when she moved to Greystone. She resented the fact that, at Dick's insistence, she had to give up her job with the state once they moved to Greystone. The long walks she took to stay trim started to get longer as she let her mind drift to dream, as Dick would later do too, about living a life that was different from her own.

Dick, on the other hand, resented Dorothy for being friendly and social with others, but cold and distant with him. As he began to worry and fuss about himself, his health and his life, he never felt that he could turn to her for comfort or help. If he felt a pain or had a worry, he often bothered anyone who was in front of him, not necessarily Dorothy. Dorothy could ignore him or wave him off, denouncing his fears and worries as nothing more than immaturity.

༄

By the late 1960s, Greystone, and the life they lived there, started to wear not only on Dorothy but also on Dick. Unlike his father, whose life crashed when he lost thousands of dollars in the Great Depression, Dick's own insecurities rose to the surface slowly. Tired of blowing into the same handkerchiefs he'd been using since he was a child, he started popping as many as ten cold pills a day, hoping the old mucus would finally dry up and disappear. He rubbed Vicks VapoRub balm inside his nose to clear up his sinuses, even though the bottle's label clearly warned against internal usage.

When he had a hernia operation, Dick worried incessantly, badgering an administrative secretary at Greystone about how much he dreaded undergoing the procedure. "You want to know what it's like to have pain? Try having a baby!" the secretary, Irene Danner, told him.

But Dick was stubborn, particularly when it came to believing what he wanted to believe. After his surgery, he took a train ride to Florida for what he said would be a "time to recuperate," leaving his wife and daughter behind.

Dick had long tried to hide his insecurities from his wife and daughter. By the 1960s, he started to give up. He and Dorothy grew even more distant, and after Dede married in 1959, Dick and Dorothy often appeared stony and cold with each other, rarely showing any personal affection and choosing to address each other by their full, first names, "Richard" and "Dorothy."

Dorothy, for that matter, was no longer the social bird of her youth. She grew more detached with not only Dick, but everybody. She showed an emotionless detachment with Dede, keeping her distance and showing little of the love and devotion that children naturally seek. Dorothy demanded the same formality she had with Dick, telling Dede that she should be called "Mother." As Dede got older, Dorothy wasn't the type of mother who would go dress shopping with her daughter, or leaf through the Sears catalog and suggest Christmas presents, or try on jewelry together at the stores in the wealthy neighborhoods of Morristown. Instead, Dorothy would go on walks and disappear for hours, leaving her husband and daughter behind.

Dick and Dorothy tried to reignite some spark, going on long trips with each other, including driving to Florida. Dick thought he could appreciate the beach the way he appreciated Bay Head in the 1920s and Miami in the 1930s. When they arrived, Dick would often disappear; he wouldn't be found until hours later, hunched over in the bar or passed out on the hotel couch. Or he'd show up at the hotel room after midnight, reeking of booze.

Dick tried to keep up the image of purity he cultivated, putting it on display when he first met Stan in 1959. That day Dick demanded that Stan meet with him privately in the kitchen.

"We're temperate," he declared, before decrying alcohol as a fool's drink or a crutch.

Soon after Stan married Dede, however—when he went with Dick on walks at the ocean, or when Dick visited Stan and Dede's newborn daughter, Carolyn—Stan would see that it was all a lie. He would be surprised to hear Dick slur his words and appear unsteady as they walked on the boardwalks in Bradley Beach and Ocean Grove.

In the 1960s, Dick was still sharply dressed, clipping his pens to his shirt pocket and wearing jackets and ties as casual wear. By the end of every trip to the beach or visit with relatives, though, his tie would be loosened and his shirt unbuttoned down to his belly. His breath would reek of beer. Dorothy would look at him, seeing how sloppy he was, and shake her head.

Beer, vodka, and rum provided an outlet and encouraged Dick to push limits that once kept his marriage, his family, and his life intact. After Dede married Stan, Dick started to open up to others and confide in them. He'd talk about how his wife was doing so little to please him, how she was far too formal and obsessed with her weight to be romantic. He'd tell people that he was out to shatter those limitations that Dorothy set, even if it cost him his marriage.

‍↬

As his drinking increased, Dick's moods swung wildly and he sometimes became weepy. Unlike his mother, Dorothy offered little sympathy, choosing to go to her bedroom and read while Dick sat in front of the television with small tears beading down his cheeks.

Dick started to realize that Dorothy would never fill the emotional void left by his mother's death. He sought to vilify her, once bragging to Stan that whenever he went on long trips with Dorothy to Florida and elsewhere in the country, he headed to the hotel bar and picked up women. "I always keep women on the side," he boasted.

Once when Dorothy gave Dede a set of Lenox china, Dick got angry while he and Stan moved the set from the attic to Stan's car. "That fucking bitch!" he yelled. "Doesn't she know that these are $25 a plate?"

By 1970, Dick had come to hate his life. He detested that his wife didn't approve of his drinking and that she made a point of disdaining others who did. Dick often confided to his son-in-law about how much he was dissatisfied with her and his job.

At Greystone, he grew tired of the people who worked for him, the people who could never do the job the right way, or his way. They were the same people he often called "dumb" and "stupid." He considered leaving it all behind, but he realized that divorce and unemployment could compel him to follow his father's fate.

What he mostly cared about was his beer and "grape juice"—his code name for vodka that he kept in the kitchen cabinet in Morris Plains—and anything else that could make what he considered his empty world a blur.

When Stan arrived in Asbury Park on that February day in 1970, he found Dorothy sitting in the passenger seat of their Chevy Impala. She was subdued, staring straight ahead as she sat in the car, wearing her winter coat with the car running and the heat turned on.

Stan approached the window and peered in. Dorothy rolled it down.

"Everything okay?" he asked.

"Everything is fine," Dorothy said.

"Where is he?" Stan asked.

"He's up on the boardwalk."

Stan looked up and saw Dick, still wearing his heavy coat and hat, walking up and down the boardwalk, a blank look on his face.

"Everything's okay," Dorothy said.

Stan waved goodbye and headed back to his car, driving back by himself to Point Pleasant. As he drove away, he looked once more. Dick kept walking, back and forth, never stopping to look away.

CHAPTER 5

THE SOBERING LIFE

December 2008

IN DECEMBER 2008, I FINALLY DROVE up the steep driveway, past the empty doghouse where Dora's beloved dog, Kiska, once lived. I pulled over and glimpsed the giant, three-story "riverhouse" on the mountainside along the Delaware River.

It was a drive I had long dreaded. Ten years earlier, I drove by the house, the driveway, and the dog all the time. I was a reporter at the *Morning Call* in Allentown in northeastern Pennsylvania, and I covered the sleepy farm and suburban areas of the Lehigh Valley. I stopped at houses and farms and talked to complete strangers about the problems of the area: rivers flooding, farms being sold or foreclosed, and developers building. Down the road from the riverhouse, a man collected stumps from trees that were pulled out by their roots when developers plowed over the Pennsylvania landscape with housing developments. There were so many stumps that a small fire had started and never stopped. Repeatedly I asked neighbors and the local police the same question: "What are we going to do about the stump guy? He's dangerous!"

But I never stopped by the house that overlooked the Delaware River. It was the place we went to every Christmas when I was a boy.

It was the place where I watched my grandfather withering away, year after year.

Dora, who was eighty-five years old in December 2008, was Dick's second wife. She met him at Greystone in the 1960s or 1970s where they both worked. Her first two husbands died before she married Dick in 1976. She had a cackling laugh that we used to make fun of when we were kids. She loved small talk and intimate gatherings. At gatherings she gave updates on her life, giving full accounts of her trips and her social meetings with friends and relatives, often emphasizing what she said with a short "mm, hmm" before shifting topics.

She liked her life simple; for Dick, she was perfect. He could never really handle Dorothy's mood swings and her physical ailments. Dora was somebody who understood social graces and felt that it was better to be a part of the conversation than withdraw, even if the conversation had little to do with her life. Dorothy was formal, forcing Dick to carry on a conversation, even when he was too drunk to know, hear, or understand what was being said.

Deep down, however, Dora was complicated. There always seemed to be something behind the simple small talk, and she knew there was something about Dick that she just didn't care to let on. The rare times we did challenge her, questioning why she didn't take better care of my grandfather, why she did little to stop the alcoholism that was wrecking his body, she was always quick with an answer.

"I've tried," she said. "I've done everything I can do. But he won't do anything." And then she'd expertly turn the conversation in a sharply different direction, doing it so well that we'd barely notice.

On December 2008, I walked up the spiral, metal staircase, which still echoed with a clanging noise at every step, and pressed the doorbell. Dora quickly appeared in the glass and pulled open the sliding doors.

"Welcome! Come on in!" she said.

It was the first time I had seen her in more than sixteen years, yet little was different about her and her life. She still had a simple way about her, wearing a solid-colored shirt and pants, with her thick hair combed back. The house still had the thick burgundy carpet, and the piano was still the largest piece of furniture in the living room. The staircase was steep and tall, and the bookcases that sat near the bottom step were still there. They looked like the same furniture my grandfather's head rammed against when he fell in 1990, leading to his death two months later.

Only Dora's hair color was different, changed from a grayish black to snow white. She moved briskly around the room as she cleared a place for me to sit, much as she did when she waited on my grandfather hand and foot.

I carried my computer bag, which contained an audio recorder. I had hoped to record her and maybe even type some notes until Dora saw what I was carrying. Her dark eyebrows straightened, and she looked concerned.

"Oh, what have ya got there?" she asked, in her Canadian accent.

"Um . . . I'm just using it for my project. . . . All my materials are in there."

"Mm, hmm," she said. "You're making me a little nervous. What is it you'd like to know?"

I knew then that I'd have to keep the interview the way Dora likes everything: simple. I would have to sit and talk to her, and be friendly with her, even though at that point I was wary of her. My reason for feeling this way was never very rational. I had often been influenced by my mother's description of her as somebody who was after my grandfather's money and took advantage of him when he was losing his mind. Even when my mother's own mental health was in question, I believed her claims. My mother never understood why Dick and Dora got together or why they married just nine months after Dorothy's death in 1975. My mother never understood how they could get together when they seemed so incompatible, and rarely said anything to each other, except when Dick was in the middle of one of his episodes—fainting at public functions, getting drunk at a bar, or berating a waitress—and Dora had to come in and save him. After my mother died in 2003, I still stayed away from Dora, perhaps as a way to honor my mother and her memory.

It was clear by Dora's reaction to the computer bag that she wanted this to be more of a casual chat—a way to catch up—rather than a serious conversation. Within my family, Dora had only maintained contact with my sister Carolyn, and in her correspondence with her, she lost some of the politeness she had displayed when we got together on holidays back when I was a kid. My sister sensed a feeling of liberation, perhaps caused by the death of Dick and, even more so, my mother, that allowed her to go beyond the small talk she was famous for. She seemed empowered by the fact that we, too, knew there was something about my mother, as there had been with Dick. We all knew that my mother's behavior could be highly irrational, especially when she was outspoken in her disapproval of Dick's remarrying. Dora seemed to be genuinely interested to find out why things were the way they were.

She knew my mother had disliked her, and she acknowledged that fact when we finally sat down and I tucked my computer bag behind the couch. She said she never could understand why.

"I don't know why your mother didn't like me so much," she said. "We had done so many things for them. We took them on a trip to Europe. We gave you guys presents on Christmas."

"I think she had some resentment because of the way you got married," I told her. "It all happened so quickly."

"Mm, hmm," Dora said. "But, hey, that sort of thing happens all the time!"

As we talked, Dora talked about Dorothy—my grandmother and Dick's first wife—whom she barely knew when she worked at Greystone. She occasionally saw her walking and exercising on the spacious campus. She remembered seeing Dorothy hunched over because of her own declining health, going on long walks along the pathways that circled the old buildings, the farmland, and the acres of barren fields that served as a buffer to the surrounding communities. To Dora, Dorothy seemed aimless and hapless.

"That's where I think the mental illness comes from," she said. "There was always something about her. She used to just walk and walk endlessly. We used to see her, hunched over, and wonder if she needed any help."

Dora described her behavior as peculiar, and she tried to pin my mother Dede's mental illness on Dorothy's side of the family. Not on Dick. When I countered that claim, Dora twitched her nose and shook her head.

"No, I don't think so," she said. "Like I said, there was always something about her. . . . Your grandfather couldn't really tolerate that kind of behavior."

She talked about the troubled relationship Dick had with my mother Dede, portraying him as the one who knew better, the one who had grown frustrated first by her behavior, rather than the other way around.

"He had warned me about your mother," she said. "He told me, 'Watch out for her, because she has a lot of thoughts about things.'"

I started to feel some resentment. *She's blaming this on Mommy?* I thought. *How dare she! Didn't she know Grandpa? Maybe Mommy was right about her.*

I reached over, dragged my bag to me, and pulled out a folder that contained all my materials for the book that I was writing. The folder was growing rapidly as I kept finding new information about people, whether I was gathering it from the cemetery records or getting it from an interview.

At the top of my stack were the copies of death certificates I obtained from the New Jersey Bureau of Vital Statistics. I had copies of the cards I obtained from Evergreen Cemetery and the newspaper obituaries reporting the gas-asphyxiation death of my great-grandfather, great-great-grandmother, and great-uncle. "They were all on Grandpa's side," I said. "That's what makes this so interesting. It's like there's this path of self-destruction, and it runs all on one side of the family, right straight through the Winanses."

Dora put on her reading glasses and scanned the articles quickly. She looked more befuddled than surprised, staring carefully at the words through her lenses.

"Right," she said, pausing. "Well, your grandfather's father died because he lost a lot of money in the stock market."

"Right, I've heard that too," I said. "But look at how he went about it."

I reached across the coffee table and pointed at paragraphs in one newspaper article that I had highlighted with a ballpoint pen. I showed how Edward Winans, my great-grandfather and Dick's father, took every step possible to ensure that he would die quickly.

"Look at how meticulous he was—he did everything he could to slam the door, plug the cracks, and stop the gas from going outside."

"Mm, hmm."

"And look at how his mother went through the same thing," I said, pointing at a copy of the *Elizabeth Daily Journal* that was on the bottom of the paper stack. "I mean, how could that be a coincidence?"

Dora leaned back against the couch, slipped off her reading glasses, and looked away, glancing at the staircase to the left, with the bookcase. Her eyes then shifted back to me.

"Well, I don't know, Tom," she said. "Do you think maybe there was something there?"

"I think there was," I said.

Dora took a deep breath. She stared down at the articles and then looked up.

She started to talk about Dick. Only this time, she showed a willingness to concede. She talked about how she expected something completely different, how she had hoped to live a life of retirement that would include trips and growing old with a loved one. She had been robbed of that opportunity twice, with her first two husbands dying too young. Before their quick courtship in 1976, she knew Dick only a little, seeing him as the stoic, tall, slender, handsome, and strong-willed administrator at Greystone who inspired people with his image, if not his personality.

He kept himself in shape, walked off the extra pounds in his middle age, and was picky with his diet.

Dora liked being married, and she shared Dick's passion for money. Like Dick, she never really had it when she was growing up in western Canada. Unlike Dick, she spent money once she got it; her husbands made good livings as businessmen, and one of them helped build her Pennsylvania house. The house was more ski chalet than residence, with an angular roof and a Dutch-style brown façade. She liked to go on cruises to exotic places, but she also maintained her bond with Canada, often going back to where she came from to see family and explore nature.

She expected to grow old and die with Dick. But a few years into the marriage, she knew it couldn't be that way. She realized that his drinking dominated his life. He embarrassed himself and anyone who was with him as his health and his sense of appropriateness disappeared.

She believed my mother Dede did what she could to sabotage the marriage by staying away and by making comments about Dora behind her back or directly telling Dick the marriage was "ridiculous" and nothing more than a money grab for his new bride. But Dora also knew that it was more than that. Dick did just as much to drive away his daughter—and anybody else, for that matter.

"Believe me, I know," she said. "I lived with it for fifteen years."

"Why wasn't there anything done about it?" I asked, referring to treatment.

"Mmm," she said. "Well, you know your grandfather. I did mention it to him sometimes, but he didn't want any part of it."

I pulled out other documents, stuff I had printed from computer websites. We talked about how Greystone was once merely a large holding cell, a place where patients didn't go for treatment within its large, hollow hallways and pale rubber rooms. People went there to waste away and die. Many of those who worked at Greystone shared this experience. Some staff members became unhinged as they dealt day in and day out with the despair of seeing people walk around the hallways like zombies and hearing the screams of people locked away.

"Believe me, I know it," she said. "I saw it."

✍

Dora was a music therapist, and she treated hundreds of patients at Greystone through holistic means, using instruments as a way to soothe their pain. Despite her plainspoken ways, she knew about mental illness and she studied it. She had earned a degree in psychology, but she got an even better education by going to work every day, taking a musical instrument into a dayroom and playing Mozart to the patients who sat in stiff chairs, staring blankly.

She knew about illnesses and the effectiveness of certain treatments. She even knew about the *Diagnostic and Statistical Manual of Mental Disorders* (*DSM*), the guidebook that the American Psychiatric Association used to identify and name behavior deemed "mental illness." When we talked about it, I had just learned about it myself; my book-writing class instructor at Columbia had required me to study it, because he figured it would give me a sense for the history of mental illness that paralleled my family's life. He thought it could point to how ignorance was the driving force for the poor treatment of my ancestors; older versions of the *DSM*, for example, identified homosexuality as a mental illness, but not bulimia or anorexia.

The more I delved into the history, the more I could see that my instructor was right.

Back when Dora worked at Greystone, obsessive-compulsive disorder was treated more as a minor neurosis than as a full-fledged illness. In the 1970s, when she met my grandfather, the *DSM* identified the symptoms of obsessive-compulsive disorder (OCD), but still omitted the potential long-term effects. Dora admitted that even as she treated people every day who suffered from extreme forms of the disease, she had no guide, no playbook, and no strategy for handling people's specific issues. If there was a problem with a patient, she would simply call for help. Either patients responded to her music therapy or they simply sat there, murmuring to themselves or zoning out entirely.

The very thought that my grandfather, given his stature as a mental health care administrator, might fall into an OCD abyss never occurred to her—even as she witnessed all of his symptoms.

"Your grandfather had his routines," she said, her voice breaking slightly. "He could be soooo stubborn! I would tell him things and he just wouldn't do them."

What I couldn't understand, I told her, was how someone who worked there—especially somebody like Dick, who had one of the top positions at Greystone, but also somebody like her—couldn't see it themselves and steer themselves or their loved ones away from destruction.

I noted that, beginning in the 1970s, people who suffered from schizophrenia, OCD, and bipolar disorder were finally able to find treatment away from the gray walls of Greystone. In the late 1990s, the US Center for Mental Health Services reported that the number of organizations providing twenty-four-hour inpatient and outpatient services more than doubled in the United States from 1970 to 1998—just as the number of beds at psychiatric hospitals was cut in half. Psychotropic drugs were available to help Dick live a long and healthy life.

"You know your grandfather," she said. "He never would have gone for it."

"Did you ever suggest it to him or say anything to him about it?" I asked. "Did you ever look into any programs that could have helped?"

"I made a suggestion one time, that maybe he should seek counseling," she said. "He didn't want any part of that. . . . You know your grandfather."

"Yeah, I do."

"Mm, hmm."

Then Dora gave me a sheepish look, bowing her head slightly and staring at me silently.

"Geez, I don't know," she said. "Do you think mental illness was involved?"

I looked at her straight in the eye.

"I think so, Dora." I said. "I think so."

Dora told me that Dick's alcoholism ruined her marriage. She recalled with embarrassment the times he passed out in public places. She recalled with humility how she expected to get a strong, confident man who pleased state officials with his tough, frugal management of the Greystone personnel, a man who had buses drive the poor in Newark to work for cheap as orderlies on the Greystone grounds. She recalled her hope in getting a man who had a sense of humor, who often recalled the practical jokes he and other sailors played on the officers when he served in the war.

For the next four hours, we shared many stories as well as our regret that things hadn't been different.

"It really is a shame," Dora said, over and over, her eyes welling up with tears.

December 1978

Dick's thick, swollen legs dragged along the thick, burgundy carpet. His face was red and puffy, and his stomach bulged over his belt. His arms were weak and lifeless, hanging limply off his shoulders. His eyes were glassy and wet, with tears welling up inside them. But those tears weren't falling. Not yet, at least.

We sat in the riverhouse, just days after Christmas, watching him move slowly from the living room to the kitchen, where he reached underneath the kitchen sink, popped open a bottle of the "grape juice" and swallowed nearly a quarter of it in one swig. Repeatedly, he moved back and forth, from the room where my family sat to the kitchen.

Just a year before, at the last Christmas family get-together, his face had been narrow, chiseled, and sharp. His skin had still been tanned from his many trips to the Jersey Shore and Florida with Dorothy. He still always wore a tie tightened up to the button on his collar. Even then, he liked to drink big gulps of "grape juice" and "ale." He kept his not-so-hidden beverages in a kitchen cabinet, next to the dishwasher detergent underneath the sink. He moved with a brisk easy gait that made his trips to the kitchen barely noticeable.

In December 1978, Dick was moving, but he was mentally gone. The effects of cirrhosis and hepatitis C—diseases he may have kept secret from everybody—took hold of his body. The tall man known for his thin legs, who once took long, high strides even when walking across a room, couldn't get his legs to stretch more than a foot apart as he walked across the carpet. The man who took showers three to four times a day now seemed to go days without washing any part of his body, and emitted an odor that smelled like urine.

Gone was the man at Greystone who ran a tight ship. Technically, he was still working at Greystone, but he was using all his vacation days until his retirement, which would be official after New Year's Day in 1979. Now, he looked less like his fellow Greystone administrators and more like the patients. He still had the pens clipped to his shirt pocket, the same ones that were in every staff photo that filled his photo albums alongside the pictures of Dorothy and Dede on the beach. But his shirt was now a large, stained flannel that was always pulled out of his pants. Tucked slightly in the same pocket was a handkerchief that hung out low, one that he pulled out continually and blew into like a bad horn.

Before Dorothy died, Dick often drank until he looked like a walking corpse. But he did it in front of Dorothy, rarely in front of anybody else. Even as his health declined and the belly over his belt bulged, people only thought of—and chose to remember—the man with the dapper suit and ironed tie, not the drunk one who was weak, sad, and slow.

At sixty-five, Dick didn't care anymore. He didn't care if he looked like the homeless people who were packed inside vans in Newark and hauled over to Greystone where they'd be locked up in rooms that had barred windows and smelled like urine. He didn't care that the drinking made him virtually immovable and prevented him from doing what he enjoyed doing more than anything: sitting on the beach with his shirt off, tanning in the sun.

All he wanted was his "grape juice," and to my family, Dora was a willing accomplice. To my family, their coupling remained a mystery. She loved the mountains; he liked the beach. She was cheerful and laughed often; Dick was cynical and no longer laughing. She was stable and confident; Dick was mentally ill and, most of the time, drunk. She always claimed that she barely knew Dick when he was married to his first wife and didn't date him until a few months after Dorothy died. My family thought differently; my father, in particular, was skeptical, given Dick's boastings a decade earlier of having dalliances while Dorothy slept during their long Florida trips. Ironically, when it was later discovered that Dick had hepatitis C, my father believed that it only proved that Dick's boastings were at least somewhat true, given that the disease is often sexually transmitted.

My family saw Dick's marriage to Dora as not one of love, but one of revenge. When Dick's first wife, Dorothy, announced just a few years before she died that she was leaving the hundreds of thousands of dollars in bonds to Dede, her daughter, Dick separated from her emotionally, if not physically, refusing to accommodate her and provide extensive assistance when her own health declined. Instead of being around the house and helping Dorothy as she struggled to sit or move, Dick often took one of his drunken trips to the shore, disappearing sometimes for twenty-four hours or longer. Often, the only way Dorothy knew where he was going was when she got a call from the police telling her Dick had a fender bender with another car. In one case, he left for so long that the police went looking for him; they found him at his Ocean Grove house, sitting on the porch, drunk.

My family thought Dora was the final straw, the final kick in the pants at Dorothy and, ultimately, at my mother too. Dick made it clear that when he died, Dede wouldn't get a dime; Dora would get everything that was his. In fact, Dick, once so devoutly tight with his money, appeared to begin spending the money he had worked so hard for on himself and his second wife.

When he and Dora married, Dick also still had his inheritance from his cousin Edwin Baldwin; now, Dick felt more inclined to spend it, and Dora went along. They went on trips to Europe, cruises to Alaska, and lots of places that were certainly more expensive and luxurious than the Jersey Shore rentals in Bay Head and Bradley Beach that Dick had frequented since he was a child.

Our lives and their lives became so separate that the only time we saw Dick and Dora was when we visited the riverhouse, three hours from our home in Point Pleasant, each year at Christmas time. They were usually staged affairs, with my grandfather mostly silent and Dora, ever the small-talk lover, doing the talking.

But even the Christmas visits were never quite like the one we had when I was eleven in 1978.

Thanks to that Howard Hughes flick, moments of odd behavior no longer got by me. Watching a wounded, puffy-faced bloated man who said he was my grandfather was significant and educational, just as my mother's long bathroom visits, her repeating of phrases and words that annoyed my father to the hilt, and her piles of Wash'n Dri towelettes told me a lot about her. It was sad, but it was ridiculous. It was pathetic, but it was also repulsive. Now I knew that my grandfather, this decrepit man who shared my genetics, *was* Howard Hughes. Like Hughes had been in his day, my grandfather was on the downside of his life, and the downside was steep. Like Hughes, he let his body go after so many years of protecting his physical image, as well as his emotional image. He lived like a homeless man, except he had the protection of Dora, the riverhouse and—like Hughes—the money to prevent him from ending up in the street.

This recognition, this in-your-face moment of clarity, came at a time when I began to recognize my own insecurities, and I started to wonder if what I saw happening to him, as well as my mother, was something to be handed down, and this was a look into the crystal ball of my future.

Could this be me? I thought. *Could I grow into this? How do I stop myself from going there?*

As we sat in the living room, waiting to be seated for dinner, my brother and I kept watching Dick as he shuffled from the kitchen to the couch. Between nips of the juice, he was pretending to clean up, picking up crumbs and little pieces of lint on the burgundy carpet in the living room and throwing them away in the kitchen garbage.

He walked by Dora often, but Dora barely seemed to notice. She sat in one of the living room chairs and kept up her small talk, which was usually along the lines of "Well, we haven't had our first snow yet," "I had to take the dog in for shots last week," and "I visited with my son yesterday. . . . He's doing fine."

Something about it all seemed to ignite something in me and my brother, who was then fourteen. I can't remember where or how it started. But one of us just started giggling. And giggling. And giggling.

The more one of us snickered, the other snickered more. We watched Dick sluggishly move from room to room, swinging one arm like an ape, and carrying lint and crumbs in his hand. It was ridiculous.

"Stop it!" my brother whispered to me, but he said it between his own smiles and laughs. He kept ducking his head under his hands and choking on his own laughter.

This wasn't like a visit to a nursing home, where the afflictions of the elderly are sad. This was a man who, beginning with the Florida trip two years earlier, had become downright goofy. This visit seemed like a natural continuation of what we saw in Florida, where he created his own circus and did everything he could to make people think him a fool, not pity him for being handicapped and pathetic.

We wondered to ourselves why nobody seemed to notice us right away as our giggles consumed us. Or at least they pretended not to. The more people talked small-talk, the funnier the scene was.

These people are talking about food and trips, and here is this old man walking around like a gorilla, I thought. *This is ridiculous.*

But Dora was sharp, and she knew where this was heading. She knew she had to stop us before we actually *had* a circus. As much as she resented my family's resentment toward her, Dora still strove to be accepted. She knew that a fight would end any chance of that ever happening.

Dora adeptly found a way to weave the matter into her small talk.

"Somebody's got the giggles," she said, before moving the conversation into something about her own grandchildren and how silly they can act at family gatherings.

My brother and I froze and then looked over at my mother and father. My father nodded, and put his hand up, waving slightly as if to say, "Okay, that's enough."

My mother, however, stared at both of us, her face still and icy. She glared at us for a second or two, the same way she had glared at me when she burped at the picnic table a few years before when my father had yelled, "Say 'excuse me'" to my brother before pinning him against a tree.

She glared for only a few seconds and then returned to the conversation. She had her public face back on, the one that masked her own obsessions, and she could match Dora's small talk as well as anybody.

As much as my mother resented Dora, she wasn't interested in a fight either. She saw my grandfather slipping away, and deep down, she didn't want him to go. My mother occasionally talked about how she had always wanted something more out of him than what she got as a child. She wanted a father who would take her seriously and could connect with her emotionally. She wanted more than the mental health administrator who disappeared all week and then tried to make up for his absence on the weekend, at the beach, displaying his goofy sense of humor. As he walked around with his gut bulging out, she knew that that opportunity was almost gone.

The conversation resumed, and then it didn't seem so funny. My sister, who was eighteen, also glared at us. Perhaps more than anybody, my sister felt a kinship with my grandfather, going back to the days when he took her to the Asbury Park boardwalk and bought her ice cream. She was the only one who could see the moistness and the tears that were constantly in Dick's eyes, that began to fall and then slid down his cheeks when we sat down for dinner. The more Dora and my mother talked, the redder his eyes got.

"This is actually really sad," my brother whispered to me, just as Dick wiped the sides of his eyes with a napkin. "We'd better stop."

⌇

Of course, Dick's slide began much earlier, even when he had the command and respect of his peers. People who had official positions in state government—lawmakers, health care workers, and the like—appreciated his attention to detail and his efficiency. They were impressed with his stature, his presence and his ability to show a stubborn resiliency, especially when he appeared at state legislative hearings in Trenton to back up his reasons for disputed personnel decisions. At those hearings, he rarely backed off, appearing stalwart and convinced on everything. He displayed the same kind of stubbornness he had with my mother whenever she wanted to take the car, but he wouldn't let her. Or when she wanted to drive to college instead of taking the train, but he wouldn't let her. Or when she wanted to visit Stan when the two were dating. But he wouldn't let her. On each decision, he showed little emotion, only dictating his reasons one by one and raising his voice only slightly.

Drinking became Dick's pastime in the late 1960s. By then, he was rarely tending to his garden at the Greystone house. He wasn't going to see Dede, my mother, very often, although that choice was mutual. The worse he got, the more fractured his relationship with his daughter, his only child, would become, just as his relationship had fractured with Dorothy.

If he had free time, he drank. If he wanted to go anywhere, like the beach, it had to involve drinking. Before he even got in the car, he had to be plowed, even if it meant getting into fender benders every few months. Somehow, he kept escaping trouble, even when the police had to drive him home and tow his car away.

❧

Dorothy's fall and her resulting neck injury in the late 1960s was, for Dick, the tipping point. She went to doctors and had surgery, but little could be done to help. She kept walking, but she couldn't walk far, or as far as she would have liked. When she did walk, she was often very slow. She insisted on walking some of the same paths she had followed around Greystone for years, even though she was hunched over, her hip twisted slightly and her body leaning to the left as she struggled to walk for miles at a time.

Her chest was in pain, and she went to see cardiologists in Morristown and elsewhere, but there was little they could do either. Dorothy was developing heart disease, and the stress she felt living with Dick could have made her heart fail. With Dick either working or driving to God knows where, Dorothy spent much of her time sitting in a chair, occasionally smiling but doing little.

When Dick was at the Greystone house, he wasn't really there, because he'd drink and do something that, to Dorothy and others, was crazy. When he actually agreed to do something with Dorothy, it had to be at the shore, and it had to involve drinking, and it had to involve women or looking at them. It had to be like that day in Asbury Park in 1970, when Dorothy sat in the car as Dick roamed the boards, drunk.

After that day, Dorothy called my family's house in Point Pleasant more often, usually when Dick was out in the car drinking and then getting himself into an accident. Dorothy kept worrying that someday Dick would leave and not come back. At this point, it wasn't so much the thought of something happening to Dick that worried her. It was the thought of being alone and uncared for.

❧

In her final months in late 1975, we visited Dorothy, my grandmother, both at the Greystone house and in the hospital. My brother, sister, and I often had to sit in the waiting room and wait for my mother and father to return. I'd watch my feet dangle off the chair, not even touching the ground, and I'd make circles with my feet as I listened to my sister and brother talk. They'd talk about my grandmother and things I didn't know or care about. I only knew that the hospital was bad, and I only cared that what was happening made my mother sad. In those days, my mother was getting sadder. I knew that if my mother was sad, I would be sad too.

Whenever our parents returned, my mother's eyes would be red, and she'd be wiping at them with the boxes of towelettes she stuffed inside her pocketbook. Then she'd force a smile and announce to my father, "Let's go out to eat. . . . Can we do that, dear? . . . Can we go out to eat? . . . Can we? . . . Can we go to a Howard Johnson's? . . . Can we go out to eat dear? . . . Can we always go out to eat, dear? . . . Promise?"

In those visits to the hospital, my grandfather was often far away, either at home, working, driving, or at the liquor store. He would not keep a bedside vigil. He would not hold Dorothy's hand as she slowly slipped away. Occasionally, Dorothy went home. When we visited, she tried hard to be polite and asked many small-talk questions, but nothing more. Her face was so wrinkled, it appeared to be ready to cave in. Her speech was slow and plodding. Her niceties seemed a little forced, as though she was trying too hard, and she often groaned as she tried to move her body in her chair.

In her final months, she tried to maintain a bond, even build a better relationship with my mother. The formality she had with my mother, the emotionless detachment, was lost. Dorothy's phone calls and pleas for help had changed that. She was honest and upfront with my mother in her final months and weeks, even if the words were often hard to utter. She drew no lines regarding how she should be talked to or even whether she should be called "Mother."

She often told my mother, in so many words, that she always loved her best. She was the one who lived with her, she reminded her, and along with her own parents, Dede's grandparents, took care of her when Dick was away. Even though Dorothy, too, was working, she was the one who was around more often. It was Dorothy's parents that took care of her when neither Dorothy nor Dick could be there. Not Dick's. She was Dorothy's child, she reminded her; not Dick's.

In one visit at Point Pleasant, after Dorothy had struggled mightily to get out of the car and walk up the sidewalk to our house, Dick openly berated Dorothy for not speaking to him "respectfully"—probably after Dorothy once again got on his case for his excessive drinking. With Dick drunk most of the time, and Dorothy's heart failing, neither was interested in creating an image of perfection anymore.

Just after he yelled, Dorothy turned to Dede, and to Carolyn, then a teenager standing next to her mother. And Dorothy told them, "Don't worry; when I die, you'll be taken care of."

Dorothy died on December 18, 1975. I came home from school that day and saw my mother standing in the living room, her eyes red and full of tears. She was sniffing slightly.

"Thomas, I have to tell you something," she said.

"What's wrong?"

"It's about your grandmother."

"Oh no," I said. "Is she dead?"

"No, no, she's not dead. . . ."

But I knew she was, because my mother then started to bawl like a baby. And then I cried, hard. I couldn't even hear what my mother said after that, because our mutual crying was so loud and deep. Somehow I got my mother to spell out what happened, what was wrong with my grandmother, and where she was and, yes, to admit that she had indeed died. My mother held my hands as she wept; it was the tightest she had held them in years. With her leg wobbly, she seemed to be leaning on me for support.

Days later at the funeral home in the Morristown area, mourners wept, frowned, and sat, looking forlorn as my grandmother's body was laid out. My mother sat in the chair, and in between small talk with relatives, wept silently as she looked at Dorothy in her coffin.

My grandfather was moving quickly, greeting people and showing a smile that few had ever seen when he was sober. He was full of energy, moving briskly from room to room, greeting those who walked in and helping with the planning of the event.

I sat in another room and watched the goings-on from afar. I was eight years old, and it was the first time I had ever seen a dead person. When I got a close look at her body, I was scared.

"Oh, my God!" I called out as I ran over to my father, grabbing his legs as my whole body shook. He took me to the room off to the side and put me in a chair. I still had a view of Dorothy, however distant.

My father was relatively calm, showing his soft side, the side he rarely showed because he was so often aggravated by mother's repeating, washing, and bathroom-hogging.

"See? It's just your grandmother," my father said to me. "It's nothing to worry about."

"But she's dead," I said. "She's dead. That can't be healthy."

"Okay, okay," he said. "It's just a part of life."

I leaned against his knee and bobbed back and forth, looking at the body out of the corner of my eye. I saw my grandmother's wrinkled face. Her eyes were shut and her mouth was a long frown. Even then, I could sense the toll of something, the effects of stress that could have brought her down. I saw the effects of what my mother whispered to my father whenever she took a call from Dorothy, pleading for help in calls they tried hard to keep from us. I already had an inkling that I was looking at a woman who, at sixty-five, died unhappy.

I was still shaking and bobbing when, almost out of nowhere, my grandfather appeared next to the casket. He stopped and planted a kiss on Dorothy's lifeless mouth.

I felt a feeling of disgust. "Why did he do that?" I asked my father.

He brushed it off. "That's a tradition," he said. "People do that when somebody they know dies."

Maybe, I thought later. *Or maybe he was drunk.*

We just never knew.

༄

His sentimentality seemed to end with that kiss. As he displayed in Florida, just months after Dorothy's death, Dick relished his freedom, drinking and dating at every turn. He was less serious, less sullen, and more playful, enjoying a good laugh, even if it was at his own expense. On the Florida trip, he had laughed at his own singing, sometimes stopping himself in the middle of the Air Force theme song—the one with the line "Off we go, into the wild blue yonder," which he repeated over and over—to chuckle to himself, over and over.

Whenever he saw my mother, he'd grab her and make fun of her weight. "There's a lot of you," he'd say. As Dora would do later, my mother played it off, at least publicly, laughing a little before walking away. Instead of going after Dick, she'd vent to my father. "I think it was terrible that he said that, don't you think so, dear? . . . Don't you think it was terrible that he said that? . . . Do you think I'm fat, dear? . . . Do you think I'm beautiful? . . . I'm beautiful, aren't I, dear? . . . Promise? . . . Promise to love me best of all?"

But the freedom soon gave way to sadness, particularly after he married Dora in September 1976. His new wife was surprised by his sudden sadness. To Dora, Dick was a playful man with a sense of humor who was willing to flirt with her and ask her out whenever she stopped by Greystone. She sensed, in their brief courtship, that he was somebody who was looking to, finally, have a little fun in his life after enduring a long, not-so-happy marriage. Dora hoped he would acclimate to her way of living the life she had known as a hunter while living and camping in the wilds of western Canada and would be ready for the next adventure.

Instead, she found herself a character in a soap opera, a caretaker to a dour, declining man who wanted little out of his life than going to the bar or liquor store. She found herself playing nurse to a man whose every move seemed to teeter on danger, even death. As he approached seventy, Dick started to have blackouts, forcing Dora on many nights to wrap her arm around his shoulder and walk him up the steep riverhouse staircase to his bed.

He kept up some of his hobbies, tending to a small garden he kept in the back of the riverhouse, where the wooded Pennsylvania forests extended for miles, and even cooking for him and Dora. He even enjoyed making Dora his specialty from his childhood—pineapple upside-down cake. During the Christmas visits, Dick had many moments of lucidity. When my brother announced that he was going to Rutgers after his high school graduation, Dick pulled out a miniature set of flags—including the American and Rutgers flags—and started waving them in the air, marching his swollen legs up and down. He often recalled his days at Peddie, laughing at some of the boyish tricks he and others would play on each other and sometimes on the administrators. We were a little stunned by his candor—particularly toward certain groups of people that, during his days as a Greystone administrator, he had defended.

"Even though we joked around, we always had respect for the officials," he said. "Not like today—not like these hippies and blacks you see on the college campuses. The blacks have no desire to help themselves."

He once bought a gun—an old-fashioned six-shooter—and showed it off to my brother. "This is the kind of thing you need to defend your property," he said. "We live out here in the woods, so we're sitting ducks out here. It's just like the way things were during the war—you had to have something at your side because you never knew if the Japs or the Germans would creep up on you."

While he was showing my brother how to clean it, Edward's face wrinkled with displeasure. "Oh no, don't tell me you're one of them?!" my grandfather said, laughing.

He was always offering to provide money to us, something he never did when Dorothy was alive. He continually pitched the idea of sending me to Peddie for high school. "The best time of my life was at Peddie," he'd say. "There was never a better school, never a better faculty that supports the students. I think Thomas would fit in well there—he's very smart."

One time, I got tired of him talking about it. I said, "Well, I'd go, but we can't afford it." My father shot me a look, showing a little anger and embarrassment. Dick said, "Well, I could pay for it. I've said that before." My father shook his head at me and responded. "Well, no, that's not it," he said. "Let's just see how things go over the next couple years."

Dick had similar talks with my sister, offering to send her to art school because he believed she had talent. He would take her up to his bedroom and show her the beach paintings he had from his cousin Baldwin. "It really is beautiful, isn't it?" he said, tearing up. "I'll always love the beach. It's the most beautiful place in the world." He would look at Carolyn and tell her how much she reminded him of Dorothy when she was in her twenties. He would speak of the days when he and Dorothy went ballroom dancing. "I hope you can find a good way of life," he said. "But your father never inspires enough confidence in you."

As each year passed, he moved further away from my family. Previously, he had regularly accepted invitations to graduations and milestones in all our lives; by the late 1970s and early 1980s, he was refusing all of them, choosing instead to stay at the riverhouse, tend to his garden in the backyard, and sleep after drinking alcohol for breakfast and lunch.

He finally relented in 1982, when Dora coaxed him to attend my brother's high school graduation. Only he didn't last long; just moments after he got out of the car to waddle up the sidewalk to our house in Point Pleasant, Dick tilted to his left and tumbled into one of the two tall evergreens that stood there.

"Oh, God," my mother said as she watched the spectacle, staring out the big picture window that extended across most of our living room. Waddling on her own bad leg, she hustled through the front door and peered out as Dora picked Dick up, wrapped his arm around her shoulder, and walked him toward the door. He sat on the couch, looking dazed. He acted as though he had no clue what had happened.

"It's okay. . . . It's okay," Dora said. "Everything is fine. Everything is fine. My kids pick him up all the time."

ᴣᴖ

Two years later, my parents did something we never thought they'd do after the Florida fiasco: they agreed to go with Dick and Dora on a European vacation funded by my grandfather to celebrate their twenty-fifth wedding anniversary.

This time the idea made more sense. They would do this on their own. My sister was working as a nurse at a hospital. My brother was in college; I was in high school. They wouldn't have the burden of shielding their children from my grandfather's drinking. They wouldn't need to deal with both children and an old man who behaved childishly, as they had in Florida eight years before. They would go to Europe, a place they had never been to. They would fly. They would go sightseeing and go to restaurants without guilt, because somebody else was paying for it. Even as they prepared, they were calm and seemed to look forward to the excursion. Even my mother's repeating seemed to abate as they got closer to the day of departure. Rarely did her questions go beyond this: "Do we have to leave early in the morning? . . . What time in the morning, dear? . . . Do we have to leave early in the morning?"

In Europe, however, trouble happened right from the start. Again, it was all about Dick. He was nasty with flight attendants aboard the plane on the way there, complaining that his drinks were mixed wrong or the food was terrible. He fought with waiters in Holland, complaining about the food and the service. He was nasty with Dede, but even more so with

Dora, telling her to "shut up" and even threatening to leave her whenever she teased him after he spent too much time at the bar.

He walked with a cane, moving slowly as they moved from ship to ship, from tourist attraction to tourist attraction. Throughout the trip, he wore the same clothes over and over, and didn't do much to clean himself, smelling like the bathrooms where he spent a great deal of time—even more than Dede did. He sometimes yelled "shut up" whenever Dora talked to him and made small talk, avoiding any talk about his gut, his gait, and his sideburns that were as bushy as his thick eyebrows, with white and gray hairs straggling out.

When he wasn't around, complaining, he was at the bar, drinking.

"That's where I always know to find him," Dora told people. Dora was often left with my mother and father, as always, the master of small talk. They just never talked about Dick.

The lowest point came aboard one of the cruise ships. After a night of heavy drinking, Dick blacked out—this time, my father later found out, to the point that there was a fear he would lapse into cardiac arrest. It happened while Dick was drinking alone. No one seemed to know what happened until the next day. No one knew, except for a doctor aboard the ship who, according to Dick, "worked a lot to revive me last night." After telling the story at breakfast, Dick even chuckled a little, kept eating, and kept harassing the help.

⮩

All of them—my father and mother, in particular—returned from Europe, drained. But my parents never let on how they really felt—not to us, at least. My mother only told us about the "wonderful time" she and my father had. They touted their souvenirs, which were beer steins and a cuckoo clock. By nightfall, my mother had returned to her habit of repeating and driving my father crazy. Life went on.

Afterward, Dora insisted on another family trip; she was still trying hard to forge a connection between herself and us. Dora may have been looking for more than family companionship; in her subtle way, she seemed to be looking for help, a buffer, or even an aide, of sorts, to help her deal with Dick when Dick was at his worst.

My father, perhaps long before anybody else did, could sense the trouble Dora was experiencing behind the small talk. At Dora's urging, and with my father's blessing, my brother and I accepted her invitation to go to the riverhouse by ourselves to stay for a few nights and ski at the local Pocono Mountains slopes.

Initially, I was hesitant.

"We're going to stay with grandpa for *three days?*" I asked my brother. "What happens if he goes for a jog in the woods?"

But after I saw how my parents were able to tolerate two weeks with them, and even report back about the wonderful time they had, I agreed.

Indeed, the more I thought of it, the more I looked forward to it. I had skied twice before and enjoyed it. But my brother Edward had a different plan in mind. Ever the idealist, he saw the trip as an opportunity to cure the family cancer. The image of my grandfather, wearing his blue blazer and falling into the tree just before his high school graduation was still fresh in Edward's mind. He wanted to deal with the problem, maybe even solve it. If he could do something about Dick, he thought, maybe he could ultimately snuff out all the problems of our family that, it appeared, had gone completely out of our control.

"I don't think you're going to be able to do anything about it," I told him. "He's too far gone."

"We've got to get to Dora," he said.

Dora, he believed, was the real culprit, the one who was preventing Dick from finding a normal life, not Dick himself. He, too, had heard my mother talk of Dora as a gold digger. He saw Dora as someone who was enabling, or even encouraging this behavior, and he believed the way to stop it was to talk to Dora.

My father drove us to a Howard Johnson's just outside Phillipsburg, about ten miles south of the riverhouse. There amid the string of restaurants and shopping malls of the clean and drab suburbia we knew, we sat in a booth by the window with Dora and my grandfather. Unlike the European vacation with my parents, this trip would be bland and simple, allowing my grandfather to indulge himself in his routines.

Sure enough, my grandfather almost immediately went to the bathroom after we sat down, and—like my mother—treated it as his sanctuary. He escaped to the bathroom frequently during our trip, staying for half-hour intervals. The minute he left at the restaurant, my brother sensed an opportunity.

"I'd like to talk about Grandpa," he said to Dora.

My brother was nervous, and his voice shook a bit as he talked. I could see beads of sweat forming around his hairline as he tried to look Dora in the eye. All the bluster he had earlier—back when he wanted to charge in like General George Patton and demand that Dora change her caretaking—was gone as soon as he started talking, and he beat around the bush without getting to the point.

When Dora replied, he was virtually silenced.

"I know, I know," Dora said. "Just think about what I'm going through."

Dora acknowledged that Dick had issues. She knew that more could be done. She said she wanted to get him help, but Dick refused. She threw everything in Dick's lap, talking about his stubbornness and how his resistance to treatment was practically insurmountable. She practically painted herself as a flawed hero, emphasizing her own efforts—however little—to get him help and revealing her own sense of helplessness when she found it impossible.

"I've tried," she said, "but there's only so much you can do."

Dora said Dick was enjoying his life now. Yes, she said, he certainly could treat himself better. Yes, she said, he drank too much. But Dick was an old man now, a man who had lived a life of hardships. He had money and he had a supportive wife. He was getting something from her, she said, that he hadn't gotten in a long time—especially from his first wife Dorothy and his daughter Dede: love.

"Generally, he's okay," she said. "He eats well. He sleeps well. The doctor says he's in decent physical shape, considering. But he gets along well."

As she talked, she ate her dinner, picking through her plate with her fork. She talked as she chewed, only taking sporadic breaks. Not long after Dora started talking, my brother backed off. I chimed in occasionally, but I felt just as hopeless. We felt better, at least, that we had talked about it, and we were relieved to finally hear from Dora and see behind her usual small talk. But we also felt we had hit a wall, a barrier to knowledge and solutions, and we still had no idea how we would ever get to the other side.

The conversation ended long before Dick returned, back from his long stay at the bathroom. We didn't stay long—Dick, still a picky eater, ate a small dinner before we headed north. As we walked out, and Dora struggled to help Dick get into the car, I leaned over to my brother and whispered to him, "What do you think?"

He shrugged and whispered back, "Not much I can do." It was as though he was repeating exactly what Dora had told him.

Going back to the riverhouse, we stopped in Belvidere, a sleepy, riverside Jersey town just miles from their home. It was the only nearby town that had stores, even if the stores looked as though they were on their last legs. Besides a supermarket, where he'd pick up food for supper, Dick's favorite stop was the liquor store on the main drag, perhaps the largest business in this small, historic town along the Delaware River.

Edward and my grandfather walked in, while I waited with Dora, standing outside the car to get some fresh air. I then heard loud noises coming from inside the store. I walked over and saw Dick yelling at the clerk. Dick had brought my brother in to help lift the cases of booze, and he became enraged when Edward was told to leave because he wasn't yet twenty-one years old.

"What do you mean, I can't bring him in here?" Dick said. "That's the stupidest thing I've ever heard."

Dick told the young clerk who he was. "I know every official in this state," he bellowed. "I could have you fired on the spot. I ran the largest hospital in the country. I know everybody there is to know."

Dora overheard it, too, and walked in. She paid the man and helped Dick carry the cases out to the car. As Dick continued to mutter, Dora tried to change the subject.

My brother walked toward me with his hands in his pockets.

"This is sad," he said.

The trips and the attempts at togetherness stopped soon thereafter, just as they had stopped after Florida. Outside of the annual Christmas visits and giving them presents on holidays, we made few attempts to seriously share our lives with Dick and Dora. Though we did invite my grandfather, he went back to skipping graduations, missing my own high school commencement in 1985, and my brother's college graduation the following year.

My family had little desire to repeat anything that happened in the past. Though little was said, it was certainly understood: my grandfather was the symbol of family despair, a smart and accomplished man whose once slow self-destruction was now on the fast track. He didn't hide his own sense of it, even once confiding to me during a Christmas visit. "I don't have much longer to go," he said, just after he showed me the garden plants that were still growing in his backyard. He still had pride in them, he said, even though he had little pride left for himself.

ॐ

The end finally came in 1990. Dick could no longer control his bowels. He began to defecate fairly often in his pants, and Dora found herself cleaning him much more than he ever did himself. He also became much more silent, and his mood turned into something like a constant stupor, his face becoming blank and barren. He barely acknowledged anybody who came into the house, including Dora's friends and relatives who visited much more often than we did.

By that time, Dick usually watched some television with Dora, and then slept in the downstairs bedroom by himself, avoiding the steep stairs that he could no longer climb on his swollen, wobbly legs. One night, in December of that year, he surprised Dora: He decided to head upstairs, and go to where he used to sleep with her. She watched him go.

The steps were steep, forming a seventy- to eighty-degree angle. Dick slowly moved from step to step, using his cane to guide him along. Just near the top, however, he froze, lifted his arms up from the railings and held them high. He then closed his eyes and popped his mouth open as his feet began to take flight, taking his body with him.

Dora tried to run over and stop him, but it was too late. He rolled down the steep flight of stairs, slammed his head into a small bookcase and cracked his brain stem.

We all wondered how he lived to seventy-seven. We wondered if he would find a way to get himself out of his misery, much like his father, grandmother, and uncle had. With this fall, he did. Whether he did it on purpose or not, we would never learn.

But when my father heard Dora's version of the story many years later, it was one of the first questions he asked: "Do you think he did it on purpose?"

ᴣᴘ

Dick survived for two months on a respirator. He finally died on February 15, 1991, and when he was buried, he was isolated, as he so wished, in Dora's graveyard with Dora's two other dead husbands, far away from the relatives he once said he loathed, the ones buried near Dorothy in Ewing Township, New Jersey, as well as his own Winans clan who filled up the family plot at Evergreen Cemetery in Hillside, New Jersey.

The funeral was a simple one; many more people seemed to be there for Dora than for Dick. At one point, it seemed like there was nobody else there for him but us. No Greystone personnel; no World War II veterans. Just us.

The service, held at a funeral home with a small seating area, had none of the trappings of a ceremony that would celebrate a long, accomplished life. There were no pictures of Dick in his sailor suit, standing next to Dede when he came home on an occasional weekend during World War II, smiling, as he played with her pigtails. There were no pictures of Dick with Dorothy, even though there were hundreds of them in his own album, standing in the same black swimming trunks he always wore in Florida and at the Jersey Shore.

The ceremony was led by a pastor who said little, if anything, about the accomplishments of a man who served in World War II, who was a top administrator at a large psychiatric hospital. Indeed, the service was entirely religious and the sermon was short. At the end, Dick was whisked away in a hearse that transported his body through Belvidere, and then the burial some ten miles to the east, where he had a simple, black gravestone that read "Winans."

On the way out of the graveyard, my mother, who had been largely stoic and unemotional toward the death, started sobbing, as did my sister, calling out loud, "He was a good man! I don't care what anybody says! He was a good man!"

My brother and I looked at each other, ready to scratch our heads. We had never been more confused by what we saw. We thought of all the heartache he helped bring about, particularly the way he had treated my mother and everybody else. At the time, we saw him as just some hypocrite who got what he deserved.

"I'm not going to cry," Edward said.

CHAPTER 6

THE HISTORY

December 2008

I VISITED THE EVERGREEN CEMETERY in Hillside again, only this time I had to contend with freezing, twenty-degree temperatures and a stiff sideways wind. Despite the bright sunshine, the ice was thick and the frozen ground was as stiff as a concrete floor.

At least now, I thought, *I'll be able to see the plot.* The first time I had been there, just weeks earlier, the Winans family was buried in a rain-drenched mud pit. That day, the sun had set, the rain was pouring, and the view was a watery blur. I barely had any memory of what the site was like, whether it was maintained, or even if the graves were marked. I had stepped out of the car for a minute or two, felt the big, cold raindrops pelting my jacket and pants, taken a few underexposed photographs, and left.

Now, despite the freezing temperatures, I could study the site, take photographs, and write down every name I saw. I hoped to get a better sense of the Winans family than what I had read on three-by-five-inch index cards.

The characters in my plot were emerging. I needed these characters—these people from my family—to come back to life and help me solve the jigsaw puzzle of my own life and its history.

I needed any and all insights into their lives. *Were there tombstones? I thought. Were they buried together? Or were they like my grandfather, who didn't want to be buried with anybody at all?*

The first time, I found the tombstones by luck. On this cold December day, I walked into the cemetery office and talked to the women who were sitting in the cubicles. One of them pulled out an eight-by-eleven-inch cemetery map and pointed to a letter and a number. She circled the plot on the map and pointed through the door toward the icy downhill slope. "Go down that hill, where all that ice is running," she said. "Follow it, and when you get around that last hump, look to your left. That's the Winanses' plot."

I got back into my car, feeling the wind punch against the windows as I drove down the paved path. The fields of tombstones and yellow grass were empty, except for a greenskeeper in a truck who drove along the narrow empty paths, stopping every minute or so to brush the snow away from the markers, and reposition some American flags the sharp breeze had blown off.

The damp wind felt colder than twenty degrees, creating layers of ice on my windshield that my wiper blades pushed away. On this well-lit day, I could see everything. I could see what seemed like hundreds of tombstones marked "Crane." I remembered the family legend that Stephen Crane, the renowned author of the 1895 Civil War book, *The Red Badge of Courage*, was a cousin whose family was from Elizabeth, New Jersey. As soon as I saw the name Crane, I could feel myself getting closer. Indeed, many Winanses graves—though not the ones I was looking for—were mixed in with the Crane plots, lending credence to the legend that the two families shared ties.

As I saw the numerous grave markers that read "Crane" and "Winans," I had a sense that Elizabeth, which was a beaten city by 2008, a city named after the English queen but now filled with ninety-nine-cent stores and pawn shops, was once a close-knit community, where family members grew up together and were laid to rest beside each other.

In a way, the city reflected the plight of my family, crumbling to ruins after enjoying years of wealth and excess. Elizabeth lost its wealth as the richer families fled to the suburbs, and the problems of New Jersey's urban areas—such as substance abuse and crime—invaded the city and the local schools in the 1950s and 1960s. The stately mansions grew old and became condemned relics. The big stores and companies, such as Singer Sewing Company, moved out of the area, with nothing to replace them.

What was left, other than the downscale downtown, was a collection of houses turned into multiple apartments and people on welfare living in crammed spaces. The homeless problem in Elizabeth was more than double the state's average: census statistics and homeless advocacy groups reported that 15 percent of the city's population in 2008 had no home. Services to treat them—including mental health and drug rehabilitation—were becoming scarce.

But at the Evergreen Cemetery, just outside the Elizabeth city line, the city's sense of community was preserved.

I saw the "I" sign again and made a somewhat sharp left turn. I started to look down the hill to my left, and then I saw it. I pulled the car over on a large patch of ice, pulled out my Nikon camera, and walked over to get a look. "Winans" was inscribed across the front flat marker. Behind it was my family.

Just a few feet beyond the family stone was my great-grandfather Edward's black-and-gray marker. Like the others, it was small and fading, listing simply his name and the date he died. Next to him was Elias Crane Winans, Edward's father and my great-great-grandfather, who had his Civil War unit inscribed below the name and date.

I touched each black marble stone and felt the frost-covered ground. Each stone was planted in the ground, face up, except for two. One, a large, white tombstone that listed the family's names with birth and death dates—was laying flat on its face; I tried to pull it up, but it was too heavy. The second, next to Elias's grave, was Frederick Winans' upside-down marker with the death date of October 4, 1928. I tried to move this stone back, too, but it also was stuck in the ground, only this time, it was too cold for the ground to give way.

I guess nobody cared about this guy, I thought.

Next to my great-grandfather Edward, there was nothing for his wife, Grace, my great-grandmother, who was listed as being buried there too. Instantly, my thoughts turned cynical. *I'll bet Grandpa had something to do with that,* I thought. *He probably didn't want to spring for the tombstone.*

On Edward's left was his mother, my great-great-grandmother, Lydia Winans. Like the graves of her sons Frederick and Edward, her marker offered no inscription other than the date: October 4, 1928.

ॐ

I headed to Route 1 and plodded through the traffic congestion to the Elizabeth library. I saw people standing at street corners, dealing with the cold by putting their hands in their pockets. One man was kicking chunks of ice that were scattered over the sidewalk. He kicked the ice toward a wall, trying to break it into tinier pieces, as though he had nothing better to do.

I thought about all the times I had driven through Elizabeth and ignored these same images because they're symbolic of urban New Jersey. I, like so many of the state's residents, chose to ignore things that I felt I couldn't change. Now they resonated with me. *I came from here?* I thought. *My family came from here?*

I walked through the large library doors and looked inside. The 100-year-old stone building had hallways that were tall and long and a reference desk as wide and round as a carousel. The white stone walls were pale but stately and clean. *Christ,* I thought. *This is the nicest building in this godforsaken place.*

After seeing neighborhood after neighborhood with houses that were falling from the roof down and seeing people walking in the street, talking to themselves, this library felt like an oasis. It felt like the Elizabeth I was beginning to learn about, the city that was named after the Queen of England and reflected the royalty and wealth of her majesty until the late nineteenth and early twentieth centuries. I thought of my family and how they must have envied this life.

This is what they wanted, I thought. *They wanted the colonial life with the stately charms.* From what I was learning, however, their plight brought them closer to the man kicking ice on the street corner.

I went upstairs and fished out of the drawers of microfilm a box labeled "*The Elizabeth Daily Journal*, 1928." I sat at the machine nearby and strung the film through, then turned the knob and watched the fuzzy black and gray pages fly by. Every once in a while, I slowed down and saw ads for Chesterfield cigarettes as the roll slowly slipped through the summer months into October. Many of the articles' words were small and faded. Some of the articles were blurry and silly. "Mrs. Jones' Dog Is Lost" read one.

But I only cared about one headline and one article—if there was one—so I zipped through much of it, slowing down only occasionally. *The same day!* I thought. *This had to make news. I can't believe this! Keep going . . . keep going.*

As I got to the fall months, I rolled more slowly. I debated with myself regarding the date to land on. *Maybe it didn't make the paper until the next day*, I thought. *Maybe I should flip forward—maybe to October 10, and then go back.*

I rolled up to October 5, 1928. The words were splashed across the top, bumping against a smaller headline that reported on the 1928 World Series. The headline was bigger than any headline that day, and on most days.

"Woman, Son, Dog Are Found Dead of Gas in Home," it read.

Lydia, my great-great-grandmother, and her eldest son, Frederick, were together, with the dog, gassed to death. Lydia, the article said, was on the couch; Frederick and the dog were on the floor.

This was their choice, I thought. *It had to be.* I rolled back in my chair, folded my arms, stretched my legs forward, and stared at the screen. The words were as clear as a *New York Times* banner headline on the Internet, and they were as loud as anything I had ever seen in a supermarket tabloid.

I could feel my gut roiling again, and the stomach gas from lunch rolled up into my throat. I ate little that day because I was just so hell-bent on getting this done before nightfall. I thought of that day in 2003 when I told my story to Mary Ellen Schoonmaker, the *Record of Bergen County* editor who encouraged me to pursue all this and how research and writing about my family's history had felt like the perfect therapy as I grieved after my mother's death. Instead, it was giving me gas, and affirming my biggest fears about myself and my family.

I'm nuts, I kept saying to myself. *I'm fucking nuts.*

I rolled my chair back toward the machine, and read the story, repeating the same line in my head. *It's not your fault*, I thought. *It's not your fault.* As I thought, I read it over and over. I then found a follow-up article that painted the scene with some detail.

I called my father and read the headline.

"Oh, God," he said. "Really? Wow! . . . I can't believe it!"

"Yes, it's true."

He paused, then sighed. "You know, your grandfather never said anything about this."

જ્જ

In the weeks that followed, I talked to nearly 100 psychologists, psychiatrists, law enforcement personnel, criminologists, and anyone who could analyze the information. I wanted to know more. *Was this merely a coincidence? Was it an accident?* I thought of the September 11 airline hijackers and what psychologists had told me before when I had written stories and columns for the *Record of Bergen County* on the cause of suicide.

Not all people who kill themselves are crazy, I thought. *It could have been an accident. Or it could have been planned. They could have been simply lonely. They could have been sick.*

I leaned toward a circumstantial, even cynical, interpretation of the event. Death likely brought horror, but also relief to the Winans family. On October 4, 1928, Elias was long dead, and Edward was beginning to lose control of his professional life. Frederick and Lydia, it appeared, had few resources available. Based on what was described in the *Journal* and what I saw in a picture the newspaper had published, they lived in a very small apartment house that was, even then, in a rough side of the city. They were old. Lydia's other son, Edward, died the same way, five years later. It's quite possible they found no other way to help alleviate the anguish they felt after suffering through emotional pain and financial loss for much of their lives.

Their deaths were, quite possibly, the only solution to their problems. When Lydia, Frederick, and Edward died in 1928 and 1933, family problems were not talked about openly, just as they weren't talked about in my family forty years later. Suicide, in particular, was considered very shameful. Few reference guides were available to help law enforcement and mental health professionals identify and treat cases of what were often described as "lunacy" and "moronic behavior."

There was no *DSM*, not until the 1950s. Many people were locked away rather than diagnosed and treated specifically for their disorder. Many people were housed in psychiatric hospitals—or what were then called "asylums"—and handled by underpaid, unqualified attendants rather than receiving regular attention from professional therapists, such as psychologists or psychiatrists.

Indeed, psychologists told me that the pattern of handling people with mental illness in the 1920s and 1930s was unchanged from the way treatment was handled centuries ago, when patients were put in tanks of ice-cold water, shackled to dungeon walls, and spun in chairs. In the early twentieth century, lobotomies were given to people as a way to sedate those who were suffering and to prevent seizures.

133

The Winans family appeared to show little—if any—interest in the treatment options that were available. Living in their small cities and suburban towns of New Jersey, they also appeared to have little access to care. The state had two main psychiatric hospitals during the first half of the twentieth century: the Trenton Psychiatric Hospital and Greystone. Other forms of clinical and outpatient treatments were available, but they were either far away or too expensive.

Back then, mental health professionals and law enforcement routinely misidentified cases of mental illness that could have yielded useful information and perhaps prevented further tragedy. Though Lydia and Frederick's 1928 deaths were ruled an accident, criminologists and mental health professionals who, at my request, reviewed the case in 2009, said the scene raised questions that could undermine the credibility of the police's decision.

Although no note was left and no motive was found, the timing of the incident, the position of the bodies, as well as the family's history made the event seem more purposeful than accidental. In those days, many police officers and coroners avoided terming a suspicious death a "suicide" so the family wouldn't feel shamed. They also avoided reaching out to mental health professionals who could have reached that conclusion.

Now psychologists and psychiatrists provide assistance to law enforcement authorities in investigating a possible suicide at a crime scene. Police and medical examiners also have since developed checklists that assist investigators as they walk through a death scene and determine whether a suicide has taken place.

⁓

Over time I grew frustrated by the lack of information I was getting. Even with the news articles I copied and the interviews I conducted that explored the minds of the mentally ill, I still lacked a connection with anyone in my family who came before my grandfather. I knew little about them other than the fact that they died, a little too early and a little too accidentally. Barely anyone who was alive knew who they were, let alone why they did what they did. I got copies of census records from 100 years ago that were handwritten and barely legible. I sent letters out to many government agencies, requesting information on births, deaths, illnesses, military history, psychiatric history, or anything else remotely connected to the story. Barely anything was returned to me. What did come back said little more than "application denied" or "no information is available on this subject."

I spent many hours researching Ancestry.com, but much of what I got was too vague and too loosely connected to my family. The one character in my story who intrigued me more than anybody was Frederick, my great-grandfather's brother, and his name popped up from time to time on the website. I found he had held a job as a wallpaper hanger, but not much other information on his professional and personal life. After seeing how his tombstone had been trashed, I wondered if this was a man who struggled with his life much the same way my grandfather, great-great-grandmother, and mother had struggled with theirs. The tossed-over tombstone was, at the very least, symbolic.

Ancestry.com and other websites provided enough information for me to obtain his birth certificate from Elizabeth City Hall. There was nothing about his cause of death or details from his life history. Unfortunately, the certificate simply stated his name, date of birth, and little else. It listed him as "married," but said nothing about a woman whose name kept popping up on Ancestry.com: Matilda Winans. She was identified as living with him in the Elizabeth area in the early 1900s. In April 2009, I made a death certificate request for Matilda and for each her three children, none of whom appeared to be alive. I didn't hear back for months.

Then I had to slow down my pace on my book, as pressure from the *Record of Bergen County* mounted. The newspaper was transforming as it tried to acclimate to the web and digital media. The demand on reporters to produce stories every day was getting bigger as the newspaper suffered through a severe industry-wide slump. Reporters were being laid off by the dozens as the Internet took away much of the content—advertising—and as a result, the revenue that kept newspapers afloat and profitable. The more I got involved in my book, the fewer stories the newspaper got from me.

As I was winding down my graduate studies, my editors asked me to meet with them in my office in Trenton. I had been moved there in February 2009 when the *Record of Bergen County* decided to combine its statehouse coverage with the *Star-Ledger*, New Jersey's largest newspaper. I was expected to produce stories on New Jersey government and its never-ending troubles with its bloated budget and political corruption. But I spent much of my time combing the Evergreen Cemetery, searching through microfiche in libraries and trying to write paragraphs for my never-ending book.

My editor, Deidre Sykes, sat at the table and was blunt. "You've been AWOL," she said. "We call you on some days, and you don't answer the phone."

I defended myself, of course, saying that I simply forgot to turn on my cell phone some days. But Deidre, who could be happy and jovial one moment and dry as a bone the next, batted away my excuses.

"If we're going to make this bureau work, we need everybody working as a team," she told me. "We can't have that if you're God knows where. You have to start working as part of the team."

I put the book down for several months to focus on the newspaper. I even considered bagging the idea of writing a book altogether. Writing the book was also taking a toll on my wife and children. They barely saw me because I spent much of my time in cities like Elizabeth or working on my laptop in my attic bedroom, trying to put just the right words and phrases together so the book made sense. While working on the book, I felt I could do little else. The book had a hold on me. The ghosts of my family's past were haunting me, and I needed to find out why—or I needed to find out why I should care.

࿊

I always considered writing as a form of therapy. Sometimes I wonder if writing could have saved other members of my family. I wonder if they had put their thoughts into words and created a diary of their experiences, the obsessive thoughts that dominated—and ultimately destroyed—their lives could have found a form of relief. Maybe my grandfather could have lived a life of fitness, allowing him to run up the stairs to his bedroom for a good night's sleep when he was seventy-seven and not fall backward into a crumbled, crushed heap.

I took up writing early, at age six, putting together a newspaper for an imaginary professional league I created using a toy hockey game. I had game standings, box scores, and stories that kept track of every game, every goal, and every save. I developed a passion for reading and writing about sports, and as I entered my teen years, I read all the New York and New Jersey papers I could get my hands on, scouring for any report, statistic, or friendly fact that reported the up-and-down saga of the New York Mets baseball team. I kept track of every average, and I fretted if the Mets didn't have a single player batting higher than .300. I kept track of the attendance at the Mets' ballpark, Shea Stadium, and felt depressed whenever I watched games on the TV and saw whole sections of the stadium empty.

My first professional job came at sixteen; I got paid $10 to write a story on my cross-country running team with its 10-0 record. From there, I worked as an editor, with a salary, at the Rutgers University newspaper, the *Daily Targum*, before launching my full-time career in 1989 at the *Princeton Packet* in central New Jersey. For the next decade or so, I bounced around small to medium newspapers until I joined the *Record of Bergen County*, in January 2001.

Going to the *Record of Bergen County* was my best move. It was the first, and maybe the only, paper I ever worked for that gave writers a voice. Until then, I had never really had one. My voice came alive after the September 11 attacks, where every snapshot of death and ruin demanded a wide range of vocabulary. The newspaper demanded that we go beyond the standard, stilted language of press releases and news conferences. These stories needed analysis, depth, and just plain good writing. Instead of writing eighty stories a month—not an unusual load at some of my former places of employment—I concentrated on one big piece that would be blasted across the front page and that would probe the issues of the terrorist attacks more deeply.

Over time, I won awards and received praise. But something was always missing. After seeing what happened to my mother, I developed a passion for the subject of mental health. Writing about it gave me a chance at self-reflection. This book was the missing piece. This story had to be more than about me. It would be the generational link of symptoms that connected me with my family and my past.

Throughout the spring and summer of 2009, I continued stumbling and digging through libraries, graveyards, and Internet websites to find the slightest glimpse of a family in peril.

⌇

A break came in June. I got a letter in the mail from the California Department of Vital Statistics. It was a death certificate for Clarence Winans, who was Frederick's oldest son, and who had died in 1986 at the age of eighty-seven. Clarence's son was listed as the informant, and his address was listed in the Los Angeles area, where Frederick's wife— and *yes*, it was his wife—Matilda moved with her three children after, I would later learn, she decided to leave Frederick.

I found the telephone number for Clarence's son, Stewart, through an Internet-based research database and called him up while I was sitting at a Wendy's, eating dinner after a long day of work in Trenton. He talked in a low voice and gave me short responses when I asked him questions. I told him about the family and what had happened to them.

"I really didn't know much about my grandfather," he said of Frederick Winans. "I didn't know him at all."

I nervously stuttered as I mentioned mental illness and how that may have been a part of the family's DNA. I worried that he would slam the phone down on me, thinking I was some sort of telemarketer or crackpot who loves to prey on the elderly. He had just ended a family party, he told me, and he sounded tired. I was prepared for the possibility that he would reject my probing. But he did nothing of the sort.

"Yeah, we've got that in the family," he said. "My father was a big drinker. He also had shock treatments."

Shock treatments? I thought. *Are you kidding me?*

I thought about Grandpa and my mother and everybody else in the family who suffered from mental illness. Nobody ever went that far. Of course nobody ever got treated either. Shock treatments were a common form of treatment for anybody before advancements were made with psychotropic drugs in the 1950s and 1960s. *Still,* I thought, *he was the first to do it. . . . or maybe the first to admit to it.* I didn't know much about Clarence Winans, who would be Frederick's eldest son, and Stewart offered me few details. But it was one of my most enlightening moments in the book's process.

Stewart told me about his daughter, who also had been going through a similar personal, family research quest. Lynne was living in the Los Angeles area and she had been interviewing people for years—including Frederick's son Clarence, before he died—and was posting the information on the Internet. She was still in touch with her aunt, Elsie Winans, who was married to Merrill, who was Frederick's youngest son and Clarence's younger brother. She had pictures of a boat cruise Matilda took when she finally got fed up with Frederick's ways and fled to California with her three children.

I talked to Lynne on the telephone and we e-mailed each other. Lynne had reams of information on almost every Winans family member, save for my immediate family, whom she didn't know existed. I helped her fill in the information, but there was one piece of juicy information contained on her family website that seemed to tie everything together for me.

"Frederick was apparently an alcoholic," she wrote.

Aha! I thought. *That's what I needed to know. That's the link I was looking for.*

She also told me about her son and how he was having issues similar to what my oldest child, Tommy, has experienced, as well as symptoms experienced by others in the family. Her son and mine had shown symptoms of sensory integration disorder, in which a person shows hypersensitivity and overreacts to excess stimulation. There was even some thought that both of them could have Asperger's disorder, an autism spectrum disorder in which people show significant difficulties in social interaction. But neither was proven.

The more I talked to Lynne, the more I realized this: *The proof is right here. Maybe this is all worth it after all. Maybe we can learn something about ourselves. Maybe our children can deal with their issues head on, and early, and never have to live through the same experiences as their ancestors.*

***

Later in the week, I felt inspired enough to drive over to the Elizabeth apartment where Lydia and Frederick had died. I wanted to see the inside, to size up the rooms and the layout of the floors. I wanted to see how trapped Lydia and Frederick could really be. I wanted to see whether they could escape the gaseous odors that filled their bedroom.

After I knocked twice, a man with wild eyes opened the door.

"What is it?" he barked. He had no shirt on, and a friend behind him was hunched over as he moved around, much the way my mother was hunched over ten years before.

The sun was setting, and the man mumbled answers as I asked him questions. He wouldn't let me in. I was disturbing whatever privacy he wanted to have at the moment. Behind him I noticed the wood was decaying and the paint was chipped all over the house. There was no wallpaper; in fact, much of the sheetrock that would finish the walls appeared to be missing. The living room and the bedroom looked small.

I got back in the car and I opened my laptop. Words flowed out. I felt the despair of the house, then and now. I could see the small rooms, the wooden walls and floors. I could see behind the tall, gated fence that seemed almost as high as the porch. *This was the end of a long journey*, I thought. *And it began with a dream that failed.*

That dream came from a Civil War veteran by the name of Elias Crane Winans, an Elizabeth man who seemed to hope that adventure would rescue him from modesty. I would learn about Elias after talking to Lynne, who had talked to those who knew what little there was known about him. I would learn that he was much like my father, a man who apparently married into mental illness and never successfully found a way to manage it. Ultimately, he suffered the same fate as his sons, Frederick and Edward: he died too young.

May 1867

Had Elias Crane Winans stayed in his home city of Elizabeth, he could have helped extend the family's wealth and success by doing what others did: owning a big piece of land and farming on it, or owning a local business and becoming a city official. Had he not been angling to stake his own claim, he could have had the stability of his parents— both of whom were established farmers who provided food for the local grocers and apparently benefited from the town's growth during the industrial age. The population of Elizabeth grew from 11,000 to 73,000 from 1860 to 1910.

Indeed, thousands of single-family houses sprang up in the late 1800s after I. M. Singer established his first sewing machine factory on Newark Bay, locating it on a thirty-two-acre plot that was the former site of Crane's Ferry and employing a workforce of 6,000 people. Home builders were also responding to the rise of the Elizabeth Seaport, which became one of the busiest ports in the country, attracting Standard Oil and the US Navy to locate its ships and machinery there.

Many, like Stephen Crane, the author of the best-selling book *The Red Badge of Courage*, were buried at the Evergreen Cemetery, which was established in 1853 and designed to fit the emerging aristocratic ways of Elizabeth culture. Local clergymen and business leaders designed the cemetery serpentine carriage and pedestrian paths. Some of the original plots were surrounded by decorative wrought-iron fences with gates.

Elias's parents were buried there, as were many of the members of the powerful Winans and Crane families who helped found Elizabeth in the 1600s. In the 1800s, many of the people who moved to Elizabeth, started a business there, raised a family, and died there chose Evergreen, undeterred by its costly price and impressed by its classic style.

Even though the cemetery was actually in Hillside, many considered Elizabeth a "rich town" because of Evergreen, as well as the large, colonial-style structures such as the city's library. Also most houses there had a kitchen, which was an unusual find in central and southern New Jersey in the nineteenth century. Restaurants and bars that made their own beer sprang up nearby, and the first ice-cream soda was invented, locals say, when a local grocer dumped a splash of ice cream in a patron's drink after he complained it was too warm.

Sports were popular with the elite and successful, too, and bicycle clubs came into vogue in the latter half of the nineteenth century. Dozens of young men engaged in long rides into the country, wearing one-piece athletic wear as they rumbled along the city's cobblestone roads. Many Elizabethans eventually grew frustrated about the condition of the roads, so they bought second-home cottages at the Jersey Shore where they could enjoy long, wide, flat roads with no traffic.

Elias wanted to go beyond the dull but profitable farming life that his parents, Nathan and Mary, had established in the Elizabeth area. He wanted to achieve the kind of success that could eventually give him the money he needed so he could live in one of Elizabeth's stately mansions, the same ones people marveled at whenever they rode into town. They appreciated the many Victorian homes that were built in the 1800s, filling the vacant land along cobblestone streets that were lit with gas lamps. Like Elias, many were starry-eyed about Elizabeth, but not about farming.

The day before his twentieth birthday, Elias joined the US Army's Company K, Ninth Infantry Regiment, and fought for the Union in the Civil War. The group was heroic and successful, but it had its share of troubles. The regiment had more Springfield rifles and ambulances than any other unit when it left for the battlefield on December 6, 1861, and helped make the Northern blockade of Southern ports effective. But several of its boats sank or ran aground on sandbars after strong gale-force winds struck just after they sailed south from Maryland in January 1862.

Elias never rose above the rank of private, and he was twice hospitalized while fighting deep in Confederate territory. He apparently suffered wounds that limited him and, later in life, forced him to rely on a wheelchair to get around.

After he was discharged on August 31, 1864, Elias became a respected member of Ulric Dahlgren Veterans Post 25, a veterans' group named after a Civil War colonel who died in battle in 1864. He and other Civil War veterans were subsequently greeted with adulation: the city erected a monument on Broad Street dedicated to the soldiers that carried this inscription: "To the Soldiers and Sailors who Fought to Preserve the Union, 1861–1865."

Like Elias, many wanted the "dignified" life, a goal that the residents of the "Queen City," as some called it, yearned to reach. Even with his Civil War record, however, Elias showed few skills beyond what he had learned at his family farm. His dreams of wealth and prosperity would ultimately die when his eighteen-year-old girlfriend, Lydia Shotwell, became pregnant. They were married on May 15, 1867, and about four months later, Frederick, their first child was born.

Elias's family weighed down his life from the moment Frederick was born. While his cousins lived in mansions and four-bedroom homes throughout the 1800s, Elias and Lydia were forced to raise their children in a small rented apartment on Liberty Street. Irish and German immigrants living in single-room units—packing as many as ten people in each space—were his neighbors.

Lydia displayed few if any labor skills, forcing Elias to find painting jobs—even if he had no choice but to push himself on local streets in his wheelchair or walk with a limp as he carried a small number of his painting tools around the city.

Lydia had grown up in privilege. Her parents were farmers, too, and owned a great deal of land in Rahway Township. When she had children, she stayed home, keeping to herself. Going into the city to shop was a responsibility that fell on Elias who, despite his limited mobility, found a way to get around town because of his painting jobs. He was assisted by the horse carriages that provided a taxi for local residents, but he also had Frederick and later his second and third children, Edward and Mary, to help push him in his wheelchair whenever it was necessary.

It's quite possible that Lydia was one of many spouses of Civil War veterans who suffered from the anxieties generated by the conflict. Researchers have found that Civil War veterans who saw more death in battle than those who didn't had higher rates of postwar illness—and their care was not handled by hospitals and clinics the way soldiers were treated in the twentieth century. After the Civil War, that job was left to the spouses, primarily wives, who had to deal with ex-soldiers who were pushing themselves in wheelchairs or still bleeding internally because of the wounds they suffered.

Younger soldiers, such as Elias, were more likely than older ones to suffer mental and physical problems after the war, which had taken more American lives than any other war. That possibility increased even more if the soldier was physically wounded in battle.

Lydia appeared to be almost reclusive after her youngest child, Amy, died of rheumatic fever in 1893 at age fourteen. The family couldn't afford a funeral, so they had a short ceremony at home. The Ulric Dahlgren Veterans Post 25 provided assistance with the arrangements.

Ironically, Elias chose Evergreen as Amy's gravesite. It didn't matter that it was one of the most expensive and exclusive cemeteries around. If there was one thing he could control, it would be the family's final resting place. He scraped up around $125 to buy a family plot near Stephen Crane and the many other Elizabethan aristocrats. He still hoped he could make up the money by establishing a successful painting business, and he hustled hard to get the rich and powerful to hire him.

༄

As the children grew, they began to display behavior that Lydia and Elias showed no ability to control. Frederick, for one, liked to hang out at the Elizabeth train station, staying away from the family and out of his mother's shy, but watchful eye.

Indeed, Union Station was one of the busiest stations in the nation, serving both the Pennsylvania and Central railroads. Presidents, including Abraham Lincoln, stopped there en route to Washington to greet crowds of well-wishers. It was also a place where carriage riders, and eventually car drivers, feared they would hit somebody because of the numerous grade-level crossings along the nearby roads.

For others and, presumably, Frederick, it was also a place to go to when they needed to sober up before going home and seeing their families. Local residents feared that people who liked to hang out at the station would get hit by a train if they drank too much and wandered into the streets.

When he left school in the 1880s, Frederick appeared to be qualified for little more than what his father offered him. Elias tried to give his son a direction, hiring Frederick as a "wallpaper hanger" for his painting jobs. But Frederick often returned to the train station, and that is the place where people often found him.

Indeed, Elias could offer little to help Frederick, especially since his war injuries worsened and limited him even more as he aged. In the 1890s, Elias, then in his fifties, was confined mostly to his wheelchair, and his heart was starting to fail.

Eventually, Frederick's brother Edward, who started a career as an insurance broker in the 1880s, hired Frederick as a clerk and Frederick appeared to find stability. In 1892, he married Matilda Frick, a hard-working, independent-minded daughter of German immigrants. Shortly thereafter, Frederick moved out of the family's Liberty Street apartment and relocated to neighboring Union Township, where he and Matilda began to raise their three children.

But after a few years, Frederick was back to hanging out at the train station, back to drinking and staying away from his wife Matilda, who raised their three children virtually on her own.

Matilda eventually realized that Frederick was becoming helpless and hopeless. She was a devout Episcopalian and didn't pursue a divorce. She wanted Frederick to abandon his perch at the station and be the father he was supposed to be. But she became less hopeful as time went on. Matilda didn't want anything getting in the way of living a normal life with her family.

If that meant leaving Frederick, so be it.

⁊

Matilda was born in a home full of children and with a strong sense of family values. Her father was a tailor, and he taught her the tricks of his trade that would help Matilda grow up to become a fine seamstress. While Frederick struggled with drinking, Matilda ran a two-story boarding house in Elizabeth, but she made much of her money by going to the homes of the local wealthy and staying with them as she sewed expensive dresses and suits. She stayed with these families for days, taking her three children with her as they played in the spacious yards. Many of the homes had beautiful gardens.

In 1915, Matilda finally gave up on Frederick, taking her three children to California and separating herself from her husband forever, though she stuck to her religious principles and never divorced. Matilda's journey to California began when she and her children stepped aboard a steamship in New York called the SS *Maumas*, which transported them to New Orleans. From there, they climbed aboard the Pacific Limited's Sunset Southern train and headed for Los Angeles, where she started her own seamstress business that was even more profitable than the one she had in New Jersey.

Once in California, Matilda had some of her household furniture and personal items shipped from New Jersey, including a bird's-eye maple dresser and chiffonier that would stay in with the family for years. She left Frederick with little furniture. Indeed, Frederick had no steady work.

Just before she left, Matilda's sixteen-year-old son Clarence was pulling his eight-year-old brother Merrill in a wagon along the busy streets near the Elizabeth train station, when Clarence suddenly stopped and pointed toward a man in the distance. They acted as though they had rarely, if ever, seen this man.

"Merrill!" Clarence said.

"What?"

"That's your father."

For the rest of his life, it would be Merrill's only recollection of his father.

~

Money was tight for Elias, too, in his final years—one of the many hardships facing Civil War veterans and their families was the inability to regularly secure medical benefits. That had been a problem since the war, when some of the regiments were not paid for as long as six months. The most glory Elias ever achieved from the war was the fact that he could call himself a veteran and have the name of his unit chiseled into his tombstone at Evergreen, which he insisted would be his final resting place.

With little money to spend, Elias worked nearly until the day he died of a heart attack on August 13, 1903, at the age of sixty-one. His body was buried next to that of his youngest daughter, Amy. Like the services for his daughter, the family couldn't afford a funeral for Elias. So the services were held at his Liberty Street apartment.

Members of the Ulric Dahlgren Veterans Post 25 appeared once again, wearing their full Union uniforms to honor their "comrade."

~

As Frederick got older, he still drank too much and he still liked the train station too much. His only resource, his brother Edward, had moved away, traveling the state and working hard on his job as an insurance broker just as the Great Depression set in.

Frederick moved in with his mother Lydia. They lived together in a small South Street shingle house in Elizabeth that was divided into two three-room apartments. The quiet pair lived there through the 1920s, maintaining a polite but rarely social relationship with those who lived in the long row of neighboring apartment buildings that were rising up in Elizabeth's busy downtown. They lived on Elias's meager military death benefits as a matter of survival.

On October 4, 1928, a neighbor detected a gas odor coming from Lydia's apartment. He called police, who quickly arrived with an ambulance and a doctor. Forcing their way in, they opened the door to the kitchen and adjoining bedroom.

There, they found Lydia on the couch and Frederick on the floor. Their dog was lying in the center of the room.

All three had been dead for several hours.

In the kitchen, gas was flowing from a burner, and its smell filled the kitchen and the bedroom. Days later, they would be buried in Evergreen, nearly completing the cycle as the family's final resting place.

CHAPTER 7

THE BLUES

January 2009

I SAT IN THE OCEAN GROVE HOUSE with my father, Stan, who leaned against the back of the couch. It was the same house that my grandfather Dick had owned when we were younger.

Back then in the 1970s, the place was pasty white, with layers of filth caked on the floors that Dick never cleaned. Now the house was my father's; he had laid carpet nearly wall to wall and thrown out the 1950s Frigidaire refrigerator.

The place became my father's refuge when my mother gave him fits. Like Dick, he went there whenever he couldn't take the nagging and the repeated disruptions of what was left of his normal life. My father retired from his principal's job in 1995, soon after my family inherited the house after my grandfather's death, and Stan suddenly found himself competing for space with my mother. He had to deal in a more intimate way with the same things we had dealt with for years: my mother's sighs of exasperation and "tsk, tsk" sounds she made whenever someone lurked in the kitchen, getting near the boxes of cookies and the frozen cake she wrapped with aluminum foil and electrical tape.

He had to cope with things all day that he had dealt with only at night for years. Instead of hearing the repeating for only a few hours at a time, he now heard it as an all-day affair. From the time they woke up, her repeating was constant; my mother indulged in driving my father mad.

"Do you love me best of all? . . . Promise?"

He heard it over and over until he escaped to Ocean Grove, taking walks down at the beach or catching a film at a second-run movie theater in nearby Bradley Beach.

Since my mother had died in 2003, my father now lived with a woman who made him happy.

"It's so good to be with somebody who is normal," he said over and over. They lived most of the time in Manchester, New Jersey, a town about an hour south of Ocean Grove, sharing their time with the thousands of others who lived in the many planned senior housing developments that were springing up in southern New Jersey. Ocean Grove, as a result, no longer needed to serve as his refuge. Instead, it was an occasional vacation spot, or a pit stop for a job he occasionally worked as a night-time desk person at a nearby nursing home. It was no longer a place to run away to. It was no longer a place of necessity. It was simply a place of peace.

Still, even as we sat within the seemingly peaceful surroundings, I knew this was the hardest interview I had to do. I would have to take my father back to the 1970s and 1980s when there was little to no peace. We would have to recall the trips to Florida with my grandfather. We would have to remember the trailer visits to Pennsylvania. We'd have to recall why, when it was my mother who burped, he chased after my brother and pinned him against a tree. We'd have to talk about why my father hit all of us, especially my brother. This, I knew, wouldn't be a pleasant day, and I fully expected to see the same anger that I had seen when things were not very pleasant in the past. Right away, as my father sat on the couch, folding his hands together as he awaited the first question, I reassured him: sure, there were people who were victims of his behavior. But my father was a victim too. He wasn't born into this family. He did not share the DNA. He had his own issues growing up. I told him that I had learned that mental illness has many victims. Those who suffer the worst effects of it are not always the people who suffer from the mental illness directly. The worst sufferers are often the people who care for them, the people who give every bit of themselves to make sure people who suffer from schizophrenia, bipolar disorder, and OCD are healthy, safe, and alive.

I told my father that I owed my life to him. I could not imagine life without him, acting as the buffer we needed between ourselves and my mother. I couldn't imagine living without the strength and courage he displayed when we had no one else around to provide it. He tried as hard as he could to shield us from the trouble my mother was causing. Yes, he swept things under the rug. Yes, his discipline sometimes went too far. But I knew that he wanted us to live as normal a life as possible. He tried to provide a rock to counteract my mother's erratic, unstable, and unreliable behavior. Many times, he failed when he lost control and turned his anger toward somebody, like my brother, who was not necessarily the cause of it. But he tried.

When I had my issues with eating disorders, back when I was in college in the 1980s, he was the one I turned to for reassurance.

"You're going to be okay," he told me. "You just need to get some help. You're going to be okay." He was the only one who told me that.

ॐ

Step by step, we recalled the incidents of the past thirty years that frustrated my father. All my father could offer was regret. He was able to laugh about some things. But he showed a lot of frustration about his inability to help my mother. As he talked, he said many of the same things I had heard before. "If only she took the damn medicine," he said, over and over. He said he was never really angry.

"I was frustrated," he said. "I was just so damn frustrated by the constant repeating, the bathroom. I just wanted things to be normal, but she was just so damn stubborn. I tried to talk to her, to get her some help, but she just wouldn't do it. She just wouldn't do it unless you forced her into it."

He recalled the first time he saw something in my mother that was awry, way back in 1959 just before the wedding. Dede showed a possessive streak just before they got married. But her symptoms of obsessive-compulsive disorder, he admitted, wouldn't show for years. If anybody in the family did display them at that time, he said, it was Dick. My father never thought the same issues would transfer down to his wife.

"He was intolerable," he said of Dick. "He never gave your mother a fair shake. She always felt guilty about asking for help because he was so tight with his money. And then he'd lecture her for wasting it. I know he never liked me."

He couldn't blame Dede, my mother, for pulling away from Dick as she did. If anything, during the 1960s, she sought to be the perfect American wife. Few, if any, could see Dede was susceptible to what was then known as "the baby blues," but what was really postpartum depression.

"The baby blues," or postpartum depression, brought out the worst of her. Her symptoms of obsessive compulsiveness arose soon afterward.

"I did everything I could," my father said. "I took her on the trips she wanted. I took her to the restaurants she liked. But it just got worse and worse and worse. At first, I thought I could handle it and I didn't think much of it. But then it just became intolerable."

As she approached forty, Dede found solace in alcohol, following her father's pattern of self-medication. She also avoided doctors who could have treated her leg, worried that they would have nothing but bad news to tell her. She spent most of her time in the bathroom, scrubbing her hands with soap and Brillo pads for a half hour or longer.

Why didn't he leave her?

"I did it for you," he said. "I was afraid you'd be left with her. I knew the situation would be much worse if I left."

My father recalled with regret that he didn't do anything sooner. He regretted not involving the family in the decisions in her care. "I was just trying to protect everybody," he said.

He especially regretted taking out his anger on us, the children.

"There are a lot of things I regret," he said. "I don't think I was the best father in the world, and I wish things were better. I'm willing to take responsibility for it."

My father sat and rubbed his hands.

"My father used to hit me too," he said. "I guess I was doing the same thing to my own children. I regret it."

I told my father that, in a way, we were normal. We reflected a society that failed to identify the effects of trauma caused by mental illness until it was too late. Even the vaunted *DSM*, the bible for identifying mental illness, did not identify the trauma that can be caused by postpartum depression until the most recent edition, published in 2000.

Even if such information was available to him, the chances of my father or anybody identifying my mother's postpartum-related problems were probably small. Treatment options were, and remain, inadequate. Unless the person who is affected by mental illness has a support system, the typical route for someone experiencing a severe form of mental illness is the street, or even jail.

I told my father that he was a hero to me because he somehow endured living with my mother, and by doing that, he kept her alive way longer than she should have. He protected us from living the same life of despair. He stayed with us when it would have been so much easier to flee. Because we educated ourselves, we hope to be ready for what may come up in the future, especially if we start to experience the same kinds of symptoms my mother had lived with.

"Write what you need to write," my father said. "I've got nothing to hide. I'm not proud of what I did. But I've got nothing to hide."

December 1983

My father's face was red, and his teeth were clenched as he backed my mother into the bedroom, raising a hand and shaking it in the air. His arm, from the finger tips to the elbow, looked like a flyswatter, ready to swing at a pest.

"I ought to let you have it!" he shouted. "I want to let you have it!"

"No, no you won't!" my mother said. "No, don't do it!"

He kept charging, moving past the doorway into the bedroom, disappearing from my view as he backed her all the way to the bed. I stood in the bathroom, just a few feet away, watching intently.

I was getting ready for bed, putting on a T-shirt that I'd slipped into, a comfortable, cotton one that would let me sleep the whole night. I wanted to be ready for Christmas day. I slept in a stiff, narrow bunk bed, one that was hard to roll around in. The smallest things bothered me: If my shirt was too tight or my underwear too loose or the fabric of clothes abrasive, I couldn't sleep. If I heard noises in the bathroom next door or from another part of the house, I couldn't sleep. If those voices turned into the sounds of a brawl, as they did that night, I wouldn't be able to sleep for hours.

I thought I had seen the last of this. For some time, with my sister out of the house and my brother at college, my parents had somehow found a way to live with each other. My father appeared ready to finally accept the repeating, the hand washing, and what he often called "possessiveness" and "obsessiveness" that had ruined so many dinner-table conversations and cast a cloud over every trip. Twenty-four years into their marriage, my father realized that the repeating was as much a part of his daily routine as it was my mother's.

He even learned to enjoy the trips to restaurants and the stay-overs at campgrounds that had created so much heartache in the past. Parking a trailer near Reading, Pennsylvania, and driving there every other weekend during the summer eliminated many of the tasks that had been necessary for the long trips.

To my father, it was better than going to the beach. Since my mother's accident at the beach in 1973, we rarely went back. The times we did go, my mother stayed far away from the water, sitting in a lawn chair and watching the water roll in.

Indeed, by the early 1980s, the only trips we took were to the trailer. With my brother Edward in college, my father seemed to breathe a sigh of relief, too, as if a long headache had finally come to an end. As he got older, Edward challenged my father, never letting him win an argument and rarely ending a confrontation without it becoming physical. They were similar, both of them temperamental, demanding, strong-willed, and stubborn. My brother was moving onto adulthood, and he was the same size and probably even stronger than my father. If my father's final thing to say was "Just do as you're told and shut up," Edward would often retort "I just feel that it's important to defend myself." My brother viewed his words as courage; my father saw them as insulting and disrespectful. They often ended these exchanges with my father's fist cocked and his teeth clenched, proclaiming, "I ought to clobber you!"

With the children gone, my mother found a way to improve her own life, even as she became mentally and, in some ways, physically worse and worse. Her injured knee was a contorted mess, and her limping gait became more and more labored. Year by year, her back became so severely hunched that her head hung close to her knees as she walked. Her repeating became longer and more redundant, even taking on a few twists and adding some vocabulary.

"Promise to *hold* and love me forever?"

"Yes, yes," my father would say.

"Promise that?"

"Yes, yes."

"Promise to talk nicely to me forever and ever?"

"Yes, yes, yes . . . what else?"

"Promise that we can go to the trailer forever and ever? . . . Promise?"

Every now and then, they had a "normal" conversation, always initiated by my father.

"The Democrats want everything," he'd say. "Reagan just wants to do the opposite of what Democrats did for years, the things they did that ruined this country. They want to tax and spend."

My mother would nod her head and say, "Yes, you're absolutely right," until the end, when she would merely repeat what my father said, and then repeat it again.

"Reagan just wants to do the opposite of what Democrats did for years, right, dear?"

"Right," my father would say. "Exactly."

"The things they did that ruined this country, right?"

"Right."

"They want to tax and spend, right?"

"Right! That's just what I just said."

"But they want to tax and spend, right?"

"Right!"

At home, the bathroom was no longer just a long pit stop. It was my mother's address. She'd wash her hands anywhere from a half hour to an hour, running the water constantly. Then she'd limp out to the kitchen, her head bobbing low and her right arm swinging back and forth as she waddled over to the sink, where she'd wash them again. Then she'd open the refrigerator, often using a towel when she grabbed the handle, and pull out the food she was ready to eat. She often left her own dinner on the plate so she could throw it out later. Instead, she'd fill herself up with chocolate-chip cake whose package had three long strips of strong, black electrical taped wrapped completely around it. She'd remove each strip one by one, picking them off with her fingernails and washing her hands in between. She'd grab a beer, pour it in a tall glass, throw out the can, and wash her hands again.

Then she'd go to one of the upper cabinets, pull out a bag of potato chips that had been sealed with three pieces of clear Scotch tape, set it on the table next to the beer and cake, and wash her hands again. In all, it took her nearly two hours to wash up and eat what looked like a late-night snack but really was her dinner. She'd consume all of it by 1 a.m., usually downing another twelve beers before passing out at the table, her head down flat next to an empty potato chip bag.

Ironically, all that, however, didn't stop her from finally getting a job, her first since she was a kid. My mother sold Avon and did it well, becoming one of the top sellers in her region. She even found a way to do it while realizing her own limitations, doing all of her selling over the telephone and having the customers come to *her* house to pick up the stuff, not the other way around. Whenever anybody balked, my mother used her best charm, smiling as she told them over the telephone that "this would be best for everybody to come here," "you're a busy woman; you don't have to wait for me this way," and "if you have any questions, you can just knock on my door and I'll answer them." It worked every time.

In 1983, my father also moved on to a more lucrative elementary school position, once announcing with pride, that we didn't "have to rub two nickels together" anymore. He no longer had to worry about the heating bill regularly exceeding $100 a month, especially when my mother routinely turned the heat up to eighty degrees. Whenever my father complained or even tried to change the setting, he got an earful.

"Can we keep it at eighty degrees? . . . Can we keep it at eighty degrees forever and ever? . . . Promise that you will?"

If there was anything my father had in common with his in-laws, it was this: he didn't like change. He had a job, he had a car, he had three children, and after locating in Point Pleasant Borough in 1959, he never moved from the town he called home. Yes, my mother's problems were legendary, and they had taken a toll on him. But, by the early 1980s, he seemed to find a way to tolerate them. "Yes, dear" was his magic phrase.

At this new school, however, Stan had to deal with bigger pressures, more demanding teachers, rougher parents, and a tougher curriculum. In the fall and winter of 1983, the pressure began to wear on him. The things about Dede that he had grown accustomed to were annoying him again. Indeed, they grated on him even more than ever, and his rage seemed to reach a level we had never seen.

I never saw my father hit my mother, and I don't believe that he did. But on Christmas Eve in 1983, he came close. When I saw him back my mother into the room, his hand raised in rage, I had to say something. I saw my father's clenched teeth and his tight body. I thought that, if he didn't hit my mother, he surely would have a heart attack, an aneurysm, or some by-product of the stress he was feeling. Surely, then, my worst fears would come true. I'd have to live with Mommy by myself.

Just as they disappeared from my view, I yelled. "No!"

My father turned around, marching out of the room into the hallway to face me as I stood in the bathroom. His teeth were still clenched, his face beet red.

"What did you say?"

"I said leave her alone!"

My father stomped into the bathroom, lifting up that hand again. Just as he raised it and pointed it toward my face, my mother peeked in and called out.

"No, dear, no!" she said. "He was just trying to help."

Her pleas didn't work. He swung his hand, but he missed my face. Instead, his elbow struck me under my ear. His arm kept going, and wrapped around the rest of my head. Instead of actually hitting me, the force of his moving arm pulled me to the ground.

"No, dear, no!" my mother said.

I sat on the bathroom floor while my father stormed out, heading toward the family room, where he popped open a beer, sat in front of the television, and brooded for hours. I went into my bedroom and stayed there without sleeping. I used to have to hear the whole makeup routine in order to get to sleep. This time, I knew it would eventually end the same way as always.

"Do you apologize?"

"Yes, yes."

"Are you sure?"

"Yes, yes."

"Do you love me forever and ever?"

"Yes, yes."

"Promise?"

"Yes, okay!"

"Promise that you'll love me forever and ever?"

"Yes!"

I knew I would get no apology, but even if I did, I didn't care. For once, in fact, I didn't care if they ever apologized to each other. I just lay on my bed, inserted the earphones from my Sony Walkman in my ears, and listened to Led Zeppelin.

For once, I didn't have to listen to "promise me you'll love me forever and ever" to get to sleep.

⁓

In my immediate family, the late 1970s and early 1980s were tough. Money, and the lack of it, had a lot to do with that. The job of handling an obsessive wife, temperamental children—who sometimes displayed some of the same obsessive tendencies as their mother—and financial worries often put my father over the edge.

At dinner, my father often sat at the table, ranting about all things political, physical, and financial. For years, he ranted about Democrats— "Carter and his good old boys are going to ruin to this country"—and defended Republicans—"All Nixon had to do was say, 'It was a mistake. It shouldn't have happened,' and they would have forgotten the whole thing." The older he got, and the more the difficulties of his marriage and his money weighed on him, the more he displayed his frustration toward all those who couldn't help him.

Back in the 1960s, Stan had been more hopeful and optimistic, often playing and laughing with his children and keeping a positive outlook even as the world burned around him.

"Everything's going to be okay" was his favorite thing to say. "Relax. You have nothing to worry about."

By the late 1970s, however, he started to develop an edge. The nurturing young man who carried his children wherever they went, who sat with his daughter Carolyn, and often watched television for hours, was now a frustrated middle-aged man who wanted out of his life, even though he knew there was no easy way to get there.

He started to say things that were not-so-obvious insults. "No one *ever* helps me!" he would say. "I do everything around here. No one *ever* helps me." His rage, which had flared up occasionally, now would linger for hours at a time, either causing him to rant about the world or roar toward anyone who dared to challenge him. Few dared to do so; even my mother would nod in agreement whenever he raged and would often refrain from her repeating until he was done with his speech. She often sat silently when he turned his anger toward the family.

"Everyone is so lazy around here!" he'd yell.

Sometimes, he turned it toward himself. "I should have never been born," he said, from time to time. "Think about it. I was born with an eye defect. I had to be operated on right after I was born. God was supposed to take me right then and there. Ever since then, I've lived a life in hell. I should have never been born!"

In 1980, my father was forty-four and unhappy. He wanted to get my mother to a psychiatrist, but with a full-time job and a house full of kids to raise, he knew that following through with that idea required a lot more energy than picking up milk at the 7-Eleven. Instead, like a lot of families who were, as he said, "rubbing two nickels together," Stan was living moment by moment. His goal was to get to the end of the day, the week, the month, or the year. His goal was to keep the family together, and any sort of change, any sort of radical shift in the dynamic, threatened to make things even worse.

By 1980, my father felt as though he had nowhere to go, nowhere to turn. He felt trapped in his chair in front of the television, sipping on his fourth beer can.

"Dear?" my mother asked, chuckling a little.

"Mm, hmm."

"What's on television?"

"The news," he'd say. "What is it?"

"Did something happen?"

"No," he'd say. "Go ahead . . . What is it?"

"Um, some of the meat touched the kitchen counter and I didn't clean it beforehand. Do you think it's okay?"

"Yes, I'm sure it's okay," he said. "Everything's going to be okay."

"Are you sure it's okay? . . . Do you think I should throw it away?"

"No, I don't think you should throw it away!" he'd yell back. "You're going to throw my hard-earned money into the trash? That's all you ever do is waste, waste, waste!"

"No, I'm not going to do that."

"Waste, waste, waste," he'd say. "That's all you ever do is waste, waste, waste."

"Um, dear, do you promise to talk nicely to me?"

"What, are you starting in on me again?! I told you not to throw it away, goddammit, so don't throw it away."

"I won't. I won't," she said. "Um, do you promise to talk nicely to me?"

"Look, don't start in on me."

"I won't," she said. "Promise to talk nicely to me?"

"Yes, I promise," he'd say. "Now don't throw it away."

"Will you love me forever and ever?"

"Yes!"

"Promise?"

"Yes!"

"Should I keep the meat?"

"Oh, goddammit, yes!"

"Okay," my mother would say, before turning back to the kitchen and promptly throwing away the meat.

Moments like this drove my father to our second bathroom, a small room next to his family room chair, where he stared at a mirror and yelled at himself. We rarely could make out what he said; when he walked out of the bathroom, he acted as though nothing ever happened.

Even as my father raged, my mother did little to change. She kept a secret bank account for herself that she filled with thousands of dollars she earned from Avon. As my father struggled to pay for food and bills, she offered nothing to assist, spending whatever money she had on the clothes that stuffed both her closets in their bedroom. Her closets got so crowded that she started filling the one I shared with my brother, forcing us to store our games, toys, and books against the wall, on our desks, under our beds, or—in some cases—sleep with them in our beds.

"Pick up this messy room," my father would yell. But there was no place to put our things between the blouses and the pants that filled our closet.

In August 1980, my father got a mysterious call. It was from his brother, my uncle Al. They hadn't seen each other in nearly five years. Whenever the idea of going to see his brother Al popped in his head, Stan had to quickly erase it, knowing that he didn't have the time or energy to do so. He was too busy being a caretaker for his wife, thinking he could ultimately solve her problems himself. He thought he could solve her problems himself, because she would never want to be treated.

On the phone, Al was bewildered. His daughter Catherine was getting married the following month. Why hadn't Stan replied to the invitation?

"Invitation?" my father replied. "Wedding? We had no idea."

They didn't talk for long. When my father got off the phone, his face was blood red. He was on fire, and he stormed after my mother.

"You knew about this, didn't you?" he yelled.

"Knew about what?"

"Don't lie to me!" he said. "You knew about Catherine's wedding—how else can anybody explain this?"

"I didn't know about that!" she said. "I swear—I didn't know."

My mother could usually get away with a lie, but this time something in her face gave her away. Sure, the invitation could have been lost in the mail. But my mother was home all day. She was the one who got the mail. She was the *only* one who got the mail, leaning on the sidebar of the storm door as she reached for the box, always afraid to have her bare feet touch the cold, dirty ground.

"You knew about that invitation!" my father said. "You just wanted to go on another goddamned trip to Pennsylvania!"

"No, that wasn't it. . . ."

The fight got worse. My father called her "fat." She called him an "asshole." They both yelled "fuck you." My mother even dared to say he couldn't "put out," that she could never get him to be a real man, let alone a real husband.

"You've ruined my life!" he yelled. "You've ruined everything about my life! Why don't you just die?"

It was, perhaps, their fight of all fights. It went on for hours, deep into the night. I worried about another night of sitting there and listening to my brother snore, while I hoped and even prayed that my father would finally give in. But the yelling was so loud and the insults so vicious, that even my brother couldn't get to sleep.

"God," he said. "Maybe this really is it. I think they're serious this time. I think they're going to get a divorce."

"I don't know," I said. "They always find a way to patch things up."

"Yeah, but listen to the things they're saying," he said. "This is a really bad one."

By 3 a.m., however, it was over. Once again, it ended with the usual routines. But this one fight, more than any other, cut deeper. For a while after that, I wondered if there was something truly evil, even criminal about my mother. We knew she was crazy. We saw the kinds of things crazy people did. We knew they operated without limits. What wouldn't stop her from going too far? We had seen Charles Manson portrayed in *Helter Skelter*. We had seen Howard Hughes portrayed in a movie. We had seen how they destroyed themselves and, in Manson's case, many others. What would stop my mother from doing whatever she needed to do to get what she wanted?

I was thirteen and I felt more detached from my mother than ever. The soft-spoken voice that I had known as a small child had disappeared. The nurturing, caring loving soul who bought me animal crackers to make me happy when I was in kindergarten was now sealing all of the sweets away from us. Occasionally, we shared a light moment, but she often spoke to me with anger. She got upset at me whenever I lingered too long in the kitchen or did anything else to cross her path.

"Thomas, it's time for you to get out of here," she'd say.

"I need to get something from the refrigerator!" I'd shoot back.

"Um, Thomas, talk respectfully to me, okay?" she'd say.

"Okay, okay."

"Do you love your mother best of all?"

"Yes, yes."

Despite his angry ways, I worried more and more about losing my father. We worried more than ever when my father went through a health scare of his own, even though he had been healthy all his life. He had high blood pressure, and the doctor worried about his heart. He took medication, but the medication had a side effect that made him sick. One time when he took it, my father thought he was having a heart attack.

"This is it. This is it. The end of a miserable life," he proclaimed.

I saw my mother roll her eyes, and I thought, *doesn't she care? Doesn't she realize she's the one who did this to him?* I started to have thoughts, even dreams, that she would do whatever she could to get her way, even if it meant hurting or killing. I was only thirteen, but I feared going to sleep.

ॐ

Those fears scared me more and more, even though they never really lasted. In a matter of days, my mother could wipe them away with her smile. I used to think that *The Mary Tyler Moore Show* theme song was written for her: "Who can turn the world on with her smile."

My mother wanted, more than anything, to be loved by her family. She wanted it unconditionally, perhaps because she never really got it from her own parents. She had no friends. She had very few relatives. She really had no one to turn to but us, and she demanded constant affirmation of our love, even if it meant being very annoying.

Other than love, my mother cared about little else than keeping to her routines. Every now and then, however, she would allow a little tiny glimpse through the window to her soul. She dreaded getting old, so she colored her hair with the brightest blonde hair dye she could find. She pasted several layers of makeup on her face. Sometimes, she'd hear a disco song being played on TV, and jiggle her crooked hips, moving her arms and legs.

"I love disco. . . . Don't you, dear?" she'd say to my father, who'd look at her like she'd lost her mind.

Every now and then before I went to sleep, my mother and I would talk. She told stories of her childhood and recalled the lush grounds of the Greystone campus.

"It really was a beautiful place," she said. "You could see the mountaintops in the distance everyday, whether it was clear or not." She talked about going to the beach with my grandparents and how much she enjoyed swimming far out, to the point that the lifeguards had to blow their whistles to call her in. "I really loved to swim," she said. "I used to swim all the time. It is such good exercise. I didn't mind going too far, because I knew what I was doing. Those lifeguards didn't need to worry so much."

One night, when I was about twelve, she talked about our first dog, Honsie. This dog lived barely two years, dying in 1968 when I was only one. But for my mother, everything about him was so vivid, so clear. She leaned against my bunk bed, relieving pressure on her leg, and told me word for word about his death.

"He had been sick for weeks," she said. "I had to carry him off the couch and sit him on some newspapers in the backseat."

"He couldn't walk?"

"Not when he was sick," she said, shaking her head as she remembered. "He was such a good dog. We potty-trained him very quickly. He would go right on the newspapers. Then he would run outside and chase after the rabbits. He was very fast, but very loving."

"How did you know he loved you?" I asked.

"He loved to sit in my lap," she said. "I used to scratch him behind his ears. Dachshunds love it, I guess."

"Why did he die so fast?"

"They didn't have a cure for heartworm back then," she said. "And we didn't know. . . . He was so limp and lifeless, we just thought he ate something bad. We waited a little too long."

Tears started to fill her eyes. "We took him to the vet, and they said he had heartworm, and there was nothing they could do about it," she said, choking up a little.

"Nothing?" I said.

"Nothing. I just remember taking him to the vet that one last time, and he looked so lifeless," she said. "It was such a shame. Such a shame."

She then sobbed. "It was such a shame! Such a shame," she cried out. "I loved that dog so much!"

I grabbed my mother's hand and felt her chapped skin. It was a rare moment, her letting me touch her. These moments were rare, but they were good. They made me feel secure; they had me feeling as though I was with her, sitting on her lap again, snuggled up against her chest.

⟩

More than anything, my father didn't like to be challenged. No one challenged him more than Edward. Even when Edward said nothing, my father was so accustomed to his challenges that he'd try to preempt them.

In a dinner table rant about guns, he'd say, "Stay out of this, okay?" before my brother even opened his mouth.

"I didn't say anything!" my brother would shoot back.

"I said, stay out of this!" my father would repeat.

If my brother—or anybody else, for that matter—spoke favorably about a Democrat, my father would say, "Democrats just want to tax and spend. You don't know that because you don't work."

My brother would respond, "That's not true—I know just as much as you do about being an American citizen."

"Just shut up," my father would retort. "You think you know everything about everything. Just shut up."

My brother's phantom "burp" at the dinner table, and the consequences, was one of many moments when my brother saw himself as the wrongly accused, and he protested loudly about the injustice. It also marked a turning point in his relationship with my father, one that was downright scary. No longer did my father just threaten to put Edward into a wall; he put him there literally, and he didn't care if the plaster cracked or the pictures popped off their hooks in our bedroom. No longer did he just threaten to put him into a tree; he'd pinned him there, showing a look of rage and punctuating it with clenched teeth.

No longer did my father just get in his face and shout down my brother's voice. He punched him in the arm, hard enough to hurt. He started to punch him so much that Edward worried about his safety.

My brother was three years older than I, bigger and much stronger than I was. He had a great, hearty laugh, just like my mother's. But he more often showed the seriousness of my father, and even his grandfather, in his face. He rarely cried, but he often yelled, and he wore his anger on his sleeve. He was highly intelligent, and his thoughts and words displayed it. The tone of his voice, and the words he used to prove a point, were often unintentionally condescending. Just one glance at him or listening to a few things he would typically say often led to misinterpretation. No one misinterpreted him more than my father. My brother was the abused "meathead" my father needed as a target, since he was too afraid and too tired of challenging my mother.

Beneath the toughness, however, Edward was soft and sensitive. I considered him my best friend, and for a while, maybe my only friend, since my shyness was often a big obstacle in my life. He saw what my mother was doing and how it was bringing the family down. He saw what it took away from my father. My brother tried to fill in the gaps. He taught me how to play baseball. He played board games very competitively, often reveling in beating me in Monopoly and Scrabble. He and I learned how to play basketball together.

♊

My brother resented my silence during his battles with our father. "You're just being a mama's boy again," he'd say to me. "Why do you just stand there?"

"I'm sorry. I'm sorry. I promise that I'll say something the next time," I'd say back.

"Yeah? I'll believe it when I see it," he'd say.

My behavior at home was an extension of how I was at school. Many of the kids—particularly those with a lot of street smarts—could sense the same thing my brother did, that I was lifeless wimp. From kindergarten right up to my high school years, I cried whenever anyone looked at me with anger and teased me with malice. I would hear, "Aw, poor, Tommy" from teachers and my parents whenever I complained to them that I was being teased. They, in turn, complained to the school, or even directly to the kids themselves and the kids' parents. But getting adults to fight my battles for me only fed the resentment of the other kids. I was labeled as a "faggot," a "queer," and a "homo," and the more I complained, the worse it got.

My brother witnessed this when I joined the cross-country running team during my freshman year of high school. One of my teammates—a guy who was friendly with my brother—watched as I tired easily during my first practice and dropped out of my first run. He called me a "faggot," smiling at me as he said it to another teammate, who also laughed. I told my brother, who was also a teammate, and he talked to the two guys and smoothed everything out. But later Edward lectured me on the value of being tough and told me that what I got was probably what I deserved.

"They're only calling you a faggot because they can," he said. "They think you're too much of a wimp to fight back."

My brother wanted me to fight, not only at school, but also at home. "You're the favorite one, you know," he would say. "You get everything you want." He needed an ally against our parents.

Finally, during my freshman year of high school, I spoke out. One evening my brother and I were laughing in our bedroom. I stood silently as my father threw open the door and started in on my brother. He had misinterpreted our raucous laughter for fighting.

"I ought to clobber you," he told my brother, who was backed against the wall. My father raised his fist and gritted his teeth.

"Go ahead . . . take me," Edward said, staring at him defiantly as my father drew his face close to his.

Edward tried to walk away, but when he did, my father grabbed him in a headlock and, like a linebacker in a tackle, thrust him toward the wall. A ladder from our bunk bed was between Edward and the wallpapered plaster; my father drove Edward into the ladder so hard that he cut his back on the dull edge of the wood. A sharp, square hook on the ladder went into the wall, forming a two-inch-long hole in the plaster.

"Look at what you did!" my father yelled.

I stood by the doorway, about ten feet away, but I could see the hole. The hook went in so strong, like a hole-puncher, it made a clean square. My brother reached for his back, lifting up his shirt as he struggled to look around to see how much he was bleeding.

"Hey!" I called out as I stood in the doorway, looking right at my father.

My father turned to me, his face iron-tight. "What?" he yelled back.

"You leave him alone," I said.

My father's face got meaner. I could see the beads of sweat dampening his forehead. A patch of perspiration was forming under his chin and around his T-shirt collar.

"You shut up!" he yelled. "You stay out of this!"

"But he didn't do anything," I shot back. "He didn't do anything!"

"I said shut up, or I'll clobber you too!" he said, raising his fist back at me, then putting it quickly down.

After he stormed out, I saw my brother, still pulling up his T-shirt and twisting his head so he could look at his back. He didn't say much. He didn't thank me. After years of silence, he didn't need to.

ॐ

When my father hit me on Christmas Eve 1983, it was not the first time. It had happened almost the same way, more than a year earlier, during the summer of 1982. Again, it involved my brother. This time, I did nothing to start it. I merely watched as my brother fought back, trying to defend himself again for something he hadn't done. I don't remember exactly what the fight was about. All I remember is what my brother said. A condescending defense to an accusation drove my father insane. They were arguing about misinterpreting what each other was saying, but my brother was trying to explain that words—even bad words—can mean

172

two different things. "Well, it's not a question of semantics" was the line that enraged my father so much he backhand-slapped Edward across his nose, causing blood to gush down into his mouth.

"Hey!" I yelled as loud as I could. I was standing in the hallway, back by the bathroom, about fifteen feet away from the living room, where my brother wiped the blood streaking down from his nose with his hand.

My father turned toward me and backed me into the bathroom. As I stood against the window along the back wall, he backhanded me across my head, hitting me with his elbow, not his hand.

I crumpled to the floor and sat there for a few minutes as I heard my brother outside, standing on the sidewalk, yelling.

"That did it. I'm leaving!" he said. "I'm leaving this godforsaken place!"

"Good," my father said. "Go ahead and go!"

I walked toward the living room and saw my father leaning outside the storm door, yelling at my brother as Edward struggled to stop his nose from bleeding onto the sidewalk. My father then walked out and handed him a handkerchief, and Edward wiped his face as my father walked back inside.

I stood in the living room and looked at my father as he passed by me, heading toward the family room.

"Are you okay?" he said.

"Yes, I am," I said.

༈

I never thought I'd see it again, but there I was, a little over a year later, on Christmas Eve, again crouched down in the bathroom by the window. As my father stormed back to the family room, I could only think of vengeance. I looked forward to Christmas morning, but not for the presents I was about to receive. I only had revenge on my mind.

That morning at about 9 a.m., I walked out to the living room, and saw a new watch for me under the tree. It had a stopwatch that would be good for running, something I had asked for since I was starting to train much harder in cross-country. I saw new gym shorts and clothes that I'd wear for practice on the team.

I didn't open any of it. Instead, I sat on the floor, slumped slightly forward, folded my hands together into a ball and rested my chin on it as I sat, glumly, and watched everybody else open theirs.

My father, in his pajamas, tried to engage me. He looked like he wanted to turn back the clock about twenty-four hours at least and try one more time to be the dad he always wanted to be, the Norman Rockwell type.

He pulled out the watch, studied it, and held it up to my face.

"This will be good—now you don't have to time yourself on the oven clock," he said.

"Right," I said.

He kept at it for nearly an hour, thrusting the watch and the clothes my way, and insisting nicely that I open them. Even my mother encouraged me, since she was the one who had bought the clothes. Finally, I opened all of them very quickly. "Thanks," I said, quietly as I tossed the wrapping paper to the side.

Eventually, my father caught on. His guilt was obvious; he just didn't realize that I needed more. I needed more than a Timex being held up to my face.

He sat on the rug, watching the others rip wrapping paper. "Come over here, Tom," he said.

I hugged him limply, raising my hand up to my eye.

"Daddy will always love you, okay?" he said. "Daddy will always love you. Everything is going to be okay, okay?"

CHAPTER 8

EATING DISASTERS

February 2009

MY BROTHER WANTED TO HEAR the tape. He wanted acknowledgement.

He wanted to hear the whole three hours. He wanted to hear remorse. He wanted to know whether my father felt what he felt, that Edward had often taken the brunt of my father's anger and frustration.

I told him I could download the audio of my father's talk onto a disc and send it to him.

"Good," he said. "I would really appreciate that."

But as the days went by, I held back—and continued doing so at my wife's suggestion. I started to think the same way she did, that it would merely open up old wounds that didn't need to be reopened. My job was not to exploit a frustrated but well-intentioned father; my goal was to provide a mirror for other families to look at and to identify many of the same things they are going through when they have mental illness in the family. Ironically, as weeks and months went by, Edward didn't ask for it again. I started to think that maybe he, too, realized it was time to move on.

With Edward, I felt I was learning more by watching him than listening to him. I was looking at a man who appeared to find balance, who had found a way to address his issues well while finding a way to live his life and to help others live their lives better than the way he lived his.

He wanted to project an image of stability, something he strived to do for so long. But he came to realize it was just an image. What he always needed was something deeper, something that would allow him to confront his insecurities and address them head on. The product of his self-exploration was starting to show: six years after my mother died, he was looking healthier and happier than he ever had. He had stopped making himself vomit.

I was proud of him, but I envied him too. I had my issues with eating disorders. I always felt as though I lacked his strength. Besides his psychologist, my brother felt the best person to deal with his issues was himself. I, on the other hand, always dumped my feelings on others, so friends and families had to share my pain as I lost weight, starved, and then purged myself, off and on for fifteen years.

Edward still showed anger. But he had his own family now and seemed to want to focus on the present rather than the past. He was forging a new life instead of repairing the old.

⸻

By the time he turned forty-five in February 2009, Edward had detached himself from many of us, settling in Maryland, about 400 miles from the rest of the family. He found a profession for his analytical mind: science. He enjoyed growing yeast in Petri dishes. But he was also doing something he had yearned to do all his life: photography. In 2010, when I was hired by Patch.com, a division of AOL, Edward came aboard, too, and took pictures for the Catonsville, Maryland, Patch news website. He found joy in the simplest stories and photographs, such as a book fair in a library.

In his forties, Edward was going through a period of self-reflection. One of his children—his youngest son, who was born in 2004—was diagnosed with attention deficit hyperactivity disorder (ADHD), and his up-and-down, crash-and-burn personality was at times too much for the family to handle. For a while, Edward and his wife wouldn't admit publicly that the problem was bigger and deeper than misbehavior.

Soon, however, Edward learned the value of humility. Ultimately, he and his wife came to the conclusion that an intervention was needed. Eventually, Edward had to reconnect to our family's past and remind himself of what could have happened had we diagnosed the issues of my mother and grandfather earlier.

Edward remembered how intelligent they were and how we often kicked ourselves for not finding a medication, a form of therapy, or any psychotropic approach that could have helped them lead happy, productive lives. He decided that his son needed medication and special services.

When we talked about my book, he gave me near carte blanche to write about anything and everything. He even talked about more than I had thought he would. He talked about his son, and how he was trying to deal with him now so his son wouldn't have to deal with certain things later. We talked about the past, although Edward didn't seem to remember much about what had happened to him so many years before. Perhaps he didn't want to.

"Geez, you know, I don't remember that. You have a much better memory than I do. I must have blocked it out of my mind," he would say.

I reminded him about the infamous burping incident, the same one that made my father laugh.

"Yeah, I remember that—yeah, that was ugly" was all that he would say.

✺

Our initial discussions took place in January 2009. A month later we had a more serious, probing interview. It took place on the phone, late at night; we were both yawning through a conversation that we knew we had to have.

By then he had grown very frustrated with his son's behavior, and he started to worry he would never find the right treatment for him. Frustrated, the old Edward came out—the one who always sought justice in every argument—as he talked about how he and his wife were considering firing his son's medical professionals.

"I made the decision that I was not going to let my son end up like Mom," Edward said. "I think about Mom, because a lot of people want to stay away from my son because of his behavior. That's exactly what happened to Mom—and look what happened to her? She died alone."

Edward said he couldn't be sure that his son's issues were ADHD, just as he couldn't be sure about what he may be suffering himself. He wasn't satisfied with psychiatry's penchant for putting diagnosis and treatment "in a box," which was one reason he never sought extensive therapy for himself.

"I never even felt closeness," he said, referring to his relationship with our father. "I feel like there's not much of a bond there. He's always been a loner."

He remembered how my father took my sister to a Yankees game in 1972, just before George Steinbrenner knocked Yankee Stadium down and renovated it. At eight years old, Edward was a huge Yankees fan, and he couldn't understand why my father wouldn't take him.

"Was I a difficult child to deal with?" he asked.

When he talked about his eating disorders, he said he did it to prevent himself from getting fat, not to stay thin. I challenged him on that, wondering if the eating disorders were a product of his self-loathing and low self-esteem.

I drew from my own experiences and wondered if he internalized as much as externalized. For someone who was never afraid to say how he felt, Edward always seemed to hold back. He seemed genuinely surprised when I told him that his behavior inspired me, particularly during my high school and college years. I felt Edward could be loud, and he often challenged my father. But as he got older, those cases became more rare. He, too, learned that—for the most part—it was better to shut up than shout out. I learned from him, more than any other person, the value of hiding aggression.

Perhaps my only release was to vomit, because it was the only thing that I felt gave me a sense of control when times were rough.

October 1982

I pulled out the Gatorade packets, tore off the corners, and poured the powder into my mouth. My tongue felt a tingle from the white crystals before I swallowed them. Some would stick in the back of my throat, choking me slightly as I tried hard to swallow.

During cross-country season, this was my lunch ritual. I walked home from high school each day, closed the door to my bedroom, and downed a packet of dry powder. Many times, it would be the only thing I'd eat all day, since I usually stuffed the meat, potatoes, and vegetables from my dinner in my pockets and later flushed them down the toilet or socked them in a secret storage place, such as my old train toy chest that I got when I was in kindergarten.

The Gatorade was supposed to be mixed in water, but water and food were making me feel sick. I thought they were bad for me. Every time I ate, I felt tightness in my stomach. I felt pressure in my bowels. I didn't know if these feelings were real or imagined. All I knew was that I *felt* them and that was enough.

I saw things on television, the horrible news stories on cancer and ulcers. Every time I felt a cramp or a pang of nausea, I worried that something horrible was happening to me. I feared I'd become one of those bald-headed children I saw on the news, the ones with the rare forms of stomach cancers who had to have fund-raisers to pay for their medical bills. I'd hear their stories, how they detected their sicknesses soon after feeling a simple, small twinge of pain. I had those twinges all the time, or at least I *felt* I was having them.

I was growing, and I was getting tall. But I felt uncomfortable with myself. I saw myself as this gangly, sickly child who was too weak, too fat, or too nauseating to get a date, have a lot of friends, or even have regular social contact with my peers. I had strong feelings for girls, but I felt imprisoned. I was too busy trying to appease my family and deal with the negativity between my mother and father and between my father and brother. I was becoming the one who was getting in the middle of things, trying to stop them from killing each other. In high school, I spent too much time worrying about myself, looking at myself, and thinking about myself, hoping all the troubles would go away. I was hoping somebody could come and correct it all for me and show me what it was like to be a human being who could survive.

$$\backsim$$

When I was younger, I used to go to my father and ask him questions: Why is there a bump on my finger? Why do I have cramp down low? Why do I feel weird? He always said something that made me calm. "You're fine. Everything's going to be okay, okay?"

As a teenager, however, I started to lose faith in my father's voice. Soon after taking his new job as principal, my father was angry again, often yelling at my mother and my brother. I saw things that totally conflicted with the rock-solid image that he sought to project. *If he can't handle himself,* I thought, *how can he handle me?* I saw him as a symbol of a family that was unstable, and I saw my parents as people to be respected, but avoided.

I started to pull further away from my mother, too, just as she had pulled away from me years before. Even though she didn't want my lips anywhere near her mouth, my mother had insisted on helping me with my showers until I was thirteen, washing my hair with soap and always telling me, "You don't need shampoo. Your hair is fine." Every day, my hair was sticky and stiff from the previous night's hair washing. She also insisted that I use an acne medicine to get rid of the zits that covered my face. Instead of helping me, the liquid burned my face, and by the time I was fourteen, I had scars from the scorched zits on my cheek.

My mother also insisted that she go with me to the barber and get my hair cut nearly down to the stubble. For years, I felt it was the only way I could feel the connection I had had with my mother when I was five. So I let her sit in the back of the barber shop and order the barber to keep shaving and never mind the scissors.

I felt our connection in December 1981, when I was fourteen and my mother's beloved dog Otto died. Otto was thirteen and had congestive heart failure. She carried the dog into the vet after he had been acting limp for weeks. She came home crying, upset that they were ready to put him to sleep. "I have to go out," she announced. "C'mon, Thomas," she said to me. When we got in the car, she said, "Let's get a haircut." I agreed, and I sat in the barber's chair and let her order the barber to "keep going." I hated it as I watched clumps of my hair land on the floor. I hated the thought of what they were going to say at school, the same things they always said. "You're in the Army now!" Every time I heard that, I'd cringe in embarrassment.

३

The only people I could really trust early on were my brother and sister, and they both insisted that I take stock in myself. They told me to take my own showers. They told me to get my own haircuts. "How else are you supposed to get girls?" they'd tell me. "No wonder they point at you and act disgusted."

My brother, ever the honest one, knew little about diplomacy. Instead, he gave me the plain, analytical facts. If I found a bump on my skin, he would break down the logic.

"It could be a symptom of cancer—probably a 20 percent chance of it, but still a chance," he'd say. Then he'd see my eyes enlarge and realize the fear and panic he had stirred inside me. "Don't worry—that's a one in five chance. It means it probably won't happen."

My brother had read books on nutrition. He had watched television programs that showed how the best athletes reached their goals. He believed the right diet was the key to athletic success. He was the one who told me about Gatorade and how it perfectly sufficed as a meal.

"You have natural talent," he said. "You're a natural long-distance runner. You need to have an energy boost before you go out there. The key to that is to have the right diet."

༄

Ironically, I often felt Edward wished he could be me. He wanted to be younger, taller, and as a runner, faster. He joined cross-country to lose the weight he gained and lost, off and on, since he was a little boy. He ran the seven-mile practice runs on the flat streets that led to ocean waters, and during cross-country meets, he charged up the damp, lush hills in local parks. He went long periods without eating; if he did eat, he'd have little more than a raw egg that he cracked into a glass of orange juice. Or he'd have a glass of Gatorade; rarely would he have two.

Once during the early 1980s, my father caught Edward in the bathroom making himself vomit. Edward was around nineteen at the time, in his freshman year at Rutgers, and he had gained back some of the weight he had lost in high school. He often spent time in the bathroom with the door open, combing his hair and looking under his shirt. Just a few months into college, he looked in the mirror and hated what he saw.

"What the hell is going on here?" my father yelled at him, after hearing groans, grunts, and choking noises come from the bathroom.

"Nothing," Edward said. He marched into his bedroom and shut the door. "Nothing at all."

༄

I eventually lived up to my brother's prediction and became a promising member of the Point Pleasant Borough High School cross-country and track teams. For me, however, running was more than a sport. I had finally found something that fit me. Running made me friends. Running suddenly made me attractive to girls.

I changed from the crying little boy who was called "faggot" to a young man with spirit and strength.

Diet was an essential part of my preparation. I had practices and meets right after school, just hours after eating starchy, greasy cafeteria food. I worried more that the food I had eaten never seemed to digest properly by the time of the starting gun. I had cramps that would slow me down—sometimes causing me to stop. I started to worry that the undigested pork rolls, pizza burgers, or spaghetti were tearing up my insides as I worked my arms and legs up and down steep hills, as my feet hit the hard pavement on local streets, or as I glided along the smooth, soft grasslands of local parks.

Missing dinner was never a big loss. I rarely ate it anyway. My mother's cooking was always so bad, I either hid it or fed it to Otto. When the dog died, the toy chest became my primary hiding spot. I would check on the remnants of the overcooked hamburgers every once in a while and see bugs crawling around the surface and insides of the meat. I worried that the smell was so strong that my father would find it. He never did.

As much as my mother went to great lengths to protect her chocolate-chip cake that she stored in the freezer and refrigerator, she showed little interest in preparing, trimming, and seasoning a roast. What we usually got was a slab of meat covered with a sticky, cellophane-like film of fat. The hamburgers were burnt hard as rocks, and they had a vague taste that resembled something close to—for reasons unknown—peanut butter. I'd sit at the table, listening to my father bark at us for not finishing our meals, and then I'd see my mother was barely picking at the pile of food on her own plate. Later, I'd see the contents of her plate in the garbage. Meanwhile, a few feet away, my mother would sit drinking beer, crunching on potato chips, and mowing down the chocolate-chip cake.

When I became a runner, I started to fret that the Cheerios and the milk I ate for breakfast would do me in, so I started skipping breakfast. Halfway through the 1982 season, when I was a sophomore, my Gatorade-powder-only diet shaved two to three pounds off me each week.

I often looked in the mirror, as my brother did, and I saw my ribs pop out of my chest. I saw myself as fit. I saw myself as strong.

But as the 1982 season progressed, and the practices started at 3 p.m., or the meets started at 3:30 p.m., I didn't get the Gatorade-induced energy boost I thought I'd get. I felt tired and sapped of energy. I felt like I could barely lift my knees up higher than my waist. By the time the race started, and I ran down a 300-yard straightway on our home course, I was out of gas.

That year, I went from a varsity-level runner at the beginning of the season to the back of the pack. Eventually, I didn't even try to finish. I started dropping out of races, stopping wherever I was on the course. I would sit down in the grass or the pavement, sink my head into my hands and feel sorry for myself. *Why did I do that?* I thought to myself. *Why couldn't I finish? What's wrong with me?*

I asked my brother for help, calling him at college several times. He said that Gatorade was good, that the mixture of salt and sugars should give me energy. He endorsed my diet; I never told him how little I *really* ate.

"Just keep doing what you're doing," he told me. "Just finish what you started and you'll be fine."

"But I feel so tired," I told him. "I wonder if there's something wrong with me. Maybe I'm anemic."

"Maybe you are," he said. "Maybe you should go see a doctor and have your blood drawn."

The next-to-last meet was in Manchester Township. The course ran through the woods, following narrow paths through the dense patch of pine trees common to southern New Jersey. Soon after the start, I was running behind two guys who seemed to be weaving back and forth, not willing to let me pass. I tried to slip through on the left or the right, but the long, pine branches were in my way.

Eventually, I got angry and pushed one of them into the patch of pine trees.

"Holy shit!" the kid yelled as he stumbled and nearly banged his head on a tree trunk. "What the hell was that about?"

"Don't worry about it," another Manchester kid yelled. "I'll get him!"

"I'm sorry!" I yelled, before I ran another 100 feet. I never gave them a chance to "get me." I dropped out, fell to the ground, and cried. I had to push myself into the pine trees and away from the sandy path or risk being stepped on by the few runners who were in the back of the pack.

Eventually, I got up and walked about 200 yards to the track, where I sat at the edge of the sandy long-jump pit and sobbed into my hands. It was the first time I cried after a meet.

My head coach spotted me and came over to talk. Coach Browning was a tall, slender man whose thick mustache and eyebrows made him look like a trucker who had been in a few bar brawls. He didn't need a whistle; his voice went everywhere. Despite his trucker look, his approach was to be more preacher than coach, enforcing his law with words and clichés rather than discipline.

"You can be the best you can be," he'd tell us. "Just give the maximum effort, and good things will follow."

"This is the greatest team I've ever had to coach," he kept telling us. In 1982, we lost one meet all year, and he often praised us for meeting his "high standards of excellence."

His only real disappointment was me. At the beginning of the year, he saw me as somebody with promise. By the Manchester meet, however, he seemed to view me more as a head case and a castoff. He even gave me a nickname—"Dink"—and even though neither he nor anybody else could explain what it meant, Coach Browning used it with disdain.

"You know, Dink?" he told me as I sat there, sobbing. "We called you Dink for no apparent reason. But now you're starting to really act like a dink."

Perhaps he meant to call me stupid and useless. But what he didn't know was what I was just starting to realize. My mind was sick. What I had seen five years earlier in the Howard Hughes movie seemed to be coming true with me, just as it had with my father and mother. On that day, I would get no closer to the glory and the women that gave others stature and popularity.

Even though I had grown immensely since beginning to free myself from my parents' grasp, something about me was still standing in my way.

⤳

The person who *really* saved me, at least during my teenage years, was Bill Borden. He showed up at my house in Point Pleasant in 1983 wanting to go to the beach. That visit made him my best friend forever, because he never did stop showing up at my house, unannounced, ready to have fun. He was my confidant. We had known each other before. But when we became closer, I learned more from Bill than from anybody. I marveled at his ability to smile his way through problems. I was struck by his ability to go up to people and start talking to them. I was amazed that he could carry on a conversation with anybody—particularly women— for hours.

I was always too shy and cynical to be social. I felt insecure about the way I looked. I felt embarrassed about my family. Bill had an awkward but honest, even charming, way about him.

Bill's mission was to have fun, to smile, and to live a good life. He had no lofty expectations for himself; he just wanted to work hard, go to bed, and wake up the next morning and do it all over again.

Bill knew something about family troubles too. But he grew up with a sense that problems could be resolved. He always found a positive way to look at things, and he always believed there was a solution to everything, even when everything seemed to be falling apart.

With Bill, I learned how to keep friends. I was too embarrassed by my family life to invite people over to my house and have them witness my mother getting one more "Will you love me forever and ever?" response out of my father. I didn't want them to see her limping, and I certainly didn't want them to eat her food. But Bill didn't care. When he showed up at our door on that day in 1983, he just walked in and talked. He stayed for a good hour, talking to my mother and father. He even had a sandwich, one that contained my mother's thick, gristly meatloaf, and swallowed it nearly whole before we got on our bikes and headed for the beach. He built a bond that day with my parents and, as a result, with me.

He made my mother laugh. She seemed to be comfortable with him, and she even asked him some probing, personal questions.

"Are you still dating Diane?" my mother would ask, and Bill would then break down the history of the relationship before getting to the point.

Bill was brilliant but he could be a bit of a space cadet, which my mother and I viewed not as a character flaw but as an endearing quality. His non sequiturs would leave all of us hunched over laughing, largely because he misheard or misinterpreted something we said.

"So what are you doing tonight?" she once asked Bill while sitting in the kitchen, a tall glass of beer and a bag of potato chips in front of her.

"No thanks—I just had steak," Bill replied.

My mother laughed for a long time and didn't get close to her beer for nearly a half hour.

☙

With Bill, I developed a sense of humor. I even got some votes for class clown during my senior year of high school. With Bill, I learned how to deal with women. Until then, I could never bring myself to ask anyone out. I was so embarrassed to look in the mirror and see my braces jutting out and pimples dotting my face. I hated the cheap, thin, tight nylon slacks my mother made me wear, and I grew so tired of splitting them in the crotch. When I started to wear jeans to school, my mother protested, even engaged me in her repeating routine to get me to stop.

"Thomas, do as I say, please, okay? . . . You are *not* allowed to wear jeans to school, okay? . . . Your father and I say you can't. . . . Promise that you won't wear jeans to school, okay? . . . Promise me?" I agreed, but I wore the jeans anyway; when I came home, my mother would look at me and say nothing.

In 1983, Bill and I landed jobs at an amusement park at the board-walk. I operated the Rock-o-Plane, a Ferris wheel with spinning cars. For much of the day, I sat in one of the cars, sticking my face in the sun and getting a tan that helped wipe away my zits. Or I'd watch Bill talk to hot-looking blondes as he chased after kids while managing the mini bumper-car ride. By that summer, I had shunned the Gatorade packets, ate three square meals each day, and fit seven-mile runs in between. I started to feel strong, and for the first time in my life, secure.

That summer, I had my first date, Sherri, a small, somewhat stout girl who wore glasses but had a wide, bright smile as white as my mother's. She made it easy for me; she told everybody she liked me. After just one date, we were holding hands and going on rides. She celebrated anniver-saries of our relationship every week, giving me cutout cardboard cards that read, "Happy one-week anniversary!" and so on. On the tiny card-board pieces, she drew pictures of hearts and sunrises on the water. After she gave them to me, she'd remind me that another one was coming. "Our second-week anniversary is coming—remember that." I saved them all.

We never kissed. The one time I tried, my lips landed under her ear. She had turned her head, just like my mother did.

※

I dated Sherri for one month before she fell for somebody else. I felt as though she had done the worst thing possible, a betrayal of immense proportions. I thought of my father and how he stuck with my mother for better or worse. I saw how he put up with the obsessions, the repeating, the hand washing, and the nagging. *He can stay with her*, I thought. *Why can't anybody stay with me?*

I got the news from friends who saw Sherri spending a weekday at the boardwalk, riding the rides with her new male friend and playing the spinning-wheel games. When I confronted her about it, she admitted it immediately and apologized.

"I'm so sorry," she said.

It was just minutes before the start of the afternoon shift, and much of the staff was standing nearby, just outside the fence that sealed off the entrance to the park. We stood on the boardwalk in Point Pleasant Beach in a sparkling midday sunshine, and many workers were finishing the last of their lunches before opening the rides to the public. With virtually everybody listening in, I asked Sherri if this meant we were through. She couldn't answer.

"I'm really sorry," she said. "I didn't want it to be this way. I really care for both of you."

But for me, that wasn't enough. I needed the drama. I needed the same kind of stage that my mother and father had for their blowouts, setting things up so everybody could see and hear. With Bill standing next to me and with some of the amusement park staff leaning against the boardwalk rail filling their lunch bags with garbage, I pulled out the pile of "anniversary cards" that I had saved from our month together. I shoved them toward her nose.

"What about this?!" I shouted. "Do these mean nothing to you?"

"Oh no!" she said. "I can't believe you would do that."

She took off, running down the boardwalk, crying.

We never talked again.

༓

Afterward, I continually rationalized to myself. *I couldn't let this go out with a whimper,* I thought. *If it was going to end, I had to have her hate me. I had to turn it into a spectacle. I always feel strength in getting revenge.*

Still, after our breakup I eventually felt horrible and jealous and small. I didn't understand how something could start out so wonderfully and end so badly. Dating just didn't seem worth the fight. In the ensuing years, relationships I had with women ended similarly to the way things ended with Sherri. Virtually every woman I dated, whether for a day, a week, or a month, ended up hating me and shutting off all contact forever. I was too "possessive," they'd say, because I would call them every day. I was too smothering, they'd say, because I visited them where they worked. I was too sentimental, they'd say, because I'd drop flowers inside the mailbox at their homes. Going out on a date was like waiting for the starter's gun to go off at a cross-country meet. I'd get stomach gas that was so severe, I could barely eat. If we ate while on the date, I would pick at my food and eat only a few bites of the meat before giving up. My brain would cramp too, because I felt as though I had nothing to say. When I was at Rutgers University, I was no longer a competitive runner, so I had nothing to brag or boast about. *What's getting in my way?* I kept asking myself. *What's stopping me from being happy?*

ॐ

I didn't feel comfortable with women until I met Jessica at a Halloween party in 1986. With Jessica, I never had to worry. She loved the jokes I told. She loved the words I wrote. She loved the hugs we had. She loved the life we shared.

When we met, I was a nineteen-year-old, lanky and insecure sophomore trying to climb the ladder at the prestigious Rutgers University newspaper, the *Daily Targum*. Since the dream of being a successful athlete had essentially failed, I was trying to live out another dream I had: becoming a successful journalist. She was a naïve, impressionable seventeen-year-old freshman who was just breaking into the campus newspaper staff, though I didn't know her. At a Halloween party, a friend of mine introduced me to a petite girl with stringy dark brown hair. Like me, she wasn't wearing a costume.

"Tom!" the friend said. "This is Jessica."

Giggling, Jessica extended her red, plastic beer cup toward mine and toasted me. She had a shy but lively look. Her hair was sprayed up like Bon Jovi's, and her makeup was thick and colorful, illuminating in the dank, dimly lit New Brunswick apartment. She had a dark mole near her mouth that gave her glamour. Her smile was bright and silly, but as soon as I tried to talk over the droning noise, that smile quickly disappeared. She seemed to hate the noise as much as I did.

I tried small talk, offering the clichéd pleasantries. But I couldn't hear my own words. I then felt a rare surge of assertion, grabbing her hand and leading her to a wall in the living room, where we slid down the side and sat on the floor. Right away, I sensed qualities in her that I hadn't seen in other women I'd met or dated: She was needy, anxious, and indelibly human. I could feel her shake as we sat on the cold floor, and pressed our warm bodies against each other. She said little as we sat there, even as I occasionally tried, but failed to talk over the noise. After a half hour had passed, she finally blurted, "I'm cold!" prompting me to walk over to a bedroom, find my worn jean jacket, and wrap it around her. Then I wrapped my arm around her and hugged her slightly.

Eventually, we went outside and found ourselves walking the vacant, cold streets that led all the way to my dorm. That night it rained, and deep puddles had formed along the pavement, blocking our path. Still, Jessica's shoulders relaxed as we walked outside, and her smile reappeared. She suddenly was playful, happy, and talkative.

"I love the Jersey Shore," she said. "You're from there too?"

"Sure," I said. "I'm from Point Pleasant."

"Point Pleasant? Wow!" she said. "That's the beach. You grew up at the beach?"

"I did," I said. "Best place in the world."

"Do you surf?"

"I tried once," I said. "I got hit in the head with the board. It was a twelve-footer that belonged to my friend's dad."

Jessica laughed hard, almost losing her breath as she did. It was such a deep and honest laugh that I felt touched.

"You're so funny!" she said. "I know who you are, you know."

"What do you mean?"

"I read you all the time!" she said. "I'm so impressed with you!"

"You read my news articles?"

"You're on the front page all the time!" she said. "How could I miss it?"

"Many people do!" I said. "Most people only read the *Targum* for the comics and the sports."

"I love the way you describe things," she said. "You tell a story."

She kept laughing and giggling all the way to my dorm, swinging her arms in delight as we walked nearly a mile. Both of my roommates were at parties, so in my room we sat on the edge of my flat, narrow bed, chatting lightly as she put her hand on my knee. It felt so good, and so warm. It never felt so easy. For once, I didn't have to make the first move.

We kissed for hours. She lay on top of me and rolled her lips around mine. For hours, we moaned, hugged, kissed, and giggled.

No relationship blossomed from this—not yet, at least. For weeks, it was just like this; Jessica was a flirtation, which suited me well for a little while. She had her routines, showing up in my dorm usually on a Thursday night, getting one of my roommates to open the door and let her in. She'd sit at the foot of my bed for hours, waiting for me to come back from work or a party. Sometimes she'd talk to my roommates and let them tell stories about me. When I finally did show, the "date" would follow the same pattern.

"I read the story you wrote today," she'd say. "It was very good." Sometimes, she'd even have the story with her, and she'd read aloud the lines she liked best. Then just as she did the first time, she'd move her hand on my knee, and we'd soon find ourselves smothering each other with kisses and hugs.

⌇

With Jessica, I had control—so much so that I was the first to call it off. After nearly two months, I started to get sick of it, sick of the routines. She wouldn't do anything more than kiss. After her five or six unannounced visits to my room, I wanted more. I wanted a companion; not a groupie. I had even grown tired of her ravings about my articles. *Yeah, they're good,* I thought. *But they're bland. They're flat. They're reporting. They're certainly not poetry.* Indeed, I finally started to feel something that I had felt in every other relationship I ever had: insecurity. What had seemed so warm and charming started to seem a little hollow and redundant.

I asked her out on a real date, one that would involve dinner, dancing, and some music—or so I promised. It was the kind of conventional dating I loathed, the kind I had rarely handled well before. But I saw it as more of a test for Jessica than it was for me. I wanted to see if we could eat together. This, I thought, had to be more than a weekly Thursday-night fling.

That night, Jessica didn't show up for more than an hour. When she did, she was raging about a roommate or friend who was driving her crazy. She felt betrayed by something the other person had said about her, something Jessica had interpreted as an insult. "I can't believe she would say that about me," she kept saying over and over. "Have you ever had anybody say anything like that about you?"

She lay flat on my bed and sulked. Her thick, dark-brown eyebrows were stiff and straight, and her mouth was in a full-blown frown. She stared straight ahead, as if she were in an angry trance. "It just doesn't make any sense," she said. "Why would she say that about me? I've never said anything about her."

She lay on my bed, grumbling, stewing, and kicking her feet in the air. "Do you think I'm a bad person?"

"No, no, you're a very sweet, loving person," I said. "But, why don't we talk about this over some food."

"I want to know from you," she said. "Am I a good person?"

"Yes, you're a great person," I said. "Can we go?"

Finally, after an hour of raging, I called her on it. "I don't know, Jessica, but I've kind of had it," I said. "I've been sitting here for two hours, waiting for you to get ready and go. I got dressed up for this and everything, and I'm feeling a bit put off here."

Jessica's angry face turned sheepish. "Oh, I'm sorry," she said. "I wasn't much for going out anyway."

I sighed. *Did she really say that?* I thought.

"Well, it's probably a little too late for that anyway," I said.

"I'm sorry. Maybe we could do it next week?"

"Maybe."

Jessica moved up close, kissed me on the lips and left. "Let's do something next week, okay?" she said as she walked out the door.

But I didn't call her. I stayed away, seeing her only at the college paper, the *Targum*, where we both worked. We smiled at each other often, and we talked occasionally. I dated other people. I missed her, but I had decided Jessica had become a burden. And after a lifetime of dealing with burdens, I didn't need another one.

꒰꒱

When I returned for my junior year in September 1987, one of my first visits was to the newspaper office. One of the first people I saw was Jessica. When I saw her, I gasped.

She now was a stunning beauty, a grown, mature woman with a beautiful body. Her skin was smooth, and the mole seemed darker, even more exotic. Her once stringy brown hair with the split ends looked silky smooth.

For weeks, I found myself sitting in the *Targum* office staring at her, focusing on her hair, her skin, and her mole. Jessica knew I was looking at her, too, but she said nothing. All she offered was a slight, wry smile back, something I took as a tacit approval of sorts. She had a boyfriend, but I felt no fear. I had her eye again.

We often worked late, and as time passed, we often worked together in the *Targum*'s production office, surveying the "dummy sheets" of newspaper print that were to be published the next day. In between checking for spelling errors and using an X-Acto knife to cut the pasted-on stories that ran too long, we tickled each other, grabbed each other by the waist, and playfully wrestled. I started offering her rides home. We would pull up to her dorm, park in the fire zone, and talk.

We talked for long periods of time, discovering that we had a lot in common. We liked books and movies, especially *Star Wars*. We loved the same stuff we had loved as kids—waterslides, roller coasters, and Ferris wheels—and we agreed we would never be too old to enjoy them. She loved my jokes; like my mother, she especially enjoyed my impersonations of others. She'd tick off the names of editors at the college paper whose idiosyncrasies stuck out. Each time, she'd laugh her deep, hearty laugh.

I loved her laugh; it was a hard one that came right from the gut. She laughed until she was left gasping for air, sometimes making herself stop so she wouldn't choke. Despite her improved looks, she never seemed to care how she looked or what others thought about her. Sometimes, we'd get a quick bite to eat, and she'd laugh so hard that she'd draw looks from the people sitting at the other tables. "Shhh!" they'd say, but Jessica would keep going until her laugh was finished.

Just after the new year, 1988, Jessica dumped her boyfriend.

"We ought to be a pair," I'd tell her. "We need to be together."

It was Jessica, however, who asserted control this time, and I eventually learned why: *she* was mad at *me* for the way things had ended before. She felt blown off. She had expected me to call her, even after the date fiasco she had created. When I didn't, she felt as rejected and hurt as I ever had.

"I was having a problem, and you didn't help me!" she told me as we sat in my 1974 Dodge Dart late one night.

"But you had a fight with somebody I didn't know," I said to her. "Why couldn't you solve that yourself?"

"Tom Davis, you don't like it when people call you names, either," she said.

"You never really cared what people thought of you before," I said. "Why did you care then?"

"Because it was important to me!" she yelled, her eyes flaring.

I paused, and then I sighed. I leaned back in the driver's seat while Jessica stared through the windshield out into the night.

"Okay, it was important to you," I said. "I'm sorry. I guess I need to take people's feelings into account more often."

"If you like me, you're going to have to prove it to me," she told me. "It's going to have to be more than words. It's going to be words with meaning."

Those words finally came in March 1988. Again, we were sitting in my car in the fire zone near her dorm at Rutgers. At the college newspaper's production office, it had been a good night. I made Jessica laugh at my impersonations. I tickled her with my hands.

In the car, she pressed herself against the passenger door while I sat restlessly in my seat. I told her I was ready to make a move; Jessica, however, said she still wasn't ready, but she didn't know why.

"What do I have to do to prove it to you, Jessica?" I said. "I've done everything you've asked. I've taken you out. I've told you time and time again how much I care for you. I've been there every time you need me."

Jessica's eyes rolled around. She sat, silently, pausing for a few seconds. She was good at blurting things out, speaking her mind. This was the first time I ever saw her hold back.

"Jessica, I'm sorry," I said. "I should have been there for you. I should have helped you that night. You're right. You needed a friend, and you didn't get one."

"Mmm . . ."

"I care for you so much. . . ." I said, my voice trailing off.

Jessica's eyes met mine. "Kiss me," she said.

I did, offering a short smooch and quickly pulling away. Jessica grabbed my shirt, clutching tightly as she pulled me quickly back in. Once again, our lips were rolling on top of each other's. Jessica ran her fingers around my lips. She was like a little kid at the ice cream store, twirling her finger inside a milkshake, enjoying the feeling of getting her fingers sticky and wet. "I love lips," she said. "I love your lips!"

⌒⌒

In the months that followed, we were inseparable. I loved being around her better than anybody I had ever met in my life.

Jessica was more than a body to hug. She was a friend and a companion. She was complicated, but real. At times, she could annoy me with her obsessions and her demands that I pay attention to nobody but her. But she would also woo me with her undying honesty.

She brought me culture; when it was cold, we walked the streets of New York City and ate at restaurants in Little Italy. "I ordered you the fettuccini alfredo," she once told me. "I know you're going to like it, so eat it." We went back to Manhattan repeatedly; it was the first time I'd been there since I had gone to Mets games as a child. I'd stare at the tall, overpowering buildings. "Wow, look at that," I'd say. "I can't even see the tops of them."

"That's what I love about you," Jessica said to me, something she said often. "You're so naïve!"

When it was warm, we went to the beach. We often sat in bumper-to-bumper traffic, the kind of thing that always annoyed my family on our arduous cross-country trips. With Jessica, however, I enjoyed it. We talked. We played games. We played *Star Wars* trivia. We tried to impress each other with the quotes we knew from movies.

When we got to the beach, we'd lie on blankets, hug each other, and talk. I'd wrap my hands around her as we listened to the waves wash in. We wouldn't move for hours, getting up only to take an occasional dip in the water or rub suntan lotion on each other.

Jessica loved amusement parks, so much so that she knew where they all were, big and small. We spent many days in Seaside Heights, New Jersey, enjoying every waterslide or mini roller coaster the town had to offer. I felt like I was living the dream we had on our cross-country trips, back when I was eight and nine—I was finally doing the stuff we used to see displayed on the billboards along the interstates.

More than anything, Jessica loved writing, and she loved talking about writing. Two years after she first did it, Jessica still loved to read my news articles line by line aloud. Initially, I'd be embarrassed. *What is she doing that for?* I'd think. *They're not that good.* But she often read them with the diction and grace of a poet, punctuating words and phrases that she especially liked, as though they were from the script of a dramatic play.

One day, she did it as we lay on my bed at my New Brunswick house, spicing up an otherwise drab, dark day at the old, pale Cape Cod where I lived during the last two years of my college life. She read aloud a story I wrote for the *Targum* about ocean pollution and how it was destroying the reputation of something I loved. Before she read it, I felt a bit unsure about it, much as I always did after I had an article published. I wondered if it made sense. I wondered if I was using the right words or phrases. I worried that the subject, the words, and the lines were too cliché and unoriginal.

Jessica found a way to give it all meaning, her brown eyes sparkling as she read it. "I love good writing," she said. "It turns me on."

ॐ

For six months, Jessica was my spirit. I thought of nothing else really and did very little with anybody other than her. My family, and even Bill, were virtually out of the picture. I felt a sense of security that I never felt before.

As time passed by, however, insecurity began to rear its ugly head. Soon after our March kiss in the car, Jessica warned me about the future: she had joined a program to spend her junior year abroad in her homeland of Israel. She would be gone for nearly a year, departing on a midday El Al flight on August 11. As the day of her flight approached, the idea that I'd lose her made my stomach roil and cramp.

I was obsessed with Jessica, and as August 11 approached, I put my thoughts on paper. The poem showed that, as much as I was enjoying my life, I worried that my good fortune was about to slip away.

The clock reads 5:12
I toss in my bed; it is hot as hell
Opening the window does not help
My clothes weigh 100 pounds; I take them off
The sheets on my bed become useless, if not distracting
The hissing radiator is too loud
The bed is uneven
My roommate talks in his sleep; what is he saying?
I stare at the ceiling, and it paints a picture
It is her
I turn—she is there
I roll over—she is still there
I walk out, have a drink, go to the bathroom
She is there
My stomach turns, and she is there
I am back in bed; she is still there
And I stare
And as I stare, I think

And as I think, I stare, and stay awake
The image is still with me. The image of her
Loving, teasing
Leaving

As August 11 approached, I started to feel the deepest sense of hope-lessness. I found it difficult to eat, going back to my high school diet of only one meal a day. On some days, I would eat no meal, just drink water or soda. I never felt hungry, just nauseated from the stomach acid that churned constantly in my stomach.

"You look so skinny," my father told me, one day in late July as Jessica and I sat at the dinner table slowly eating a plate of barbeque food.

"I'm fine," I told him, just as I told him every time he asked the question. But I wasn't. In fact, I never was.

CHAPTER 9

DELIVERANCE

April 2009

THE PALE WALLS LOOKED GRAY and dark in the dimly lit room. I sat by the window, scooping from a bowl of soggy cereal. My wife lay in the bed, soundly asleep.

Kathleen could finally sleep. She no longer seemed to worry about how late I was staying up. She no longer seemed to care that I was neglecting newspaper work, so much so that my bosses were confronting me about it.

She didn't complain about me spending most nights fussing over family details that I had dug up from libraries, psychiatric hospitals, and interviews with Dora and my brother, sister, and father. She no longer tried to coax me to shut off the light and lie next to her.

Kathleen saw my sunken, sleepy eyes every day and no longer complained that rest was more important than the book. We had endured two months of this intensive research together. Kathleen was either beginning to understand or she had finally given up. She knew my book was an open wound that needed to be healed. By looking back, I could move forward. I could learn to deal with my own failings in ways that escaped my ancestors. On this night in April 2009, my wife wrapped herself in her blankets and turned toward the wall.

"Whatever," Kathleen said as she looked at me leaning forward in my chair, tapping on my laptop just as she started to slip into a deep sleep.

On this night, I had waited longer than usual to get home from work. I wanted Kathleen's eyes to be shut and her snoring to be deep and heavy. I wanted a room that felt as empty and dark as the rooms I sat in twenty-one years earlier, just after Jessica left me. I wanted to be inside my young self and find out why I found relief in sticking my fingers down my throat—as many as eight times a day—and then pressing down on my tongue and choking myself so I'd vomit into the toilet.

I turned on the computer, popped up iTunes, and looked for Elton John. I used to listen to the song "Funeral for a Friend" while driving my car home from work twenty-one years earlier. I would look up at the night sky and see Jessica in the solid black, walking through JFK airport one last time. I'd think of the day she left, August 11, 1988, and I'd see her waving as I wept into my hands.

I used to turn off the song before it got to the words. I often got sick of remembering that image and seeing it wherever I was looking, whether it was in the sky, in the walls of my newspaper office, or in the ceiling over my bed. I'd see that image, and I couldn't restrain the urge to hide in the bathroom for an hour and bend over the toilet, just as my mother often bent over the sink to wash her hands.

On this night, I wanted the image back. I needed it for my book. I needed to connect what happened to me then to what had happened before, to my family. I wanted to know not so much about my grandfather, my mother, and those before them. I wanted to know about me.

I wanted to know whether the mental health people were right when they diagnosed me with eating disorders. *What if they're wrong?* I thought. *What if they exaggerated? What if this was just an isolated case? How could I be like my mother? Like my grandfather? Like my great-grandfather? I'm still here, aren't I?*

This time, I couldn't go to a graveyard and look up documents that offered a cause. I couldn't go to my mother's Greystone house from the 1950s and watch the patients walk by and think *For Christ's sake, anybody living here would crack up!* I couldn't go to the Internet and dig up information or go to the Rutgers library and read the *DSM*. I had to change course, and my journey. This time, it had to be internal, not external.

I had to connect to that time and place when the world seemed dark and the songs of my life were always slow and sad. Only I knew that world. Only I could remember what it was like to watch the first person I truly loved leave and how my reaction was so weird and strange that it scared me. I wanted to know why the only solution I could find was to get sick.

As the song moved, I could think back and feel the hard airport floor, when Jessica flew away for good. I could see the patch of gray dust balls kick up and fill the air every time I shifted my leg. The dust floated lightly, stilled by the thick heat. *Where the hell is the air-conditioning?* I thought, bathed in sweat while waiting at the JFK airport on that day in 1988.

I remembered waiting and looking through the dust at the clock on the wall. Every so often, I had to crane my neck around the crowds of people walking by, rushing to get to their next flight. I remembered thinking then some of the same or similar thoughts I had now in 2009. *Am I going nuts? Why am I watching a clock?*

August 1988

I kept my eyes on the clock's hands as they moved toward noon, closer and closer to Jessica's departure.

My mind started to fade, my eyes misty from the deep, damp August humidity that made JFK airport feel like Georgia. I saw people carrying big blue Samsonites, the same ones my parents took on our long trips to Florida and California. Every time I saw one, I thought of another August day, back when I was eight years old, when the Samsonites flipped off the car roof rack and our clothes spread all over Interstate 70 in Ohio. I remembered my father crying out, "Why? Why?" as he got out of the car, picked up the remains, repacked, retied the load to the roof, and resumed our arduous trip to California.

Thirteen years later, in 1988, the Samsonite suitcases at JFK airport looked solid and sealed tightly. They looked as though they were going a long way. Jessica had hers on the floor next to me, against the wall near her younger sister Michelle. Jessica sat on my other side, leaning against me and holding my hand as we waited and watched the travelers pass by.

My hands were so sweaty that I could barely feel Jessica's grip. We had been holding hands since we left Jessica's home in New Jersey, about two hours before. On the way to JFK airport, we sat on the hot, steel floor of her father's van, between a pile of luggage, paint cans, buckets, and a rack of tools, and we cooked in the heat and humidity.

We didn't let go of our handhold until sometime around noon, when the word came.

"Time to go!" Jessica's father declared.

As I let go, I could feel my heart start to pound. Jessica was the first girl I had ever loved. Now she was going to leave for a junior year abroad in Israel.

In the two years we dated off and on, I never had to worry about anything. It felt good to be adored again, the way I was adored when I was three, when my mother sat me on her lap, fed me my dinner, and called me "sweetheart" long after I didn't have to be handfed any more. No longer did I care about being pushed away by my mother when I was seven and how she told me that I couldn't sit in her lap anymore because she said I wasn't "clean" enough.

As we approached the boarding gate, I felt lightheaded and foggy-eyed. Jessica and I kept our hands together. *Christ*, I thought. *This is real.*

She's really leaving. I was facing a senior year without her. *What is going on here? Why does this have to happen?*

She had warned me. "I'm going on a junior year abroad to Israel," she had told me in March.

"Are you going tomorrow?" I asked.

"No, August," she said.

Good, I thought. I never had a relationship that lasted longer than two months, anyway. August was fine. August was cool. Worrying about August was like worrying about death. It was just too far away.

But there we were, August 11, 1988, walking slowly toward the gate, walking toward a goodbye. I started to cry. I felt shame again. At twenty-one, I thought I had finally learned how to stop being a wimp, just as my brother wanted me to. As we walked toward the boarding gate, my legs went limp, and my body, wobbly. Each leg felt like it weighed 200 pounds. My weeping turned into giant sobs. It felt worse than getting hit.

I released her hand and covered my face as I cried. Jessica wept too. I peeked at her through my fingers, watching her squeeze her nose and wipe her eyes.

I leaned over, grabbed her, and kissed her hard. I could feel the tears from her eyes that had pooled around her lips. Then I pulled away and watched her walk toward the security gate, wiping her eyes with her hands and still squeezing her nose.

I couldn't watch anymore. I buried my face in my hands. I felt my legs go limp again as the tears covered my face, down to the beard stubble on my chin. I looked up one more time and saw her waving. Jessica's crying had stopped. Now she was smiling.

☙

I turned around and walked back. I kept crying as I walked, each leg feeling heavier with each step. Jessica's parents and sister walked ahead. Every few seconds or so, they turned around to glance at me. I moved slowly, sobbing into my palms and feeling like I was dragging my body in a sack.

Jessica's father had his keys out, ready to hustle across the big, hot blacktop, get to the van, and get out of there. Just as we stepped outside and the doors opened, Michelle stopped. She walked over to me, looked at my face, and rubbed my back.

"It's okay," she said. "It's okay. Everything's going to be okay."

All the way to the parking lot, she walked next to me, patting my back every so often as we headed toward the van. The lot seemed so much bigger than it did when we walked into the terminal, and the van so much farther away. I didn't have Jessica's sweaty hand to hold. But I did have Michelle's touch. Every so often, the rub became a pat. I moved my hands and glanced at her face. I could see Jessica's cream-colored skin, the same soft skin that got me excited whenever I touched it.

I climbed into the back of her parents' van and sat on top of an upside-down paint bucket. Jessica's dad looked at me for five long seconds. His face looked pained. He had no tears, but his eyes were red and tired. He looked like the man I had heard about, the man who had seen war and violence, a veteran of the Arab-Israeli Wars. He had a dour, sullen face and the look of a man who has seen too much tragedy.

"You okay?" he asked.

"Sure, sure," I said. "I'm fine."

I choked back tears as we pulled out and began the long, bumpy drive back to Jersey. I wanted to be five again and yell so my mother could hear me and put me back on her lap. I wanted to yell, "I can't stop! I just can't stop!" and be that same weak kid I was growing up, the one who didn't take his own showers until he was in puberty.

With every shake of the van as it hit pothole after pothole, I thought of Jessica in the air, aboard an El Al plane, gliding across the ocean, smiling, thinking of her new country and her new life. I thought of me, going back to Jersey, going back to Rutgers where I had to study for an exam in a journalism seminar class the next day. I wept quietly, just as I had whenever my brother yelled at me for being the "favorite one," the one who almost always escaped my father's wrath.

ॐ

We got to her home in New Jersey and pulled into Jessica's driveway. I walked over to my car, which was parked in the street. I was alone again.

As I sat in my hot car, the Dodge Dart where Jessica and I had kissed, I felt empty. On the half-hour drive back to New Brunswick, I alternated between sobs and stomachaches. As I drove, watching the trees and stores pass by, I worked hard to stop every tear. Each time I did, my gut felt tight and bloated. I thought my stomach was going to pop out, right through my belly button.

In New Brunswick, my roommates were gone because it was summer break. I needed a place where I could read and focus. In the late afternoon hours, in the thick, damp heat, I had an empty house, a pile of books, and the set of sweaty clothes I was wearing.

I sat on my bed, but the twin mattress felt too low, and the springs were bulging through the fabric. I tried resting on my back and holding a book that I had barely read up to my eyes. But I couldn't read. My mind drifted back to the airport, back to the summer. I stared at the ceiling, and in the pale, white scene, I could see Jessica, running up to me on the beach, grabbing my waist, squeezing me, and pressing her face against my back.

As I stared above, I thought about bed and how we loved to lie in it. We'd be there for hours before we'd finally walk out of the room, no matter where. We did it in New Brunswick, on the same twin mattress with the bulging springs. We did it in Point Pleasant with its thin walls.

Whenever we were in Point Pleasant, I sensed the irony. This was the place where my brother got beat up whenever my father, full of rage, had had it with my mother's repeating. This is where I went to hide whenever my parents fought and I'd have to hear my father go through the makeup routine my mother demanded. "Do you apologize for what you said?" "Yes, yes," he'd say. "Promise?" "Yes, yes . . . what else?" "Do you love me best of all? . . . Promise? . . . Promise to love me forever and ever? . . . Promise?"

One time earlier that summer when I was with Jessica in Point Pleasant, I heard a knock on the door and my mother's voice coming from the other side.

"Thomas! Come out here, please!"

I walked out and saw her. "Come over here," she said.

She leaned against the couch. Her eyebrows were thick and stiff. They were like my grandfather's eyebrows, only painted on.

"Thomas, we don't want you in there, alone, with Jessica anymore," she told me.

"What?" I said. "What did I do?"

"We just don't want you in there."

"Please, tell me what I did," I said.

"We just don't want you in there," she said. "Talk nicely to me, okay?"

"I did!"

"Talk nicely to me, okay?"

"Okay, okay," I said.

"Do you love your mother best of all? . . . Promise?"

"Yes! Yes!"

"Promise?"

"Yes!"

Then I went back into the room. Jessica wrapped her arms around me tightly. I quickly forgot about my mother.

~

As I lay in my bed in New Brunswick, those visions came and went. With every vision, I could feel a burning shoot up from my gut through my ribs to my throat. *I need to eat*, I thought as I burped up stomach gas over and over. I had this idea that if I ate a lot, and quickly, that it would make my indigestion go away. Sometimes, the idea worked. Most times, it didn't.

I stood up, picked up my books, and walked out. I walked over to Skinny Vinny's pizza joint behind the Rutgers Student Center and bought a slice. I swallowed it in about six bites and then hustled over to the student center, belching up the pizza I had just eaten and feeling my throat burn.

I walked across the parking lot, through the dense air. The sun was setting; it was finally starting to cool. The parking lot was big, just like the one at JFK airport. It looked lonely, with the streetlights bouncing off the back windows of the few cars parked there. I went to the *Targum* newspaper office, carrying the pile of books in my armpit as I ran up three flights of stairs. As I approached the door, I glanced to my right and saw another door. It led to the concrete staircase and a ledge where nobody went, except for me and Jessica.

Every noise inside had an echo. I loved the echo. I loved hearing ourselves twice as we held hands and pounded on the steps as we ran up to the ledge. Then we leaned against the dirty brick wall and kissed. We ran up there whenever the newsroom got rough and the stress of putting together a college daily newspaper ran high. Sometimes, we ran up there just to hug. We'd laugh and listen to the echo.

On that day, with Jessica gone, I walked up a few steps and looked up. I saw the ledge. "Hello?" I called up. I knew nobody was up there. I just wanted to hear the sound.

I walked into the office, sat at a desk in the back room, put my feet up by the computer, opened a book in my lap, and stared at the pages. The air was much cooler, and the light was brighter. But the words on the pages were still a gray-and-white blur. I stared ahead at the blank, concrete wall in front of my face. It was pale, like my bedroom ceiling. Like all my other visions, this one came in flashes. In the wall, I saw the fancy Shadowbrook restaurant, the place we had gone a week earlier where we planned to have our last date. I had saved money from my summer job, an internship at the *Asbury Park Press*, so we could go there. I spent $200 on duck and wine. At one point the waiters walked up to our table, holding two wooden cylinders.

"Would you like some?" they asked.

"What is that?" I said.

"It's pepper."

"I'm fine," I said. "She's leaving. . . . She's going to Israel."

The servers shook Jessica's hand. Minutes later, they brought in a dish of cake. They sang to us. "I'll love you forever," I told Jessica that night.

"Oh, I'm sure you'll find somebody," she said.

"Maybe," I said. "But I'll love you forever."

Then in the fading, yellow wall at the *Targum* office, she was gone again. I cried. The office was empty, so I yelled.

"I want her back!" I yelled. "I want her back! I want her back!"

ॐ

My journalism seminar started at nine the next morning. I walked across campus, bleary-eyed and sleepless. All night I had sat upright in that same chair at the *Targum* office, weeping. The pile of textbooks and the notebook felt ten pounds heavier than it had the day before, causing my back to twist to compensate. Just outside the classroom building, the pinch became a cramp. Two books slid out from under my armpit and fell facedown on the sidewalk. Papers scattered all around, drawing looks from people passing by. It was just like that time the Samsonites tore off the car roof in Ohio, back when I was eight. Only no one stopped to help.

"Shit!" I yelled.

I dreaded this day as much as I had dreaded the day before. I hadn't read a single chapter—not even a page—for the entire semester. All the available time I had, I had spent with Jessica.

That morning, I expected to fail. I had no interest in the class. I barely had a memory of anything we had discussed during the lectures. Instead, I had visions again as I walked to class. Only this time, I saw myself the following year, in May 1989, watching everybody graduate while I stood on the sidewalk in my shorts and ripped T-shirt, sobbing again.

In class, I sat slumped in my chair. The professor passed out the exam. I glanced at the paper: multiple choice and essay. My answers were Hail Mary passes. My multiple-choice answers were sheer guesses, and my essays were bullshit.

I handed in the paper and left just as the exam period ended. I picked up my books and sprinted toward my car.

I drove south, heading toward Point Pleasant.

Traffic moved slowly as the cars squeezed through the turnoffs, U-turns, and jughandle left turns that stretched for miles. In my Dart, I could get two radio stations. One of them, WNBC 660, played "Question" by the Moody Blues. The deejay seemed to know that I was there, listening.

With each line, I cried. Then I yelled out again. With no air-conditioning, I had the windows rolled down. Into the outside air, where cars slowed up in the traffic, I yelled, "No! No!"

When I got home, I thought of my grandfather, weeping as he sat at the dinner table when we visited him in the years before. I remembered him walking along that red shag carpet at the riverhouse, a broken man. I remember how bad he looked.

I thought, *Is that me?* I wondered, *What's wrong with me? Why can't I handle these things?*

Am I him?

꒱

When I got home, my crying stopped. For the next week or so, I hung with Bill and I went to work. I worked hard to distract myself and to shove the loneliness aside, but I couldn't escape it. As summer faded, the sun fell earlier. The darker it got, the more I stayed in bed and stared at the ceiling.

Four hours of sleep in a night was a lot for me. In the weeks after Jessica left, I frequently nodded off while driving, sometimes catching myself before ramming a guardrail or a tree. At work, I fell asleep at my desk.

But in bed, at night, my eyes were usually wide open and my brain was wide awake.

Bill took me to bars. He introduced me to women. "This is my best friend Tom," he'd say.

I felt empty as I looked at other women. If I didn't see Jessica in them, not even a trace of her, I'd fake a laugh or utter a "hello" under my breath before turning back toward my beer.

One night, I drove home with Bill from a party that I hadn't wanted to go to.

"You'll have a good time." He had said it with a smile, like he always did. This time, Bill's smile didn't rub off on me. I agreed grudgingly, although I worried. *How much of a bad pill was I going to be? Could I stop thinking about Jessica even for a minute?*

I survived the party, barely talking to anybody as I stood in the corner of the small apartment, taking only a few sips from one beer bottle. We were there for an hour. Bill seemed to sense my stress, saying only, "Wanna go?"

A bunch of guys saw us heading out and asked for a ride. They were a loud bunch, laughing at everything they said to each other. They piled in the Dart's backseat, and they laughed about the tunes on the radio. I had WNBC 660 on, playing some oldie from the 1960s and 1970s.

"This is old!" they said. "What about Guns N' Roses?"

"I've got the album," I said. "I don't have the stereo."

"Fuck that shit!" one of them yelled. "Fuck it! Hey, you know that fucking song, 'Paradise City'?"

"Yeah!" another yelled, and began shouting the lyrics at the top of his voice.

With each line, I could feel my stomach roiling, ". . . where the grass is green and the girls are pretty!"

I didn't want to be happy. I didn't want to be yelling. I was thinking of Jessica and I wanted them to be silent, just as I was at the party.

"Take me down!" they yelled, raising their hands in their air and swaying back and forth. "Take me down!"

"SHUT UP!" I yelled, glaring at them through the rearview mirror. "Shut the fuck up!"

Silence fell, save for a few small giggles. I turned around, keeping one hand on the wheel but my eyes only on them.

"What the fuck did I just say?!" I yelled. "Shut . . . the fuck . . . UP!"

Now even the giggles were gone. Bill looked at me, then glanced at the guys in the backseat. Their smiles had finally dropped.

"Yeah, shut the fuck up!" he said. "Tom's trying to drive!"

⌇

In the ensuing weeks, I tried running. Usually, I got juiced by a three-mile jog. Instead, I felt sick before I even ran to the end of the block.

I worried and badgered my father with questions, much the way my mother would.

"If you don't feel well, then go to a doctor," he said.

"Do you think I have an ulcer?" I said.

"Well, that's why you go to a doctor, to get it checked out."

A doctor? Not yet. I couldn't handle the thought. I couldn't stand the vision. "Yes, you have cancer," they'd say. I had seen it coming since I was age three.

Screw it, I thought. As bad as I felt, I feared the unknown. Either I'd get over it, I kept telling myself, or I'd die. Instead, I returned to Rutgers for my senior year, hoping school, friends, and the life I knew before Jessica would return.

Before I left, I got a good sign: my grade for the summer exam was a C. For the first time I could remember, I surprised, even shocked, myself. *How the hell did I pass?* I kept asking. I couldn't figure out how or why I passed. I couldn't remember the questions. I couldn't even think of any rational way of explaining the answers. *Maybe good things were about to come*, I thought.

But as the days went by, my sickness got worse. Rutgers was the setting for all my lonely visions. Walking around campus, I could feel Jessica's hand. I could feel her lips whenever the campus bus passed by Passion Puddle, the pond by her dorm that was covered with the layers of fallen leaves year-round, and the constant gleam of sunshine on the water.

The people at the *Daily Targum* who had worked with Jessica and me the previous year kept asking, "How's Jessica?" They sincerely wanted to know. But it was the one question I didn't want to hear. It was like somebody asking, "How's the cancer?"

Most of the time, I didn't even have an answer. I considered calling her, or at least calling her family. I thought of Michelle, how she rubbed my back and made me feel good, at least for that one moment. Maybe her family could deal with me again and help.

Then just days after the semester began, Jessica's first letter finally arrived. It was pale blue, folded over and taped, with no envelope. "Haifa, Israel" was the return address.

She had been staying at a kibbutz, a commune-like setting where food, chores, and events were shared. In the letter, she talked about doing things she had never done before. She talked about those things with joy, the same way she got excited whenever we went to amusement parks and rode roller coasters and she grabbed me and laughed.

She also joked about many of the things we used to joke about. I could see her laughing as she wrote the letter. At the bottom, she told me she loved me, how much she missed me. She signed it, "Love, Jessica."

It was the last time she ever wrote it.

For a few days, at least, I felt like we were together again. *Maybe I could survive the waiting*, I thought. *Maybe I could stare at the ceiling and not dream of the past.*

Days after I got the letter, I called her family. I thanked them for the way they had treated me at the JFK airport.

"Is Michelle around?" I asked.

"No, she's not here," Jessica's mother said.

"Could you tell her 'thank you' too?"

I asked if Jessica had a telephone number. "She does, but it's the number for her floor," her mother said, speaking in her broken English. "Somebody else may answer it, but you can ask for her."

I called from my house, using the phone that hung on the kitchen wall and leaning against the wall as I dialed. I asked the international operator to put me through. I tried several times, going through the operator. After about five tries, I got a ring, and somebody answered.

"Do you know a Jessica . . . ?" I asked.

The person said yes, and went to get her. Minutes passed before Jessica answered.

Her voice sounded a little deep, and even a bit throaty. She sounded older.

"Hello?" she said.

"Um, hello? Jessica?" I asked.

Then came a pause. "Yes?" she said.

"This is Tom," I said.

"Oh . . . hi."

"Um . . . how is it going?"

"Um . . . okay."

I told her I missed her. I told her I was sick without her. I told her I was losing sleep and losing weight.

Each time, her responses were short, empty, and stale. "Okay," she said. "I'm sorry to hear that."

"I love you," I told her.

"I have to go now," she said.

"Oh . . . okay."

"I have to go," she said.

I said goodbye and hung up. I leaned back against the kitchen wall, raised my hand to my hair, and twirled it on my finger. Then I walked over to the kitchen table and sat. I stared out the window, where the sun shone brightly. I stared right into the sunlight.

I felt ill.

⤳

Two weeks later, in mid-September, another pale-blue, folded-over letter came. "Dear Tom," it started.

This letter had no jokes. It had no laughs. The tone was as pale as the white ceiling over my bed.

"I'm sorry I couldn't talk to you," were the words I remember. "But you shouldn't try to call me here.

"I still care for you deeply . . . but I've met someone else."

Then the speech became a lecture. She talked about how I should move on, find a new life. "I'm sure you'll meet someone else.

"You can keep writing to me. . . . But I'm tired of you talking about what's going on at *Targum*. You never have any questions about what I'm doing in Israel. You don't seem interested at all."

I didn't like the Jessica who lectured; I loved the one who laughed. This letter didn't make me laugh.

"You can still write to me," she said. "But try to show some interest in my life."

I refolded the letter and tucked it into my pants pocket. Until then, I had saved all her letters in a folder, spreading them flat so they wouldn't wrinkle. This time, I squished it into my pocket, practically crumpling the paper into a little ball.

I marched out the door and headed toward the *Targum* office. I felt like I had at the airport, my legs heavier with each step. The September air was warm but not hot. There was no sweat to cloud my vision. I was just plain confused. *How should I take this?*

On the way there, I saw a friend, Nina, who worked with me and Jessica at the *Daily Targum*. She was sitting on the front steps of her sorority house, puffing on a cigarette, smiling, and talking to friends.

"Hey, you!" she said, smiling.

"Hey. . . ."

"Why so sad?"

I pulled out the letter, unfolded it, smoothed it out on my leg, and handed it to her. She set her cigarette in an ashtray, and she read the letter out loud. She frowned, and then she gasped.

"Oh no!" she said.

"What?"

"You got a 'Dear John'!"

"A 'Dear John'?" I asked. "What's that?"

"A breakup letter."

I took it from her and read it again. I shook my head, placed the letter in my lap, and stared straight ahead at the student center. The sky had darkened, and the street lights were bouncing off the car windshields. Small crowds of students were walking between the cars, laughing. I felt distant, as though I were staring at something 100 miles away. I felt as though college was over. I felt I could never be happy again.

"I'm so sorry, Tom," Nina said.

"How could she do this?" I said.

"I never liked Jessica," she said. "I thought she was unfriendly. She was possessive of you."

"I actually liked that."

"Yeah, well, now she has no use for you."

I clutched the letter and walked back to my house. My legs felt even heavier and sweat started to form on my forehead. I walked inside my apartment and could smell hamburgers—one of my housemates was cooking. My stomach churned. I hurried into my bedroom and closed the door. I lay on my back. I read the letter again. And again. And again. I felt like a lawyer looking for a loophole. Did she really mean it? Could Nina have missed something?

After the ninth or tenth read, I tore it into pieces so small that there was no way I could reassemble it. There was no way I could reread it.

After a few hours, I got up and walked out to the hallway. All my roommates were either out or upstairs. The only thing left was the hamburger smell. I clutched my gut and felt a cramp rise to my rib cage. I walked over to the bathroom and sat on the seat waiting to go. But all I could feel was the cramp.

I didn't eat for another four days.

⌇

In October, I took four midterm exams and failed three of them. I was too busy in the library, reading encyclopedias and medical journals. I read research papers on colitis, stomach cancer, and ulcers. I thought I had them all.

Or I was at the drugstore buying boxes of Gas-X or Tums. I started to pop those every hour. But they just made me sicker. The Tums, in particular, went down hard. The pills were big, like flat gumdrops. One afternoon in late September, I took three. Standing next to the toilet, I could feel them stick in my throat and squeeze through my chest. My stomach was bloated and the gas burned.

I stuck my finger down my throat and puked them back up.

What have I done? I immediately thought.

Then came a feeling of warmth, almost like a high. Vomiting was a rush, a good rush.

Finally, I felt normal, or whatever my normal was. I felt the way I did before I ever knew Jessica. I felt like I did before I fell in love.

Only the rush wore off. I needed it again. I needed to be back in that place. I needed to keep going just so the good feeling stuck around. I went back to the bowl, back to sticking fingers down my throat and feeling the vomit wash through.

By mid-October, I was purging up to eight times a day. When I did eat, it was little more than bread and water. When I exercised, it was a three-mile run, just like the ones in high school, when I burned off the meager amount of calories I got from eating only packets of powdered Gatorade for four days straight.

One dreary, drizzly day as I lay in bed, I could feel the acid surging to my throat. I got up and walked out into the hallway. The house was dark, as it usually was. I searched for my roommates, running up the stairs and peeking behind the closed doors of their bedrooms. Nobody was around.

I ran back down, heading for the bathroom. I sat on the floor, slipped my fingers into my mouth, leaned over the bowl, and choked myself, before pulling the fingers quickly out. I coughed, but nothing more.

Just one more, I thought. *C'mon, Tom. One more.*

I shoved my fingers down again, this time bumping them against the back of my throat, pressing on my tongue, and holding them there until I choked. By the second try, the inhibitions were down. Any sense of apprehension was gone. I had crossed the line of trying. Now I knew I couldn't stop. I had to finish.

Then came a dry heave, that feeling when the stomach jerks up as though it's hitting your throat but leaves nothing. I shoved the two fingers down even harder, right down my windpipe, and left them there for ten seconds, preventing any air from slipping through.

Finally, I felt the bubbles filling my chest, slipping through my throat, and with one last push from the gut, filling my mouth and falling into the water.

I peeked behind the bathroom's window shade and glanced at the rain and leaves falling outside. I finally felt good, but I knew better. The good feeling was good, but it never lasted long enough to be a cure. So I waited.

C'mon, I said to myself. *Just one more time . . .*

I slipped into dreams. I mired myself in thoughts. I could hear Jessica's voice again, the soft, sultry voice that was disappearing from my mind.

I dreamed and heard her talking to her two-year-old brother, speaking in Hebrew, caressing him with words I could never interpret, but I always could tell they were kind and sweet. I could still see him smile, then run up and hug her after she talked to him—hug her the way I wanted to hug her, and gaze at her with a sense of innocence and joy. I wanted to hear that voice again, and I forced my clouded brain to replay it, over and over. I was too afraid I'd forget it.

As I sat on the cold bathroom tile, I felt that same boneless, lifeless feeling I had at the airport. I felt that crumbling feeling I had as I wiped the tears that covered my face. I had that same sense of paralysis I had as I walked to the parking lot and climbed into the back of her parents' van.

Then, as I sat alone in that lonely New Brunswick house, those visions, just like Jessica, went away. I felt the same dizziness that had been lingering for weeks, the sensation that made my head feel as though it was detaching from my neck. A sticky, pussy film covered my eyes, making them hard to close and blurring everything that was more than a foot away from my face. My lips were dry and raw.

Just once more, I thought to myself. *One more time. Let it out, one more time, and it all will feel better. Just get it out.*

CHAPTER 10

THE END
IS JUST THE BEGINNING

September 2009

GOING TO MY MOTHER'S GRAVE in Point Pleasant just after my father's wedding was a last-minute decision. This was supposed to be a ceremonious day, a day of moving forward, not backward. It was a decision my family made as we left Point Pleasant Presbyterian Church, the church of my youth, where I had been baptized. It was made just after I watched my father marry Marilyn Burke, the woman who finally made him happy.

I hadn't been there since the winter, some seven months before. The grass was still a summery green, though beginning to pale. The sky was cloudy and gray, the ground slightly damp from an early rainfall. I felt the ground that covered my mother's casket, and rubbed my hand through the weeds and my fingers through the loose dirt. It was soft and warm, just how my mother liked things. For once, I could feel good about where she was. I could feel that she was being protected.

My three-year-old daughter Anna picked up a stick and drew in the soft dirt. Then she picked the grass that grew around the square stone, rolling the blades of grass between her fingers. She was the picture of my mother, right out of my grandfather's photo albums: young, little, blonde, precocious, and a little bored. When we took pictures, she stood near the stone, forcing a smile, just as my mother did as she stood on the sands of Bradley Beach some sixty years before. When our photos were done, Anna crouched back down and again ran her fingers through the grass and weeds. She picked at the petals of the flowers we lay at the gravestone, flowers that came from our table at the wedding, and she rubbed the tiny pieces between her fingertips.

My seven-year-old, Jonathan, stuck the lens of a camera up close to the stone, carefully trying to focus on the inscription: "Dorothy W. Davis / Nov 12 1937 / Jan 18 2003." (My mother's real name was Dorothy.) I couldn't help but think back to when he was a baby in 2002 and how he made my mother smile. My mother would sit in her chair, the one she never left except to go to the bathroom. By then, she was barely more than skin and bones. Her arms and legs looked like her hands: red, flaky, and raw. She tried, but she could barely flash the bright, big smile that seemed to wash away her troubles. When confronted with Jonathan's freckled face, chubby body, and gummy grin, though, she was able to say, "I know everybody always says their kids are cute, but he really *is* cute!"

I saw Tommy, who was then eleven, bend over to look at the tombstone, studying it. He paused for a few minutes, staring intently at the stone. He was the only one of the three with memories of her alive. Few, if any, of those could be pleasant. He could still recall the night of the phone call, how his cute gesture to reach his grandparents turned into the phone call we always feared.

"I remember that—that was really weird," he told me, every time we talked about that night on January 18, 2003, when I took the phone away from him and heard my sister say, "Thomas! Mommy died!" Tommy could still remember going to the nursing home where my mother stayed whenever we couldn't keep her safe. He could still remember playing on the floor around my chair as my mother sat there talking to me endlessly about how she was fine, she was good to go, even though she so obviously wasn't. *Please get me out of here, Thomas. . . . Will you please tell your father to get me out of here? Will you please?* He could remember playing with cars between my mother's skeletal legs and the legs of her chair.

I thought of these children, staring at and playing around a gravestone on a warm but damp day, when they could have been doing something else. They could have had Dede alive, a grandmother who doted over them, who would park them in the backseat of her car and take them to the beach. Instead, they had a tombstone they could only stare at and lay flowers on. Instead of pleasant memories, they had an ugly stone marker, just like the many others that marked the members of my family who left before their time.

As I watched them and let my mind wander, I could feel the sting we had felt eleven years earlier when we took Tommy out of the hospital at just a few days old and he shook uncontrollably. The doctor said it was nothing. Then Tommy didn't smile for four months, and only rarely did during the first three years of his life. When he got older, he wouldn't play on the monkey bars if others were on it. He threw up even when he wasn't upset, causing car-seat covers, clothes, and tablecloths to run constantly through cycles in the washer and dryer.

We took Tommy to occupational therapy, because we didn't want what happened to those before him to happen to him. We wanted him to live a normal, happy life. As I watched, I thought, just as I had before: *If we were able to save Tommy and help turn him into a strong, cheerful eleven-year-old boy, what could we have done for Mommy?*

We had added another generation to the family line—more people cursed with something that makes them shake, worry, fuss, obsess, and perhaps die before their time. I sometimes worry that my children, too, are doomed. But in front of my mother's grave, I cherished how my children looked. They were so young, so clean and bright in their formal wear for the wedding. My daughter wore a bright yellow spring dress; Jonathan looked sharp in his khaki pants. I started to grieve, even more, as I realized how that could so quickly change, just as it had for my mother and those before her. But I also felt warmth in that, at least with Tommy, we were doing something about it.

I thought of my wife Kathleen, who stood with my sister-in-law near the car. I thought of Kathleen as a saint, a woman who put up with so much in her own life and then had to put up with mine. She had lost her father in the Vietnam War and was her family's caregiver when she was in her teens, watching after her mother who had suffered through a series of strokes. She stayed with me, even when she met my mother for the first time, just months before we married in August 1996, and she had to witness my mother repeating over and over what she was trying to tell my father.

Kathleen had enough sense to see something in me that I couldn't see in myself, even as I slowly recovered from the worst symptoms of eating disorders. She saw how anxious I was just before we had Tommy, and how my anxiety grew worse. She compelled me to see a psychologist as I still struggled with ways to cope with myself. She took part in my mother's care as we went through a journey of finding mental health facilities, assisted-living facilities, nursing homes, and stay-at-home health care aides, which gave us some hope, but never any cure.

Kathleen provided the intimacy, the romance, and even the security that I thought I had with Jessica, as well as the affection that I once had with my mother. But with Kathleen, there was always something more. She provided the selfless devotion that I never had, always doing what she had to do to solidify her need to help me and my mother. She realized that this experience was brutal, but also helpful, because it was a catharsis. As I watched my mother slowly die, I could see myself, and I could use the experience to turn myself toward the direction of self-help and healing.

With Kathleen, I never had to worry about her fleeing through an airport or forcing me to kiss behind her ear because she was afraid of germs. Kathleen was going to get things right, and she was going to make sure of it. In many ways, this selfless devotion made her more attractive than anyone I'd known before.

♬

I needed Kathleen, just as my mother needed me.

We met just a year before we married, in 1995. At twenty-nine, I was a little better than I was at twenty-one. By then, I had grown tired of the self-induced vomiting that once made me lose sixty pounds within sixty days. Often I forced myself to eat, and I tried hard to keep it in. Over time, I gained much of the weight back. But I still found it hard to pull myself out of bed every day and face a world that I—like my mother—found hard to fit into. I still found it hard to sit, eat, and digest. Every meal was a trial. Even as the memories of Jessica slowly faded, my fear of food, and how it felt when it fell into my stomach remained. God, I hated that feeling. Every bite made me feel full and sick. Every meal came with a thought: *Am I hurting myself?* For years, I still couldn't turn these feelings off, even when I was doing my damnedest to make sure that whatever I ate stayed in my stomach and didn't leave again through my mouth. I made a pact with myself: *Okay, have the fears*, I kept telling myself. *Just don't puke.*

I dreaded the fattiest of foods. If I ate a bite of a doughnut, I felt bloated; if I felt bloated, I felt depressed and ashamed. Sometimes, I actually would puke, just to feel free of even the smallest of bites. Then I'd feel ashamed, because I couldn't exhibit even the smallest bit of self-control, something that I promised to myself. So I'd withdraw. Most times, I withdrew to my bedroom, keeping my thoughts and my food to myself. I stayed away from people and closed the door. Instead of puking, I'd try to shake myself out of the funks.

The early 1990s were a roller-coaster ride, a trip through highs and lows where I rarely found a happy medium. I was a reporter, and I found failure as much—or more—than I found success. Some days, I broke stories; other days, I'd be yelled at for being lazy and useless. I often went to work hungry and left it nearly twelve hours later feeling empty. If the story was big, food was easy to forget. If the day was bad, food was hard to face. My meals were often the seventy-nine-cent tacos at Taco Bell or the vending-machine sandwiches at the *Delaware State News*, where I worked for a pittance for two and a half years and had to deal with bosses who cared more about numbers than humanity.

I had friends, but no companionship. In 1992, Bill had married and had children right away. No longer could we do what we had often done before: hang with each other, goof around, and talk. No longer did we have the intimacy that could only go so far between heterosexual males. All I had left were the walls of the bedrooms of my apartments—the eight different apartments I had from 1988 to 1995, spanning the Jersey Shore and central and southern Delaware. I'd sit in my apartment for hours, staring at a small $25 television set I had bought from the Salvation Army, not really listening. Instead, I tried to encourage myself. *You're fine. You're not sick. You're fine. You're not sick. Get over it. Get through it.*

I'd try to remember the stories I had learned in kindergarten, like *The Little Engine That Could. You can do it,* I'd tell myself. *Get over that hump.* Many times, I got over it. I'd go for a run and make myself feel good because I was shedding pounds. Running made my stomach feel different: less bloated, more compact.

Other times, I puked.

I dated occasionally. But every woman paled when compared to Jessica, and I went through periods when I missed her terribly. In 1989, she had returned from her Israeli trip and got a job in the publishing industry. I repeatedly talked myself out of visiting her or calling her. I often had to convince myself out of it, just as I convinced myself out of puking.

꒱

Kathleen was a gift.

As with Jessica, Kathleen's love appeared to be unconditional—except that with Kathleen there was security, trust, faithfulness, consistency, and maturity. She showed me the love I needed, just as my mother had shown it when I was three and Jessica showed it when I was twenty-one. Only with Kathleen, love was not only unconditional; it was lasting.

To Kathleen, love was new. She was a short woman with a voice that could shake an opera house. She was a teacher in the dramatic arts and had grown accustomed to yelling at stage sets full of people. She liked to call herself "complex." She was stable, but a little moody. She was gentle, but she was loud. She was rough, and even awkward and clumsy. She had smooth skin and soft, Hush-Puppy brown eyes. But she had barely dated before and knew little about what to say to a man. She was not a romantic, but she was loyal. She was not exotic, but she was pretty. She thrived on what was simple and practical. She focused on the small, trivial, and mundane things. She focused on what mattered, not what was unreal.

Our courtship was short. Our first date was in September 1995; on our second date, I said to her, "Can we visit my sick relative in the hospital?" Instead of going out to eat, we hung out with a three-year-old girl who was having seizures. We escorted the girl to the bathroom and pushed the rack that carried her intravenous tubes. Watching Kathleen hold her hand and make sure she sat safely in the bathroom, I found Kathleen the most attractive woman I'd ever known. To me, she was an angel and a savior, a person who showed devotion that I never knew possible.

Whenever Kathleen and I sat in the car together watching the small waves wash in near the beach, I'd often think about that hospital scene and have visions of Kathleen holding the girl's hand, nudging her along. It gave me a feeling of warmth and joy.

One time, the Moody Blues song "Question," the one I had heard and cried about on the way back from the airport, seven years earlier, came over the radio as we wrapped our bodies together in the car right next to the beach. Only this time, the song felt good, joyful, even inspirational. For once, there was something to look forward to, not back.

When we married in 1996, I was impressed that Kathleen's biggest worry was whether the minister would omit the line "Do you promise to honor and obey" from our vows. She insisted, over and over, that he strike it. As I stood at the altar and watched her eyes roll as the minister mistakenly uttered the words, I wondered, *Who could worry about the words?*

I looked behind her and saw my mother leaning over the pew. She was wearing a frayed sweater half-hanging over her blouse. She looked annoyed and bored. That morning, my mother had forced my father to stop six times on their three-hour drive from Point Pleasant to West Point, where we were married less than a mile from the grave of Kathleen's father. The whole way, my mother complained over and over about going to the bathroom. *Who would worry about words?* I thought. *Kathleen should look at my mother. That'll give her something to worry about.*

To Kathleen, stability mattered. The future mattered. She saw my mother for what she was, but she refused to let me follow. After we were married, she insisted that I see a psychologist for the first time, which was nearly eight years after I first suffered the symptoms of eating disorders. Initially, I refused. Kathleen and I clashed over it in our stubborn ways; in some ways, she also displayed some of the worst characteristics of my mother and Jessica. Kathleen could be tough, even unrelenting. But there was something more genuine about those traits in her, because they were always wrapped with undying loyalty and selflessness. She called on me to get help, even as she became pregnant with our first child, Tommy, in 1997, and both of us were shedding tears as we battled the anxiety we felt about the baby and toward each other. We exchanged harsh words as we let out our frustrations.

"If we're going to survive as a family, you need to confront your issues!" she'd tell me. At times, I felt as low as I had on those trips back when I

was a kid, and I heard my defenseless father give in
mother. In the end, though, I knew Kathleen was right,
up on me, she wanted to give to me.

Kathleen wanted to fix things, not run away. Kathl
about what really mattered: getting me help. I listened to ___ and
finally followed through.

On my second visit with the psychologist, he confirmed what she had
suggested. A week earlier, he had given me a "stress test." He held up the
results, which showed a chart with lots of lines and dots. The line in the
middle was "stress-free." My line was way above, looking like mountain
peaks.

"Your stress level is off the chart," he told me.

ॐ

Thanks to my wife, I could finally address me. Also thanks to my wife,
we addressed our son's difficulties, getting him help before he needed it
more.

"We're going to address these issues early," she told me. Tommy was
always so anxious, just like his family members before him. He got sick
after experiencing the slightest bit of stress. With help, however, I could
see him heal. I could see him adjust to a world that he could fit into, find
friends, and live life with some comfort. After years of this, we could
see him adapt; he went from a kid who refused to play on the monkey
bars because other children were there or who got sick after a cry to an
eleven-year-old who was secure in his choices and stable in his ways.

We addressed my mother, even as the situation became more hopeless. Kathleen inspired me to make a move just as my mother's obsessive thoughts grew worse. It had been the same way when Kathleen had
been a teenager and her mother had suffered. Her family didn't ignore
things and hope they would go away. They got help; they found a doctor in New York who saved her mother's life. I watched Kathleen, and

I felt inspired enough to finally talk to my dad, as well as my sister and brother, to finally try to get something done about my mother.

Thanks to my mother, we did something about ourselves too. My father finally started talking about her battle with obsessive-compulsive disorder and asked for our help. My brother, who was also at the grave that day in September 2009 and stood silently as he stared at the stone, got help for himself, too, and was able to find some level of happiness that he had never known before.

ॐ

On that warm, wet September day in 2009, we didn't forget. Kathleen, my brother, and his wife thought of visiting the graveyard. How my mother looked and acted when she was alive wasn't important. Having the children see her name and touch her tombstone was what mattered.

I stood there and thought of my book. Until then, I had been stuck on certain things, trying to find a way to satisfy the goals and the hopes set out by my Columbia professor for this work. I needed inspiration, particularly to write what was left. This visit, I thought, was the most important research I could have. In that moment, my wife taught me about compassion, education, and giving. "C'mon kids," she told them. "Come see your grandmother." As my daughter knelt down and picked at the grass, and as Jonathan whipped out his camera, I could feel tears well in my eyes. I hadn't cried over my mother in nearly seven years.

May 2000

After all these years of knowing, I never thought it would come to this. We were visiting on Mother's Day at Ancora Psychiatric Hospital.

My mother was wearing a stained, light-blue shirt with her name scribbled in fading black marker on the back just under the neckline. The rule of the hospital was simple: if your shirt was not marked, you lost it.

The other patients were stealing my mother's clothes, because she didn't want to touch a dirty marker that was handled by a dirty attendant and then write her own name on the dirty shirt. Eventually, the attendants marked the shirts for her, because they knew that she would have it her way. She always did.

In her small bedroom, she had no space for the $100 blouses that she had routinely stuffed inside three bedroom closets at our Point Pleasant house. She couldn't go on one of her spending sprees to Macy's or Boscov's department store with my dad's credit card—or her own credit card, the one she kept hidden from everybody so she could buy even more clothes. At Ancora, she only had what wasn't yet stolen, as well as the standard-issue blue shirts that everybody wore. A few weeks in a jaded, smelly, and noisy psychiatric hospital chipped away at her stubborn spirit; now, she didn't care what she wore. She'd slip on two of those hospital blues if she had to. She didn't care, as long as she was warm.

At Ancora, she couldn't scoot to the bathroom like she used to and smother her swollen, flaky, dried-up hands with soap for an hour. She had no place to hide: the bathroom there was just too disgusting for that, in her opinion, and the other dirty patients would hover around the door, smelling as though they needed a diaper change. Still, she couldn't run from the lingering urine odor that pervaded the hospital's first floor. She couldn't pull out a can of Lysol and spray half of the contents, masking that odor that made the tall, dimly lit, decaying hallways of Ancora even more detestable. She wouldn't touch the phone, the one that patients occasionally grabbed, grunted into, and then slammed back on the hook after it had been dangling on the cord all day.

By now, my mother had overstayed her welcome at four different nursing homes, as well as assisted-living facilities, and psychiatric emergency centers. Staying at home didn't work, either. She refused to take the Luvox medication that had been prescribed to her, even injected into her, even when she had been determined to be a threat to herself.

Two years before, she had been finally diagnosed with an illness: she suffered from severe obsessive-compulsive disorder. The older she got, the more erratic, stubborn, and hostile she became. She wasn't clean and didn't bathe unless forced. Sometimes, she defecated in her pants and sat in it for days. Those days, even limping to the bathroom had become too hard, and her worries over her bladder had become too much. Her obsessions had finally overwhelmed her, and she was in a revolt against herself.

So she could no longer be home. She couldn't even go to a doctor's office. If she did, the fear was that she would find a sharp tool and jab it into her stomach. She had worried so much about her bladder that she threatened to end her life. For years, her condition—mentally and physically—had become progressively worse. Instead of hustling around the house, limping from kitchen to the bathroom, she stayed in a chair and watched political shows all day, but with the sound turned down. She stopped selling Avon. Her body was hunched over, halfway to the floor. At my wedding in 1996, she alarmed people. She rattled on about the slippery floor outside the bathroom.

"Somebody's going to slip and fall and kill themselves," she told my father. "Don't you agree, dear? . . . Don't you think somebody is going to hurt themselves? . . . Don't you think, dear?"

She grew dependent on my father for everything. She never had been so helpless before, not even when she had her knee injury two decades earlier.

It deepened with the bladder operation she had in the summer of 1998. When she came home, she couldn't stop. She couldn't even have a casual conversation. Every word, every question, and every comment was about the bladder. "Dear, I think there's something wrong with me!" she said. "I have to have another operation done. . . . Don't you think so, dear? . . . Don't you think they messed up?"

My father took her back to the doctor, to other doctors. All of them repeatedly told her it was okay. They had fixed the bladder. It had fallen inside her body, probably because she tried so hard for so long, in so many visits to the bathroom, to push the urine out, to get rid of something she believed was dirty, even poisonous. But, it was okay, the doctors told her. The doctors had put it back.

She had several office visits with the doctor and made the same plea.

"But don't you think it fell again? . . . Don't you think there's something wrong?" she asked. "It's okay," one told her. "I'm a doctor; I know what I'm talking about." But my mother still worried and worried and worried. She could feel the stitches on her stomach, and she panicked if she felt even the slightest pull.

She worried from the time she got up until the time she went to bed. She eventually turned off the TV in the living room but still sat in her chair there. And she worried. When she stayed away from the bathroom, now afraid to push the urine out, she had no refuge. She was convinced that her bladder was broken and that the urine filling it would burst out and kill her.

"Will it kill me?" she repeatedly asked my dad. "Will it kill me? . . . Will it kill me?" The bathroom was once the best place for her to be. Now it was no longer safe.

I started to get calls from my father, pleading for help. The first time I got a call, I was stunned. *My father is asking me for help? He wants help now?* I thought.

He had retired from his job as a principal; he hoped to enjoy the perfect retirement life. Now he was asking for help because his retirement, like the rest of his life, was far from perfect.

The calls started to come two, three, even four times a week. My father sounded desperate.

"She's at it again," he said. "She won't leave me alone!" I promised to visit him, as long as he promised to listen.

One day, in the summer of 1998, we talked in the family room, the same room that had been my father's hideout, where he drank beer, watched bad TV shows, and stayed out of my mother's sight. Now, two years into retirement, my father was looking healthier. He enjoyed long walks on the Ocean Grove boardwalk, and he had lost some weight. He had stopped much of his own drinking, and his face showed much less of the rage and stress that he could never quite hide in his expression. Indeed, he was even conciliatory, understanding, patient, and humble.

"I've known for a long time," he said. "I first saw it back when she had you, actually."

"What do you mean?"

"Well, right after she had you, she couldn't leave the house," he said. "I had to go to the supermarket for her. She wouldn't even drive a car."

"What about the repeating?" I asked. "When did that start?"

"Not until then," he said. "She was a loving, doting mother. She never had any problem with anybody."

He admitted, however, that he saw early signs. When they dated, back in the 1950s, my mother had been possessive and grew jealous of the friends my father kept.

"Maybe I shouldn't tell you this," he told me, with a chuckle. "I thought of breaking it off then. I saw something there."

"Why didn't you break it off?" I said.

He shrugged. "I couldn't," he said. "I loved your mother. I really did."

He leaned back in his chair, sipping from a glass of water. It was early in the morning, and my mother was still asleep. Even though the worry made her wake up earlier than ever, her sleeping habits had changed little; at night she still had beer and chips. Mornings started at ten, with giant-sized cups of coffee.

"I know I should have done something earlier," he said.

"Why haven't we ever talked about this?" I asked him.

"I always thought I could handle it myself," he said. "I didn't want to get the kids involved. I wanted you to live your lives."

"But we *were* involved," I told him.

He sipped from the water glass again. "Yeah, well, you're probably right," he said.

He needed my help. I immediately thought of the burden. I thought of how I was going through my own hell, how Kathleen and I were adjusting to being new parents. We were living in a small apartment in Manahawkin, existing on the meager salary I earned from the *Press of Atlantic City*. I was spending a lot of time at home helping take care of him. As a result, I lost focus at work and my bosses showed little mercy. In June, the *Press* gave me perhaps the worst job evaluation I had ever received. In our apartment, there was tension. We didn't have money. We had a staircase with rotting steps, and my wife nearly sprained her back trying to carry Tommy over it. We had a picture window with leaks, and the draft came in like a breeze.

"What about Edward?" I asked my father. "Couldn't he help?"

My father wouldn't dare. It was more than just their relationship, which had never really mended since the yelling, hitting, and shouting had defined it. My father had enough sense to know that my brother, too, was struggling.

Edward was living with his wife and oldest son in Maryland. They, too, had little money and little space. Edward and his wife seemed to be feeling the stress of raising a child, too. Just as Kathleen and I did, on occasion, Edward and his wife would display some obvious tension between the two of them, particularly when their three-year-old son would act up, scream, or cry.

Edward and his wife were similarly idealistic; both enjoyed their lives after they married in 1992. Edward had never seemed happier, and he did everything he could to cater to his wife, who aspired to be a singer. But as they dealt with the problems of raising a family, Edward became more tense, nervous, and anxious. He toiled as a scientist, even though he made little money and never really liked it. He wanted more money and a happier life. Privately, Edward took his tensions to the toilet bowl, where he, too, would stick his fingers down his throat and vomit.

"He's all the way down in Maryland," my father told me.

He didn't want to deal with Carolyn, either. He and Carolyn also had had a rocky relationship. They had never really dealt with their issues either. Carolyn was living in Manasquan with her husband and six-year-old daughter. She had worked as a nurse, got married, and gave birth to her daughter. She seemed to have the most stable life of the three of us.

Carolyn also had issues with my mother, and she had never really mended fences with her, either. The memories of getting whipped with a garbage can were also still too real.

"You're really it," my father said to me. "You've always been close with your mother."

Soon after I talked to him, I called Kathleen. I told her what we had talked about. I told her my father wanted me to help, to be involved. I told her that this was, at the very least, cathartic for me. Watching my mother and seeing how she dealt with life helped me better deal with myself. In the months since she started to complain about her bladder, I started to feel better about myself. I hadn't had a stomachache in a long while. I had no desire to puke or hide. Watching my mother was the best therapy of all. Helping her helped me, and I wanted to help.

"Well, then we have to do what we have to do," Kathleen said. "It's family. Family comes first."

჻

One day in November 1998, my mother talked of suicide. Many would be scared of such a thing. I felt relief; my father did too. You can *force* someone to get help only if her own or somebody else's life is in danger, and suicidal thoughts were the signal. My mother couldn't take it anymore; the second she uttered "I want to kill myself," my dad called the crisis center at Kimball Medical Center in Lakewood.

Thus began a seemingly endless six-hour visit to the hospital. Throughout it all, my mother refused any kind of help and pleaded to go home. But the pleas that used to sway my father didn't work, and this time, he had the backing of mental health professionals, the very first to ever treat my mother. She had lived sixty-one years without ever having to see one, other than those who had walked to their offices outside her Greystone window, leading along the patients whose behavior so frightened my mother.

Immediately, she was put in a temporary facility called the Shoreline Behavioral Center in Toms River, where she would stay for two or three weeks, or until a more permanent solution could be found. When I visited there, I felt as if I was walking inside a funhouse. The patients' screams and incoherent rants came from their bedrooms and echoed through the narrow hallways. My mother usually sat with the calm ones who watched ESPN on the big TV with the volume turned way up.

When I first saw her, I was stunned: her hair wasn't washed, and for the first time in twenty-five years, the thick, blonde dye that she had used routinely since her mid-thirties to hide the gray was disappearing from her roots.

I sat with her by the TV, talking to her. She continually pleaded to go home, and the more she did, the more she hoped Dad would do what he normally did: buckle under to her pressure. I tried to change the subject, but it was no use.

"I just want to go home, that's all," my mother kept saying. "I just want to go home. Please tell your father to take me home?"

"I don't think I can do that, Mommy," I said.

"Oh yes, you can. Be a sweetie pie and tell your father I'm fine. I can go home."

"But you'll complain about your bladder," I said.

"Thomas," she said. "There is something wrong with my bladder. That's what I keep telling your father. But you know your father—he's *so* stubborn."

By then, I had fully expected my father to buckle, because he had so many times before. Only this time he was standing his ground, refusing, backed up by the psychiatrists who knew better. They even suggested that she may be bipolar and that she might need long-term treatment for *two* illnesses—not just one.

꙳

During the two weeks she was there, she kept lying about herself and talking about how she was perfectly fine, that there was nothing wrong with her brain, her head, her thoughts, her words. "I'm ready to go home," she kept saying. The longer she stayed, the better she played the part.

Several days after she was admitted, my wife and I told the attendants to slip the Luvox into her food. She wouldn't take it otherwise, we told them. Rather than say no, the attendants winked at us and walked away. Within days, her behavior changed: my mother started to show energy I didn't think she could display. She stopped almost all of her repeating, except to say repeatedly, "Take me home."

After two weeks, the social workers became convinced and were swayed by her. Where she had failed with my dad and the doctors, she succeeded with the social workers. They were usually young, impressionable, and emotional. They were stressed by never having enough beds to handle the crowd. They were too overwhelmed to handle my mother, the master manipulator, and she charmed them the same way she used to charm everybody, flashing that smile of hers that always cooled my father's rage.

They even began to sound like her. "Why can't you take her home?" they asked. "She seems fine to us. She's wonderful."

My father would respond that she was too much to handle, that she needed more help than he could provide. But they'd just respond the same way: "Why can't she go home?"

꙳

So she did—go home, that is. Only her improvement never lasted. In 1998 and 1999, my father called the 911 center at Kimball Medical

Center four separate times. Each time, she was committed to the Shoreline Behavioral Center. Each time, she would stay for two, maybe three weeks, before being sent home because they told us, "There's never enough room," or "You need to find a long-term solution."

Each time, they gave her medicine. But as soon as she left, she stopped taking it and acted even worse than before.

With each departure, we tried repeatedly to find the safe landing she needed, the permanent solution that the social workers talked about. We looked at brochures and on the Internet for some place that could give her comfort and treatment.

The first place we found was the Bayville Manor, an assisted-living facility in Berkeley Township, New Jersey, just south of Toms River. There my wife and I again nudged the aides to put Luvox into her food. Once again, we got winks. Almost instantly, my mother did better. She even started to play the piano in the recreation room and entertain her fellow residents. "You never knew your mother played piano?" my father asked me.

I was shocked when I visited and saw her banging away on the keys. She was flashing that old smile of hers. This time, it seemed genuine.

"You didn't know?" my father asked me.

"Not at all," I said as I listened and saw the delight of the elderly as they clapped along to the notes of "When the Saints Come Marching In."

༃

After a few weeks of my mother playing piano and smiling, my father decided to take her home, again. Maybe she turned a corner, he thought. Soon after, however, the old obsessions returned. The repetitive worrying over her bladder, her hands, her food, and on and on, crept back. By May 1999, she was back at the Kimball crisis center and then to Shoreline, which again was only temporary.

We had her go to a nursing home, the King Manor Care Center in Neptune, where she was housed with patients with Alzheimer's disease. Those patients roamed the hallways and sometimes departed through the fire doors, setting off the alarm. While there, my mother was always testing the limits. She bugged the aides and attendants the same way she would bug my father. "I dropped this cookie," she would say. "I think I'd better throw it away. . . . Don't you think I should throw this cookie away?" She escaped once, grabbing a taxi that would take her to Ocean Grove, where my father usually was. She showed up at the door, smiling.

"I just came for a visit," she said. "That's all."

My father started to charge toward her, just as he used to when I was young, when he was always gearing up for a fight. This time, however, I intercepted him. As I carried Tommy in my left arm—it was to be another goodwill visit with the grandparents that went badly—I pointed to my mother with my right index figure, demanding that she get back into the cab.

"Get back in there now!" I yelled.

"No, Thomas," she said. "I'm going to stay."

"I said, get back in the cab!"

"Um, Thomas, don't talk to me that way, do you hear me?"

"No," I said. "I'm not going to talk nicely. Get back in the cab."

"Thomas, talk nicely to me. . . ."

"Okay, I'll talk nicely to you," I said. "Get back into the cab!"

We went back and forth for ten minutes. The whole time, I bounced Tommy up and down as he dug his head into my shoulder. I was trying to settle him down while yelling in his ear. This time with my mother, I didn't cave. She limped back to the cab. I paid the driver to take her back to the nursing home.

༄

In June 1999, we thought we had finally found the right place. It was an assisted-living facility called Brandywine in Brick Township. It was her fourth home in five months. The new place looked more like a ski lodge in Vermont than a nursing-care facility. It had a stone façade and a slanted roof, and its windows were modern and clean. It looked like the kind of place where you could sit by a fire and drink hot cocoa. My mother took one glance at it and instantly rejected it.

"I just want to go home," she said. "When can I go home?" But my father and I thought it was perfect: the place was clean and staff members were friendly. When we first arrived, we dropped her off in her room while we talked to the administrators.

We were impressed, we told them. My only fear was simple: *Could they handle her? What kind of doctors were on staff? Were the nurses properly equipped?*

The administrators chuckled at my nervousness and my mild skepticism. One told me as I was leaving the place, "Don't worry, Tom. We'll take good care of your mother."

Within weeks, however, there were problems. Already, Brandywine was going to boot her out. My father called to tell me. He was desperate. I was incredulous.

"That's not what they told me," I told him. "They told me straight, 'We're going to take good care of her.' They have no right to do this."

Their words, however, meant nothing. My mother's constant repeating was getting to the nurses. She was hoarding food, collecting gallon containers of ice cream and eating very little of it. She collected cans of soda but rarely drank a drop. She started to use a walker, but she seemed to use it more for hoarding than actually walking. She'd pick up a Styrofoam cup of soda, and stick it inside a pouch that hung from the walker's handlebars. Then she wouldn't touch it, determining that it was too dirty to drink, just hours after she got it. The cup would stay there for days, even weeks, eventually spilling into the pouch and creating a little pond of soda.

I was still in denial. I couldn't believe that her resident status was in peril, especially when I had been told "not to worry." I telephoned the head nurse, the one who was leading the charge to get her out of there. *Maybe somebody heard this wrong,* I thought.

I thought I could easily convince her by reminding her what I was promised. The nurse's words, however, surprised me.

"You don't understand," she said. "This is not the kind of place for your mother."

She didn't tell me what that place was. "The administrator told me you'd take good care of her," I said. "You can't do this. You have to stick to the deal."

The nurse kept sighing, impatiently. "But you don't understand," she repeated. "This is not the kind of place for your mother."

After a month, my mother was out. Once again, she was home. Soon enough, my father was on the phone with Kimball, once again, getting her admitted.

⊰⊱

The only place left was Ancora Psychiatric Hospital. My father had one too many nights at Kimball, sitting there for six hours each time, awaiting the diagnosis he already knew he'd get. It didn't matter that she was doing what she always did, calling attention to herself and eliciting sympathy. My father knew that something had to be done. Finally in April 2000, at the urging of the psychiatrists at Shoreline and with the blessing of the normally passive but equally frustrated social workers, my father sent my mother to Ancora, to this isolated box, stuck somewhere in a desolate patch of scrub pines known as "Pine Barrens," South Jersey's no-man's-land. Miles down a desolate two-lane road, miles away from the nearest store or any sign of life, Ancora was like Greystone, only without the majestic buildings and the mountain view. At this place, the grass was overgrown and yellowing. The land was flat and boring.

On Mother's Day in 2000, I arrived around 2 p.m. with my then two-year-old son Tommy and my wife. No other sons and daughters

were there to see their moms. At first, I was reluctant, but my wife insisted. "You should go see your mother on Mother's Day," she told me.
"Everybody sees their mothers on Mother's Day."

By then, we had moved to Pennsylvania; I had left the *Press of Atlantic
City* and found comfort and support at the *Morning Call* newspaper in
Allentown, Pennsylvania, where my editor would allow me to spend time
to deal with my parents' situation. On this Sunday, we drove the three-
hour trip to South Jersey, some thirty miles southeast of Philadelphia, to
the box-like hospital in the scrub pines.

We arrived in the late afternoon, just as the sun disappeared behind
the pines. When we walked inside, I was struck by how empty the lobby
was. All the life was behind a thick metal door. It was surrounded by a
wall made of rectangular cement blocks, like a cellar. The door was locked
shut, so I had to pound on the window glass to get attention.

An attendant walked up and let me in. But she told me that my wife
and son would have to wait. I said I had been told I could bring my
family in.

"I'm sorry," she said. "No one should have told you that."

"But that was the whole reason we drove three hours to be here!" I
told her.

My wife nudged me. "Don't start a fight," she said.

"But can you believe this?" I said. "We drove all this way, and they're
turning us away."

"You can come in," the attendant said. "But they have to stay here."

Before I walked in, my wife pulled me aside and gave me a nod. She
told me to keep pushing, but she would find a way.

"Okay," I told the attendant, who pushed on the heavy door, letting me
in, while my wife disappeared from view.

As at Shoreline, I heard screams and moans coming from all direc-
tions. And there was more. The people walked by me, rambling or yelling about irrelevant things. They smelled too. One of them was sitting
by the phone with the receiver hanging from a hook. As I waited for my

mother to arrive, I watched him stand up and try to make a call on it. Another guy walked up and snatched away the receiver, then dropped it, leaving it dangling off the hook.

In the dimly lit hallway, I didn't see my mother right away. But I did see my wife. Carrying Tommy at her hip, she had walked around the building and found a door. The door was locked but bent, showing a little opening where the metal met the frame. All over the door, there were half-inch holes, as if it had been shot at. I could see Kathleen and Tommy through the holes. As soon as I could see them, I also saw my mother, standing alone in the hallway, staring at Kathleen through the holes.

"Look," another attendant told my mother. "Your grandbaby is there!"

My mother walked over to my wife and son, and they began to talk through the holes. I walked out through the big heavy door, then around the building and joined my wife and son.

I greeted my mother and smiled at my wife. "How'd you find this?" I asked.

"I walked to an overhang and I thought I'd see a door there," she said. "I saw this one and it looked open."

My mother had been talking to her, asking about a promise I had made days before when I announced my visit: she wanted to know if we had gone to a Wawa convenience store to get coffee. She was going on and on about whether I followed through on my promise to bring her the coffee.

"Did you bring it?" she asked. "You said you'd bring it. You said you'd bring it. Right?"

I told her we brought it. "Happy Mother's Day."

We talked through the holes. She kept going on about the coffee. She talked about how much she liked Wawa coffee. She said it had a richer flavor than the other brands.

"Happy Mother's Day," I said. "Can we talk about something else?"

She laughed in that charming way she always did.

"Your grandson's here," I said. "Let's talk about that."

Instead, she talked about getting out of there. She said she was going to grab a taxi to take her to Point Pleasant.

"Don't listen to your father," she told me. "Your father doesn't know what the hell he's talking about."

On and one she went. "Get me out of here. If you don't take me out, I'm leaving," she kept saying for what seemed like fifteen minutes. It didn't matter that I could only see her through the holes. On and on she went.

Finally, she stopped herself and glanced at Tommy. It was a cold, dead stop, and rather abrupt.

Her eyes were fixed on Tommy's face. By then, he had moved his head off my wife's shoulder and was listening to what was being said. My mother started to study his eyes.

"What color are his eyes?" she asked.

"They're brown," my wife said.

My mother, however, saw another color buried in there. "No, I can see the green," she said.

My wife was amazed. Nobody could see the green, except her. My wife had thought she was the only one who could see it.

Somehow, even through the holes, my mother knew.

ॐ

Four months later, she left. The ugly cycle started all over again. The 911 calls. The two or three weeks in Shoreline Behavioral Center. The month-long stays in the Kings Manor Care Center nursing home in Neptune. She just couldn't stay at these places long enough. When she did stay, she got nothing out of them. She grew more resentful. She became sneakier and more defiant. Her behavior was abhorrent, even if her motives were transparent.

It all seemed to be a way to bring my father back. It was more than a cry for help; it was a desperate demand for attention. In between the episodes, she repeated her intentions over and over. "I just want your father to keep me home," she said. "I want your father home. Everything would be fine if your father stayed home." She had lost control of my father; now she wanted it back.

But my father was giving up; for the first time ever, he talked to a divorce lawyer. Even after all those fights from decades before, he had never taken this step.

Ironically, the lawyer talked him out of it, saying he could lose a great deal of savings. My father knew as well as anybody: divorced or not, he was in over his head. He was stuck. He was in his sixties, and he found it almost impossible to escape the damage my mother made.

My father saw doctors and talked to psychologists and psychiatrists. He kept hoping he could find help. One psychologist sensed the despair and desperation in my father's voice and asked more about him. "Maybe you should get help," the psychologist told him.

My father never did, but he did vow to find peace.

He hired an aide and often escaped to Ocean Grove, taking long walks on the boardwalk, leaving my mother behind. But he couldn't leave her completely, not even when he went away for an hour. My mother kept calling. So did the aide, who repeatedly clashed with her. My mother fired the aide several times. Each time, my father had to call the aide and urge her to come back.

In the years past, my mother had given up much of her drinking, losing the will to do what she once did with ease. Her health was in decline. She had a hiatal hernia, turning her off of food, and she shed the fat and the muscle from her once-plump body. With my father escaping to Ocean Grove, however, she reversed herself. She often had a cab take her around town in Point Pleasant and Brick Township, where she spent more than $5,000 on food, clothes, and tall glasses of beer at Applebee's restaurant. On other days, she made daily delivery calls for pizza, sandwiches, and beer.

She usually ate and drank about half of what she ordered, and she stuffed the rest into the refrigerator. For weeks, the pizza and the sandwiches just sat there, uneaten, growing patches of mold the size of silver dollars. She usually ate and drank in her chair until she passed out, then snore until 3 a.m. when she'd wake up, walk to the refrigerator, pop open a beer, pour it into a glass, and drink again.

This went on for months. Finally in April 2001, I decided to get tough. I told my father that I wanted to be the bad guy. He had done enough of that during their entire forty-two-year marriage. Now he needed help. He agreed and told the aide to leave so I could have control of the house. I was going to get her out of there and bring her closer to me.

By then, I had moved to Metuchen, New Jersey, about an hour north of Point Pleasant, and taken a job at the *Record of Bergen County*. Once there, I started shopping for nursing homes nearby. My goal was to get her to move there and allow me to take control.

I was thankful that my wife was willing to take part. She even urged me to take this step: going to Point Pleasant unannounced, armed with a cell phone and a piece of paper listing numbers for the crisis center and the police. I was going to burst onto the scene and order my mother to go with me. She was going to go to Rose Mountain Care Center in New Brunswick.

After the hour-long drive, I walked in and saw her sitting there, with her head bent over the arm of the chair. It was around 10 a.m. and she was snoring so hard and so loud that her head was bouncing on the upholstery.

I peeked into the kitchen and saw a piece of shattered glass sitting in a pool of coffee, spread all over the counter. The coffee pot was shattered on the counter with the handle sitting on the floor.

I walked over to my mother and nudged her on the shoulder.

"C'mon, Mommy," I said. "We've gotta go."

She woke out of her sleep, blinking her eyes. "What?"

"We're going to the hospital," I told her. "We're getting help."

She screamed, then grabbed the arms of the chair, digging her nails into the fabric, as though I were going to pull her away.

"C'mon!" I said. "Let's go! We're going!"

She screamed again.

I called the police on my cell. She got up from her chair, and grabbed the house phone. As she got up, I saw a thick patch of brown where she had been sitting. It was shit. She had crapped in her pants and sat on it, perhaps for days. It had soaked into and stained the fabric.

My mother called Briggs Taxi. "I'm going shopping!" she yelled.

After I got off the phone with the police, I called back Briggs Taxi and canceled the cab.

"We're waiting for the police," I told my mother.

My mother screamed at me. "Thomas, you call the taxi back right now!"

"Look at this coffee pot!" I yelled at her, pointing toward the kitchen. "You're going to kill yourself!"

"Thomas, don't interfere!" she said. "You call the police back right now!"

As we waited, she screamed at me continuously. "Thomas, how dare you do this!" she said. "You are a son of a bitch! You call the police back right now! You call that cab back!"

With each scream, I felt pain. "I hate you for this," she said, her voice lowering, almost demonic. "You are a son of a bitch! Call back Briggs Taxi!"

I wanted her to love me. But I knew the only way I could love her and show it was to not give in.

The police soon arrived and saw the coffee pot. They had been there before; several of my father's 911 calls included a visit from police. Usually, a friend of mine from high school, Lt. Mike Colwell, helped us out so my father could admit her into Kimball. He usually called an ambulance.

But it was a Saturday and Mike wasn't there. The police officer who did appear said they had less staff. Instead, he dispatched social workers to the house. Then he left; the social workers arrived three hours later. The whole time, I sat on the couch, just a few feet from my mother, listening to her grumble and gripe, dreading that the social workers were going to arrive.

"I'm not going," she kept saying. "I'm staying right here. I'm going shopping."

The social workers walked in but they didn't sit down. They looked about eighteen years old. After talking to my mother for a few minutes, they acted as though they were ready to go. Each stood about ten feet away from her, asking her simple questions, none of which were too deep. Their own questions provided the answers.

"So you're okay?"

"Yes, of course!" my mother told her.

She was no longer screaming. Now she was showing the old charm, turning it on just at the right moment and flashing her trademark smile.

"So, do you both live in the area?" my mother asked the social workers.

I told them about the coffee pot. I didn't even clean it up, I told them, because I wanted them to see. "Look at that pot," I said, pointing them toward the kitchen. "That's sharp glass just sitting there. She could have killed herself."

The social workers turned back to my mother. "What happened with the coffee pot?" one of them asked.

"Oh, it just slipped out of my hands," she said, chuckling a little. "I can be kind of clumsy."

About ten minutes after they had arrived, they left. I stopped them as they walked off the porch steps.

"You're not going to do anything?"

"You don't understand," I was told. "She has to be endangering her own life or somebody else's."

"What about the coffee pot?" I asked.

"What about it?"

"You don't consider that a danger?"

They both shook their heads.

"I just can't believe this," I said, shaking my head. "One day, I'm going to walk in here and I'm going to find her dead—and then I'm going to blame you for it!"

They said nothing as they turned and walked away.

"And then I'll sue you!" I yelled.

Then one of them stopped, turned around, and glared at me.

"That's your right," she said, shrugging.

They got into their car and left. I walked back into the house and grabbed my phone.

"I love you, Mommy," I said. "But I gotta go."

"You're not going to stay?" she said.

"No, I gotta go," I said. "You win."

"Um, talk nicely to me, Thomas...."

"Okay, I will," I said, and then walked out the door. For a moment, I wondered if I'd ever see her again.

"My mother's dead," I told my wife, as soon as I got home. "I give up."

✢

Three days later, the police were called again. My mother had argued with the aide. The aide ran to a neighbor's house, saying my mother had threatened to kill her. The police and my father arrived soon after. Mike was there this time. Within hours, my mother was back at Shoreline Behavioral Center. Within days, she was back at Ancora Psychiatric Hospital.

✢

We pulled her out of Ancora after a month. Then we put her in Rose Mountain, the nursing home ten minutes from my house. During the summer of 2001, I visited her twice a week. My wife visited her once a week. Whenever I went there, I listened to her rattle on about how she wanted to go home, the same way she always had before. She did it so much, and for so long, that I grew numb to it. I had stock answers for everything.

"I understand," I told her. "I know. It's not the best situation."

I'd often take Tommy with me and he'd play under my chair. I'd stay for nearly an hour. Then as I got up, she'd always say something to stop me.

"So how are you, my dear?" Then I'd stay for another hour, talking about myself, before we'd start talking about her again.

Occasionally, I took her on little trips, usually over to Fuddruckers restaurant in New Brunswick, where she'd get a cheeseburger. She and Tommy, who was then three, would sit next to each other and eat the same thing. Both of them would eat it quickly. At the end of the meal, they'd both look up at me, their eyes sweet and puppy-like, and say the same thing.

"Can I have a cookie?"

For the first time in years, my mother was calm. The whole time she was at Rose Mountain, she didn't have a drop of medicine. The best medicine, we came to see, was the visits. I even had her come to the condo we had bought in Metuchen to stay and talk. She'd climb the steps, hanging onto the railing that my wife had installed for her. Then she'd sit in the living room and follow the same routine: complain for nearly an hour, notice when I got antsy, show an interest in me, and stay for another hour.

My father noticed the difference too. At the end of August, he decided to take her back. I questioned it at first. But this time, he seemed deeply committed. My wife and I had sought to remove the stress my mother had lived with for three years, ever since she came out of the hospital and felt the stitches from her bladder operation. Now my father wanted to give it a try.

At first, the arrangement looked like it wasn't going to last. Once again, my father complained that my mother was being aggravating and irritating. He even hinted that he may have to call 911 again, because it was just getting to be too much. She was still repeating, though not as severely. She was still worried about her bladder, though not as badly.

But when the September 11 attacks happened, just two weeks after my mother left Rose Mountain, my father no longer complained. Perhaps he realized there were people worse off than him. She stayed there, at home in Point Pleasant, until January 18, 2003, living relatively peacefully, and as time passed, she never said much of anything anymore.

She repeated, but she seemed too tired to continue very long. She stayed in her chair all day, watching the television, often with the sound way down. When we saw her, there was no more of the pleading. There was no more of the helplessness. She was a mother again.

She even let us kiss her again, usually behind the ear, but it was still a kiss.

⨕

During that time, my father stayed close to home and took his occasional Ocean Grove walks. He was at a movie in Bradley Beach when she called around 3 p.m. on January 18. When he returned to the Ocean Grove house, he listened to the answering machine.

"Dear, something has gone terribly wrong!" my mother said, before the line went dead. After listening to the message, my father tried to call home, but he got only a busy signal.

My mother had fallen as she tried to get the mail, leaning on the slide bar on the storm door in Point Pleasant as she reached for the mailbox. She didn't want her bare feet to touch the cold ground. But the bar broke, causing her to fall on her face. She bled profusely and a neighbor helped her up and back inside.

About a half hour later, she felt pain in her chest and called my dad. Unable to reach him, she headed toward the bathroom. On the way there, her heart gave out and she collapsed on the couch. When my sister found her, she may have been dead for two hours.

⨕

The funeral was three days later. I stood up before the gathering at the funeral home, reading my eulogy. My eyes were still red from crying.

The night before at the wake, I had cried as I watched my father bend down in front of the casket, crying himself and saying between sobs, "I'm sorry! I'm so sorry!" I hugged my father and bawled on his shoulder. "I love you, Daddy," I told him.

But I also had tears of joy: a band of editors and reporters, colleagues from the *Record of Bergen County*, showed up to hug me and pat me on the back. The newspaper had sent flowers and urged me to take time off so I could grieve. I had never worked for a newspaper where people had cared so much.

The funeral day was sunny, but cold. The snow from a recent storm hadn't thawed. People walked in wearing overcoats and fur, kicking off the snow from their shoes. I wore my jacket and tie, and carried a speech I had written. I had it folded in my pocket, ready to go.

I was the second to talk, after my sister. In the audience, I saw Bill and nodded to him. He smiled. He had taken time off from work to be there. To Bill, we were family. He had to be there.

I looked at my mother in the casket and then faced the crowd.

"In a way I am my mother," I told them. "Because we lived the same lives and suffered through the same challenges."

EPILOGUE

EVERY MORNING, I TAKE what I like to call my "vitamins." That's what I say when the kids see me roll a little white pill, an anti-anxiety drug called Lexapro, in the palm of my right hand, drop it onto my tongue, suck down some orange juice, and swallow it. "What's that?" my five-year-old daughter will say, looking at me with her little blue eyes. I imagine she's thinking, *I thought people only take pills when they're sick.*

Sick may or may not be the right word. But I'm pretty sure that without these pills I would be a very sick man. They've helped me the same way Bill helped me when I was in high school and I needed a friend—a refuge, really—from the tension, heartache, and illness of my life. They've helped me the same way my wife helped me back in the 1990s when I needed someone to point me—as well as my mother—in the direction of healing.

I know these pills have helped me through the challenges of life that I face every day, whether it's something family-related, something on the job, or concerns such as a stomachache that others may consider benign but I consider a crisis. I know these pills are no cure for whatever ails me.

Rather, they help me manage through a life that, as I said in the eulogy to my mother, has many "challenges."

I still get frustrated at things I shouldn't. I still get impatient when I should take more time. But when I take medication, I feel that I have a safety net I didn't have before. I feel more confident than ever that I can handle the stressful day-to-day life of an editor for Patch.com, which hired me to be the Jersey Shore regional editor in September 2010. I feel more confident that I can be a successful journalist and a stable parent as I manage a staff of eleven—and father two boys and a girl.

I feel that I can face my children and deal with their issues more effectively. I feel that I can work with my wife and understand her better. I can be a source of support for her, just as she has been for me.

I feel that I have an advantage my mother, my grandfather, my great-grandfather, my great-great-grandmother, and my great-uncle never had. Imagine if they all had made the same decision, taking two minutes out of their day to follow a routine that helps them go about their business. And pills certainly don't have to be the solution. Holistic methods such as breathing exercises and yoga can help people manage their way through the stresses of life, whether they have a mental illness or not.

Maybe Edward Winans would have felt a little more relaxed about this life and chosen to read a book, go for a walk, or stay with his family in Bay Head that day in 1933, rather than plugging the holes in his house, flipping on the gas jets, and breathing in the fumes. Maybe Dick Winans would have thought that taking one pill each day, or exercising regularly, would have been easier to handle than drinking a bottle of vodka or a case of beer. Maybe my mother would have felt secure enough to seek answers to her own questions rather than repeating them to my father over and over and over.

Indeed, pills aren't for everybody. When I first started taking them, in the summer of 2007, I got diarrhea and stomach cramps. I lost about thirty pounds. I told my psychiatrist, "You gave me a pill for someone who has problems with his stomach, and what happens? I have problems with my stomach! What's the point?" A lot of people can't get over the symptoms, and they give it up right away. I didn't; I stuck with it, and I even impressed my psychiatrist with my resiliency. "It's not typical for someone with your history," he said. But my history dictated the obvious: I had no choice.

Other friends of mine who have taken medication have said it makes them tired or gain weight. I have no such fears, because I always remember where I was when I first needed them and why I feel the need to continue taking them.

Indeed, my biggest worry is forgetting. I know I have to take these every day and I've read about what could happen if I stop. The depression and suicide rates of people who stop taking certain medications are very high. I've also dealt with the erratic behavior of people—particularly my mother—who didn't stay committed to a pill-taking regimen. Stopping the medicine—or any psychotropic medicine, really—often makes people so depressed that they crash mentally. They feel even more helpless than they did before they started taking it.

The only choice I have is to stick with my regimen, combining the medication with a regular amount of sleep and exercise. I often fall short on the latter two requirements. But the events that led to my decision to see a psychiatrist and start taking medication only proved how desperate and "sick" I can be when I don't have a safety net. I know that, on some level, I needed something to prevent me from going too far.

ॐ

After my mother died in 2003, I thought the story of mental illness in my family, and in my life, was over. I wanted to make sure of that, and I knew that the process of separating myself from the past and forging a new future would involve healing, talking, and revisiting. But I also believed that I had to move on and develop some sense of normalcy for my children that I never really knew.

Days after the funeral, however, I learned differently. I was driving around with my then one-year-old son Jonathan, in his car seat fast asleep. My wife was shopping; I was driving around, trying to give Jonathan a much-needed nap. But what I really needed was the time. I needed time to ponder everything that had happened. I needed to think about all the years I had with my mother, all the good times and bad, and what I could have done differently. I had to think about the final years, the bouncing around from hospital to facility to hospital, and how so much of what had happened might have been avoided. I had to think about whether we could have done anything to save her life.

I saw Jonathan sleeping in his seat, his little face under a pile of black hair. *Never again*, I thought. *Never again. Never again.* I felt as though I had let him and Tommy down. *If I couldn't protect my own mother, how can I protect them? What do I do to prevent what happened to her from happening to them?*

Suddenly I felt this burst of emotion as I was driving on Route 1 in Edison, New Jersey, watching the shopping centers and malls that fill both sides of the roads pass by. My words of regret and sorrow just poured out.

"I'm sorry!" I shouted, looking in the rearview mirror, making sure I didn't wail so loudly that I'd wake Jonathan up. "I'm sorry! I'm sorry!" I said as tears fell from my eyes.

༣

The first step of healing and dealing with the future was writing. My article on my mother entitled "Trapped by Mental Illness . . . and a Health-Care System That Failed Her" appeared in my newspaper, the *Record of Bergen County*, about four months after she died. The story recounted the events of the previous five years, when my mother suffered the most. I learned that writing always works best when it operates on instinct. When I wrote these lines, I did hardly any research. I asked few questions of others. I wrote them out of the emotion I felt at the time. I thought it was the right time to tap into it, and I had to do it then before I got too far away from these feelings. The article also served as a resource for ideas, thoughts, and phrases for this book.

She lay there, her legs wooden and stiff, eyes closed and mouth wide open. She looked like one of my 5-year-old son's dolls after he's finished with it: lifeless and done.

God, I thought, if only my mother could see herself now. She hated people knowing about her health problems. How could she hide being dead? But this moment was as much ironic as it was horrifying.

It was Jan. 18, around 6:30 p.m. when I saw her, hours after she collapsed, presumably on her way to the bathroom where she always hid in times of crisis. We believed it was a heart attack, but that was merely a guess. Not until the autopsy report was released, three months later, did we know it was exactly that. We could say we didn't see it coming. But then again, maybe we did.

To say we were sad—my father was there, as was my sister, who found her—would be merely stating the obvious. We were relieved, too. It was the end of five years of hell, five years of bouncing around . . . [mental health facilities], assisted-living facilities, and nursing homes. It was the end of five years of fighting over psychiatrists and medicines, doctors, health care aides, and nurses. Now she was home; now she was at peace.

"If she would only take the damn medicine" was one of the first things I heard my dad say, minutes after I first saw her that night at our old house in Point Pleasant. I'd heard him say that a hundred times. It was always his cry for help. Going back to November 1998, when my mother's 30-year battle with mental illness was first addressed, he would rant and rave about his inability to solve her problems, and hope that whoever was in the room at the time was listening. No one ever seemed to be.

I am writing now, partly because I find writing therapeutic. I often flashback to what I've experienced over the last five years, and I continue to second-guess myself over what I could have done differently. But blaming myself or my family would be too easy. I want the world to know what failed my mother, and how helpless and isolated my family felt as we wrestled with a mental health care system that's resistant to any sense of organization or progress.

And as I recall everything my family went through, I no longer want to be alone in feeling this way.*

From that came my "Coping" column, which I wrote for five years and which earned praise from mental health professionals and sufferers throughout the country. I established myself as a mental health care "expert," and I appeared on CBS News, WABC-TV in New York, and even *Entertainment Tonight* to talk about how the issues we faced as a family could relate to the topics of the day—such as, for example, the mental illnesses suffered by veterans of the Iraq war. I built a reputation from these stories, and in 2007, I was named Citizen of the Year by the New Jersey Psychiatric Association, a district branch of the American Psychiatric Association. In 2008, I received an Ambassador Award from the New Jersey Governor's Council on Mental Health Stigma. I also taught what many considered a groundbreaking course on mental health issues in the media at Fairleigh Dickinson University in New Jersey.

My principal achievement was being named one of six people in the nation to win a Rosalynn Carter Mental Health Journalism Fellowship in 2004. When I found out, I literally jumped for joy, nearly banging my head into a light fixture in our house in Metuchen. "I got it!" I yelled. "I got it. I got it!"

I thought I had reached the pinnacle. For years, I had toiled in journalism, and I had achieved a lot of success. But I had never had anything close to national acclaim: I was one of only six Americans to win the fellowship, which came with a $10,000 stipend that funded a project I did on the treatment of people with mental illnesses in the prison system.

---

*Courtesy of *The Record* (Bergen Co., NJ) / NorthJersey.com

But what made it really special was that I would be combining the passions of my life: writing, journalism, and mental illness. For once, I found a way to channel them all together. I traveled the country, from Alaska to Florida, visiting courts and jails and spending time with the homeless as I researched why people with mental illness find it difficult to avoid crime. I never had so much joy as a reporter, giving voice to what I consider the "voiceless," whether they were native Alaskans battling alcoholism in Anchorage or homeless immigrants sleeping under highway bridges in San Antonio.

Ironically, a fit of frustration I had may have precipitated this project. I was angry at the Carter Center people after they rejected my application a year earlier. Back in 2003, I wrote a letter to the program administrators—including the former First Lady Rosalynn Carter herself—to complain that many of the recipients were from the *New York Times* and "media that already have the resources" to cover the stories of mental illness. I even threatened to get others to boycott the program if the trend of picking the best, richest, and most familiar media continued.

When I was approved in 2004, I was assured that my letter had nothing to do with it. My credentials and my proposal, they said, spoke for themselves. But when I went to the first fellowship meeting in Atlanta in September 2004 and met Mrs. Carter, I was led to believe otherwise.

She saw me in the packed room of fellows from New Zealand, South Africa, and all parts of the United States. Mrs. Carter walked over to me and put out her hand. For a split second, I thought she was going to give me a piece of her mind.

"I loved that letter you wrote!" she told me.

"Well, thank you, Mrs. Carter," I said as I stood there, surprised that she even remembered. "I hope I didn't offend you at all. I was just trying to make a point."

"No, no," she said. "You were right. You were right."

꒰꒱

Perhaps the most stunning development, however, came earlier that same year. In April 2004, I got an e-mail from Jessica. Of all the friends I had made over the years, I thought she would be the last one I'd ever hear from again. But there it was, an e-mail that began with "Tom Davis. How are you?"

It didn't take me long to respond, and we had an exchange that was better than cordial. It was like old friends getting reacquainted. Subsequent e-mail exchanges led to a reunion a year later; we met up at a Barnes & Noble near the *Record of Bergen County*'s office in Hackensack, New Jersey, where we had tea and coffee and talked. We even laughed, and she laughed that deep laugh that used to make her hyperventilate many years before.

We talked little about the relationship we once had. We said nothing about the ill will between us that came afterward. But we did talk about what happened to me. I told her about the eating disorders and the weight loss. I recounted every little thing that had happened from the time she left to the present. She sat there listening, her chin resting on her hand, absorbing everything, her deep brown eyes staring at me. At that moment, I couldn't help but recall the letters she sent from Israel back in 1988 that pushed me away, even as I was sick, practically dying. Now at age thirty-six, she was generous and approachable. Now she wanted to know. She wanted to share.

A month later, Jessica e-mailed me again. She wanted to write about it. She wanted to talk about a kid who had a girlfriend and felt the pressures of life. His only option, in his mind, was to "puke," as Jessica put it. Indeed, the main character had a life that was sharply similar to mine, even if it didn't divulge anything about the character's adult life or reveal anything about mine. But it did provide a reflection of what was reality, and what could still be if I ever lost control of myself again.

I helped Jessica edit the book, and I allowed my life to serve as an example of what it's like to be a man, not a woman, defying the sexual stereotypes and suffering through his eating—and why it happens.

Jessica's young adult novel followed the trials of a high school kid who struggled to find love and friendship while suffering through bulimia. A literary magazine awarded the novel a bronze medal in the Best Young Adult Fiction category of its 2009 Book of the Year Awards.

Jessica dedicated the book to me.

꒜

Mixed in with the successes, however, were some more challenges, reminding me of what I had said in my mother's eulogy: life is never completely safe. As I entered my thirties, I had overcome many of the symptoms of eating disorders that had nearly crippled me in my twenties. But as I approached my forties and I experienced the challenges of working longer hours and being the father of three, those symptoms not only returned but seemed to present themselves in unexpected ways.

In November 2004, I was returning from my part-time job as an adjunct professor at Rutgers University when I reached to grab a pen from my bag; I was hoping to write a note to remind myself of a story I needed to write that day. Instead, I smashed into the back of a car—which, in turn, rammed into the car in front of it. I suffered strained chest muscles and burns from the air bag. I found it hard to breathe for weeks.

I was lucky, because I was alive. The custodian at the junkyard who handled my wrecked car took one look at the obliterated front end and then pointed at another car that didn't look half as bad.

"See that car," he said. "That guy died."

The people I hit didn't suffer serious injuries either. A month later, I paid a lawyer $500 to get my penalty reduced to a two-point ticket.

Consciously, I thought I had the matter handled. Then in late December, I started to feel a pain in my gut that wouldn't go away. My bowels became loose, and for nearly a year, I couldn't release a solid stool. I tried Metamucil laxatives and some other "holistic" remedies. None of them worked well for me.

A few doctors checked me out and told me I was fine. They said I was just nervous, noting my blood pressure was a little high. Just like the doctors from seventeen years before, they told me "it was in your head." They told me I was "burning the candle at both ends." But I started to worry and wonder: *Is this coming back? Is there some sort of stress hormone that's wreaking havoc on my body all over again? Am I getting an ulcer? Is there something in my intestines that's slowing digestion? What's wrong with me?*

Over time, my fears subsided. When we had our third and last child, Anna, in January 2006, I became consumed with her care, making sure she was fed and safe. Children always helped take the spotlight off me, and I found some level of comfort in forgetting about my own life, while devoting myself to hers.

In early 2007, however, my fears returned. By then I had applied and was accepted to Columbia University, where I planned to study digital journalism. I did that with reluctance. I had long wanted to go to graduate school, but time, I felt, was running out. I needed to go, especially with the newspaper industry starting to flounder. I needed to capitalize on the digital-media revolution, and Columbia was the place to learn.

When I was accepted, however, I worried about the challenge of having two jobs, raising three young children, and dealing with school issues all over again. I started to get the acidic burps that once bothered me greatly as a twenty-one-year-old and seemed to be more than a nuisance as a near-forty-year-old. I started to feel the same tightness in my chest that as a teenager I used to dismiss as overeating.

I started to read on the Internet to learn about esophageal cancer. Much as I had when I was twenty-one, I diagnosed myself and fed my fears. The day of my fortieth birthday, I went to New York City with my wife to see the Broadway musical *Spamalot*. I thought I could lick a possible midlife crisis right off the bat by doing exactly what I wanted to do most: be with my wife and see Monty Python skits performed on a stage.

Instead, I sat there, feeling the gas rumble in my stomach and getting frustrated by the bubbles percolating up my throat. I felt miserable, and even a visit to the Bubba Gump Shrimp Factory restaurant did little to assuage my fears. The more shrimp I ate, the worse I felt. The soda I drank made the bubbles and the burning in my throat worse. I wanted to go home and lie in bed for a month.

The feeling lingered for two months, right until my first day at Columbia. On orientation day, I starved myself as we went on a "reporting" trip through the Bronx to learn how we could apply modern media techniques to covering New York City. The whole time my stomach rumbled and rolled. For lunch, I ate no more than a piece of bread at an Italian deli that some said was "world-renowned." My head felt light as we toured the neighborhoods in a bus. I started to look at the restaurants and the other places we visited—but not for their food or hospitality. I wanted to know about their bathrooms, and I often retreated to them and sat on the pot for fifteen minutes at a time, waiting for whatever was happening outside to end. *Should I puke?* I kept asking myself.

I went to see a doctor that weekend. "There's something wrong with me," I said. "I think I have something wrong with my esophagus."

He poked around in my throat and then felt the skin above my stomach. He wrote me out a script for an anti-anxiety medication, and then gave me some samples of Lexapro pills.

"Does this help my stomach?" I asked.

The doctor pointed toward his head, tapping his skull. "This is for up here," he said.

I took the pills home, but I was steamed. *For my head?* I thought. *There's nothing wrong with my head!* I was acting like my mother ten years earlier, when she rejected doctors, pills, care, and all forms of help during the last years of her life. "What a quack" I said about him to my wife.

At my wife's urging, I took one pill, the Lexapro. For years, she had hinted that I should turn to medicine. I had resisted and resented the suggestion. I knew I had issues. I did think that, as I had eulogized at her funeral, that I was my mother. But deep down I also saw myself as different, stronger and more open-minded. I resisted and hated all comparisons. I thought I could overcome the challenges, because I knew so much more about life than she had. Taking medication, however, would still be the ultimate sacrifice; I worried that it would alter my personality and maybe destroy my creativity. I was willing to do anything—see a psychologist, visit family counselors—before taking a pill.

Still, at my wife's urging, I took it. Immediately, I got diarrhea. Instantly, I swore off it. "They gave me a pill to help my stomach, and my stomach's worse!" I told my wife.

That day, a Sunday, I sat in our bedroom and didn't leave until the next morning. During the afternoon—a warm, sunny day—I watched the kids play outside in the backyard. For the first time since I had become a father, I had no desire to be out there with them. I always prided the way I involved myself in the children, and I took an active role in making sure they learned all the things kids should do and know. I always prided myself in the way I was able to distract myself from my own needs and fears and deal with everybody else's. But that day, I didn't care. I thought I was going to be dead, and soon. I felt helpless, stuck to a swivel chair as I stared at my computer, searching for remedies and cures for a disease or illness I didn't know about.

Several days later, I attended my first classes at Columbia. I taught my first summer classes at Rutgers. On top of all that, I had to put in a full day of work at the *Record of Bergen County*, and I had to go to Trenton to pick up some records for a story I was doing on school-bus accidents.

The bottom fell out on that Wednesday. My class at Rutgers went fine; the ride to Trenton did not. I felt sick the entire way, and I could feel my stomach twist, rumble, and roll around like it had at *Spamalot*.

Somewhere near the Delaware River in the parking lot of a minor league baseball team's stadium, I pulled over and got out. I felt the most helpless I had in a long time. I started to think the same things I had thought when I was in college, when I didn't care whether I lived or died.

Maybe I can drive my car into the river, I thought. *They'll just say, "He's a bad driver. He just missed the turn."* I had these thoughts, which scared me. They weren't necessarily suicidal. But they did remind me of what had happened to me before, some nineteen years earlier, when I shoved my fingers down my throat, making myself vomit until there was nothing left inside of me. *What is wrong with me?* I kept thinking. *I can't take myself anymore!*

Once again, I thought of my mother and my grandfather, how they could be self-destructive, how they didn't seem to care what came next. Was I self-destructing too? *What is wrong with me?* I kept thinking. *Was this going to be my backward fall down the staircase, cracking my brain stem against a bookcase? Was this me, leaning on the slider on the storm door, ready to slam my face into the cement?*

I called my professor at Columbia and my boss at work. "There's something really wrong with me," I told them. "I have to deal with it. I may have to go to the hospital." I then called my wife. "There's something wrong with me. I have to do something about it," I said, shedding tears.

"Just calm down, Tom," she told me.

"You have to call the doctor," I told her. "And don't let him tell you it's in my head! It's not. It's in my stomach. I know it is."

"Okay, okay," Kathleen said, speaking calmly.

Sometimes, this kind of talk would aggravate her and make her sigh. Kathleen always had to take a few deep breaths before dealing with my emotions. This time, she spoke calmly and slowly.

"I'll call the doctor and then I'll call you back, okay," she said.

I paced the parking lot, looking at the Delaware River as I waited for her call. I started wondering how deep the river was. I wondered how long it would take to sink my car and myself. I wondered how painful drowning really was. I really didn't want to do it, and I really had no intention of doing it. But I did worry. *Will this get worse?* I wondered. *What happens if this gets worse? What if I really can't take it anymore?*

Kathleen got back to me about fifteen minutes later.

"The doctor won't see you," she said.

"What do you mean he won't see me?" I said. "That's ridiculous. I have to check myself into a hospital!"

"He wrote you a prescription," Kathleen said.

"For what?"

"For Xanax," she said.

"Xanax?!"

"Yes," she said. She even chuckled a little bit.

"Why are you laughing?" I said.

"Tom, don't do any work today," she said. "Just come home, get your medicine, and we'll talk then."

I stayed on the phone but said nothing.

"You're fine, Tom," she said. "You're fine."

᠌

I made the hour-long trek back home. Along the way, as I watched the rows of shopping centers and barren fields of Central Jersey pass by, I thought of Kathleen's laugh. Kathleen's laugh was like my father's stern declarations against fear, the ones he used against my mother, over and over, just to get her to shut up. I could hear him in the laugh, telling my mother that she was gong to be okay, goddammit, for the fortieth time. "You're going to be fine, dear, okay? Yes, I love you best of all. I promise."

Kathleen was being my dad, and as I thought about it, I realized why she had laughed. She was laughing, because I was being ridiculous. As I drove down Route 1, whizzing through the green and yellow traffic lights, Kathleen's words and laugh started to sink in. *I know what she's saying*, I thought. *I'm being my mother . . . and she's right!*

I started to feel some rational sense wash over me. I was starting to get this. I thought about the past and all the things that had happened before with me, my mother, and my other relatives. I started to see the similarities. I saw the images of the past. I started to feel clean. *Yes, I* thought. *I really am my mother, because we shared many of the same challenges. And we still do.*

I picked up the drugs and went home. I sat at the table in the kitchen and watched my wife roam around the kitchen, going about her life.

"You know what, Kathleen?" I said. "I'm mentally ill."

She stopped, looked me, and started to respond.

"No, really," I said. "I'm being just like my mother."

I pulled out the pills from the bag, opened the top, swallowed one of the Xanax, sat back in my chair and waited. About twenty minutes later, almost unconsciously, I found myself eating a bag of pretzels. I was so hungry, and I started to stuff myself with them. It felt so good.

Several weeks later, I found a psychiatrist and started taking the Lexapro.

I haven't stopped since.

ACKNOWLEDGMENTS

A LEGACY OF MADNESS IS BASED on interviews with more than sixty family members, psychiatrists, photographers, experts, friends, and family acquaintances who captured the moments and places of my families' lives. Newspaper articles and reference books were also useful in both reporting what happened to my family generations ago and recounting the history of mental illness over the past century and how research and treatment evolved.

I had lengthy sessions with my family, including Stan Davis, my father; Carolyn Delp, my sister; and Edward Davis, my brother. My cousins were very helpful in providing answers to the many questions I had about my grandfather's ancestors—some of whom moved out to California to escape the Winans family curse, but nevertheless still endured similar troubles and near-fatal consequences.

I interviewed co-workers and acquaintances of Richard "Dick" Winans, including Karl Marx, his top assistant at Greystone Park Psychiatric Hospital; Shirley Smoyak, who worked under my grandfather as a student nurse at Greystone and later became a professor of continuing education at Rutgers University; and John Lapko, a maintenance worker and groundskeeper who helped take care of my grandfather's house on the Greystone grounds and drove him to personnel hearings in Trenton, New Jersey.

I used the articles I wrote for the *Record of Bergen County* as resources, and the newspaper granted me permission to use the material.

I collected photographs from my grandfather's photo albums and showed them to historians and other professionals who provided historical analysis on the homes where my mother and grandfather lived, the clothes they wore, the paintings of Bay Head, and also the locked-down, dungeon-like architecture of Greystone where my grandfather worked and where my mother was raised. These professionals included Peg Shultz, the history program coordinator for the Morris County, New Jersey Heritage Commission; Kurt Hirschberg, Bruce Reynolds, and Douglas McVarish, all licensed architects who have studied the Victorian and Gothic styles of construction at Greystone; and Kate Ogden, a Stockton State College professor in New Jersey.

I visited my grandfather's house—where my grandmother and mother also lived—on the Greystone grounds and I took photographs inside. I also took photographs of Greystone's other century-old buildings and showed them to the same historians and professionals, who offered analysis on the buildings' dungeon-like design and style, revealing the reality of the environment that provided the setting of my mother's childhood.

I interviewed criminologists and medical examiners who provided commentary and analysis on the premature and suspicious nature of my family's deaths. They included John Howard, president of the National Association of Medical Examiners; and Julie Howe, executive director of the American Board of Medicolegal Death Investigators.

I reviewed paintings and photographs from people who captured Hightstown, Point Pleasant, Elizabeth, and Bay Head, New Jersey, and other settings in my family's life from the 1600s through the Great Depression to the present day. They include David Martin, the historian at Peddie High School, where my grandfather was a student; and the family of Dick LaBonté, whose artwork captured life at the Jersey Shore during the 1920s and 1930s.

Interviewing historians and studying the writings, photographs, and paintings of the scenery surrounding my family allowed me to extend their persona to their environment. Peaceful sand-and-sea images at the Jersey Shore were a contrast to my family's personal trauma and hardship. Personal experiences also allow me to describe the horrific psychiatric hospital and suicide scenes that serve as the ever-present but fitting backdrop to the turmoil.

I discussed the history of mental illness with members of the Carter Center Mental Health Task Force, with whom I've developed a close relationship since my fellowship in 2004 and 2005. They included Otto Wahl, a psychology professor at the University of Hartford; and Larry Kutner, co-founder and co-director of the Harvard Medical School Center for Mental Health and Media. I also interviewed my own psychiatrist who provided reference materials regarding the *DSM*.

In addition, I relied on news articles that reported the deaths of my great-great-grandmother Lydia, her son Frederick, and their dog. The October 5, 1928, edition of the *Elizabeth Daily Journal*, under the headline "Woman, Son, Dog Are Found Dead of Gas at Home," and a follow-up article on October 6, reporting the police version of their deaths. I also relied on the *New York Times* from that time period to provide weather reports for the New Jersey area when my great-great-grandmother Lydia, great-grandfather Edward, and great-uncle Frederick killed themselves. The details showed irony: each died on days that were remarkably pleasant, showing a stark contrast from their depressed lives.

For my great-grandfather Edward's death, I relied on July 13, 1933, stories from the *Times of Trenton* and the *Hightstown Gazette*, as well as his death certificate.

I also obtained and reviewed death records and US Census records for Elias, Lydia, Edward, Frederick, Dick, and Dorothy Winans, as well as my mother Dede (Winans) Davis. I received permission from living family members regarding the telling of their stories.

Sam Freedman, my Columbia University professor, served as my mentor and accepted my idea for his class. Amina Henry, a freelance book editor, provided valuable tips.

ABOUT THE AUTHOR

Tom Davis is the Jersey Shore regional editor for Patch.com and an adjunct professor of journalism at Rutgers University. He has more than twenty years of experience as an editor and reporter at various news organizations. This is his first book. He lives in New Jersey.

Hazelden, a national nonprofit organization founded in 1949, helps people reclaim their lives from the disease of addiction. Built on decades of knowledge and experience, Hazelden offers a comprehensive approach to addiction that addresses the full range of patient, family, and professional needs, including treatment and continuing care for youth and adults, research, higher learning, public education and advocacy, and publishing.

A life of recovery is lived "one day at a time." Hazelden publications, both educational and inspirational, support and strengthen lifelong recovery. In 1954, Hazelden published *Twenty-Four Hours a Day*, the first daily meditation book for recovering alcoholics, and Hazelden continues to publish works to inspire and guide individuals in treatment and recovery, and their loved ones. Professionals who work to prevent and treat addiction also turn to Hazelden for evidence-based curricula, informational materials, and videos for use in schools, treatment programs, and correctional programs.

Through published works, Hazelden extends the reach of hope, encouragement, help, and support to individuals, families, and communities affected by addiction and related issues.

For questions about Hazelden publications, please call **800-328-9000** or visit us online at **hazelden.org/bookstore**.